Breakfast with Evil and
Other Risky Ventures

Breakfast with Evil and Other Risky Ventures

The Non-essential Ashis Nandy

ASHIS NANDY

Foreword by
K. SATCHIDANANDAN

OXFORD
UNIVERSITY PRESS

OXFORD
UNIVERSITY PRESS

Oxford University Press is a department of the University of Oxford.
It furthers the University's objective of excellence in research, scholarship,
and education by publishing worldwide. Oxford is a registered trademark of
Oxford University Press in the UK and in certain other countries.

Published in India by
Oxford University Press
22 Workspace, 2nd Floor, 1/22 Asaf Ali Road, New Delhi 110 002, India

© Oxford University Press 2021

The moral rights of the authors have been asserted.

First Edition published in 2021

ISBN-13 (print edition): 978-0-19-012092-4
ISBN-10 (print edition): 0-19-012092-4

ISBN-13 (eBook): 978-0-19-099121-0
ISBN-10 (eBook): 0-19-099121-6

Typeset in ScalaPro 10.5/14
by Tranistics Data Technologies, Kolkata 700 091
Printed in India by Rakmo Press, New Delhi 110 020

... freedom is nothing but the
distance between the hunter and the hunted ...

we are not guiltless
long ago we became the accomplices
of the history in the mirror, waiting for the day
to be deposited in lava
and turn into a cold spring
to meet the darkness once again

Bei Dao, 'Accomplices', in *August Sleep
Walker*, tr. Bonnie S. McDougall
(New York: New Directions, 1990), p. 89.

Contents

BOOK III: THE WORK OF CULTURE

BOOK IV: THE CLINICAL GAZE

BOOK V: SHREDS OF HOPE

The Song of the Walkers

A Foreword

I

We were certain they would come.

We broke the idols of those who
might have stood against them, one by one.
We waited in the capital to welcome them
with goblets brimming with children's blood.
We removed our clothes to put on barks
set fire to monuments,
propitiated fire for the sacrifices to come,
changed the names of the royal streets.
Afraid our libraries might provoke them
we razed them to the ground, letting
only the palm leaves inscribed with the mantras
of black magic to survive.

But we did not even know when they came.
For, they had come up, holding aloft
our own idols, saluting our flag,
dressed like we used to be,
carrying our law-books, chanting our slogans,

speaking our tongue, piously touching
the stone-steps of the royal assembly.

Only when they began to poison our wells,
rob our kids of their food and
shoot people down accusing them of thinking
did we realise they had ever been
amidst us, within us. Now we
look askance at one another and wonder,
'Are you the barbarian? Are you?'

No answer. We only see the fire spreading
filling our future with smoke and our
language turning into that of death.

Now we wait for our saviour at the city square,
as if it were someone else.

II

My name: Lunatic.
No one asked before I was born
In which country I wanted to be born.
Now you point your gun at my head
and tell me the motherland is heaven
and I have to love it.

Sir, does the guttersnipe care
to which country the gutter belongs?
And the beggar, her street?
Does the country matter, sir,
to the one whose name figures neither
in the census nor in the voters' list?

I shall sing '*vande mataram*', sir,
though I have never seen my mother.

Don't scare me with those beautiful
descriptions of the sweet fruits and
the sweet waters, Sir!
Certainly you don't mean
the rotten fruits I pick up
and the pipe water I drink to survive?

I belong nowhere, sir.
No one is paying me to
guard your frontiers.

I am a traitor sir. Just
finish me off with the same pistol
that had put an end to the fool
who had ruined his life
to serve this ungrateful country.

Don't forget to pass on my flesh and
my blood to my starving sister.

And, dear comrades in alms,
please don't lay my body for public viewing:
a nation going round a corpse
is not a pretty sight to see.

Donate my eyes to a blind boy.
Let him grow up to see, with my eyes,
a humane paradise untouched
by your dark hatred.

Vande mataram! Praise the mother!

III

Walk, walk, walk together
Walk with the questions
yet to find an answer

Walk with the song
without a roof
Walk with the pitcher
whose river has vanished
Walk with the last leaf
of the felled tree
Walk with the consonants
of the proscribed poem
Walk with the blood
from the stab-wound

Walk, walk, along the shade
between the hare and the grass;
through the fire
between the word and its meaning
Walk in red with the sun's dreams
Walk in black with the moon's solitude

Walk against the wind's direction
Walk across the water's flow

Walk, walk,
from death to life
with a palette of colours

You are the sculptor
and you, the sculpture

Stop, and you will fall
Walk without a pause
like the Buddha leaving for Gaya
like Jesus climbing Calvary
like the Prophet flying to Medina
like Gandhi marching to Dandi.

Walk, walk on,
never look back.
Walk.

K. SATCHIDANANDAN
(Translated from the original Malayalam by the poet)

Prolegomena

Last year Oxford University Press, New Delhi, showed some interest in publishing my complete works. That frightened me. Complete works are like monuments. Except for some Indian politicians who love to unveil their own statues with extravagant fanfare, such monuments are raised only to the dead. I have been also grumbling for a while that my steady decline into respectability has become a nuisance. And what could be a more clinching proof of that decline than seeing one's complete works published in one's lifetime?

This book is a pre-emptive attempt to scan my scattered writings and produce a volume that I should be able to live with. Many of the essays and papers here were written at short notice for newspapers and journals. I expected them to find their natural burial ground once people got rid of their stockpiles of old, yellowing newspapers and news magazines. But I had to make exceptions of three kinds. First, I have tried during the last so many decades to use my forewords to locate the authors or their works in a larger cultural and intellectual landscape. I always thought the plays and film scripts of Vijay Tendulkar offered a powerful social psychology of violence and I never believed that the cartoons of O.V. Vijayan could be painlessly consumed while casually reading a newspaper over a cup of morning tea.

Second, I have been often pushed to comment upon seemingly trivial events that have signposted larger cultural and political changes. For a student of psychoanalytic sociology and political psychology, the temptation to unscramble human subjectivities shaping macroscopic social, cultural, and political changes is impossible to resist. The short essay on sugar in this collection, which can be called an ill-disguised obituary of the humble jaggery, is an instance. Let the coming generations have the final word on how trivial the trivia actually are.

Third, there are the vignettes of intellectuals whose careers were cut short by premature death or who never got their just rewards due to the vagaries of academic fashion. A Third World intellectual writer staying and working in the Third World soon finds out that there is no automatic promotions in global affairs. Even after the retirement of the Second World from the stage, the Third World remains where it always was. The desperate, compulsive attempt to deny that awareness has become a preoccupation of an intellectual class unable to see the evil around them without wearing their ideological glasses. I am not vending a formulaic self-criticism of the Third World intelligentsia, but identifying a vital strategy of survival.

Yes, I do believe that location makes a difference. The heat and the dust of the tropics, the constant exposure to the harsh, dehumanizing realities surrounding one, the brutalizing spectacle of modern nation-states trying to discipline their recalcitrant populations into suicidal foot soldiers of development, progress, and nationalism and, amidst all this, the surviving algorithm of life that still throws up immensely creative artistic and intellectual initiatives and superbly imaginative forms of resistance. Such an ambience numbs one and cruelly flattens imagination but can also allow experiments with a variety of worldviews and alternative visions of a desirable society. The South—even if it is only a mythic South, something like invented traditions and imagined national communities—lives out its past and its archives of memory here-and-now and writes its lurid future on all available wall space in each slum.

More so at a time when we are flooded by myriad gift-wrapped quick-fixes, their use-by dates smartly erased by professional spin doctors in an increasingly corporatized world. Today our nationalisms are mostly ersatz, stirred up like instant coffee at roadside stalls by smart politicians at election time. Even our cricket is no longer only a game; all elements of play are being gradually taken out of it by ultra-nationalism and business interests.

* * *

Yet, for some unknown reason, so many of us have heeded Chinua Achebe's words towards the end of his book *Home and Exile*:

> To any writer who is working in the remote provinces of the world and may now be contemplating giving up his room or selling his house and packing his baggage ... I will say: Don't trouble to bring your message in person. Write it where you are, take it down that little dusty road to the village post office and send it!

Many have alibis for not following Achebe's advisory. Mine is that I was brought up in a city that was the capital of British India for roughly 175 years out of 190 years of British rule. I grew up at that contact zone and saw the zone telescoped into the personality of my relatives, friends, teachers, the writers I read, the plays I saw, the musicians I heard, the cuisines we fancied, and the sports we followed. Often the mix was comic but sometimes awe-inspiring in its inventiveness, too. It was a location from where, if one stared at the world without flinching, one could find a vantage ground to look at oneself, too. Freud was not an accident in my life; I was looking for him for a long time, without knowing that he existed.

I have not lived in Calcutta for some sixty years now; the locus of my intellectual world has shifted. But my world still carries fragments of the now-near-mythic city. The world itself once met India at Calcutta but that contact zone now looks a small, self-absorbed one. Yet, I cannot have full access to the other worlds I navigate. In the changing demography of my intellectual life, I now converse more with myself, a lesser number of fellow-academics, and a large number of ghosts from the past. Is this change another name of aging? Perhaps. But, while compiling this book, I did find that I had tried to open such conversations earlier too, across continents, languages, systems of knowledge, and forms of silence. Sometimes they have even crossed barriers of mortality, too, as the two imaginary interviews included in this volume suggest.

The columns, essays, papers, interviews, and lectures here are not only conversations with my readers and myself, they have been sometimes preparatory steps towards my other writings. I had not thought of putting them in a book when I wrote them for newspapers, magazines, or professional journals. Some were quick responses to political events and the demands of friends and institutions I cherished. There are also a few lectures that have waited long enough to be rewritten as more serious papers, more nuanced and better annotated. In their present form, they try to retain the flavour of an open-ended public lecture seeking to initiate a dialogue with the audience.

There are here some interviews, too. Once upon a time, I liked giving interviews, especially if they promised to be intellectually challenging. Two of my published books are serial, one-to-one dialogues, one with an Iranian philosopher and the other with an Indian psychoanalyst. Nowadays, most interlocutors are journalists trying to meet deadlines and, in the world's largest democracy, interviews in newspapers or newsmagazines are now invitations to illiterate trolls and semiliterate politicians to gatecrash into the conversation. Having spent my formative years in democratic India, I am not used to weighing my words or being dreadfully self-conscious even when in public.

* * *

Usually, prefaces state the main concerns of the book and sometimes set up a frame within which even disparate sections of the book can be read. This collection is more like a miscellany held together by one person's life experiences rather than by the book's contents. At most, I can hesitantly add that these experiences are vaguely shaped by some of the major traumata my generation of

South Asians have experienced and lived with—from the artificial, manmade famine of 1943 which took a toll of three million lives, the birth of Independent India and Pakistan at a cost of more than a million lives in a frenzied, decentralized, 'popular genocide'—as Mahmood Mamdani puts it—accompanied by a massive ethnic cleansing that displaced roughly twenty million in its first flush during 1946–48. And just when we thought that we in our middle age were destined to live in placid, unheroic times, came the Bangladesh genocide of 1971 and the Sri Lanka's protracted, brutal civil war (1983–2009), followed by the unending daily dose of violence in Pakistan, India, and Afghanistan.

You cannot even start building a humane society in South Asia without confronting that living past. I have in mind not the archived, historicized, manageable past that allows one to get on with life with a few annual days of remembrance. I have in mind the past that is the stuff of our nightmares and lives in our shared memories, myths, and legends. It is the past that comes alive whenever we go to a psychiatrist, a guru, or a shaman or whenever we look inwards, face-to-face with our solitude, counting the lesions we carry on our souls. Ghosts of that disowned but obstinate past are the invisible invitees every time we seek to negotiate an international treaty with our neighbours or try to justify new forms of censorship and surveillance to strangle political dissent.

I am primarily a child of the twentieth century. Even when I dabbled in future studies, that initiative was embedded in the culture of its time. Something was obviously missing from such studies. For, they did not prepare me for the twenty-first century. I remain mostly a spectator of this century. Certainly I did not anticipate that in the second decade of the twenty-first century, a large number of creative artists, writers, film-makers, journalists, and political analysts will be turned into mute spectators of India's grand entry at the high table of international relations. Many who had taken the vivacity and longevity of Indian democracy as granted are suddenly finding their voices choked, visions ridiculed, and self-confidence shattered. In something that did not happen even under British colonialism, a Tamil writer, Perumal Murugan, under attack, not only disowned and withdrew from circulation his 'controversial' book in 2015, he disowned all his earlier books and declared himself dead, saying 'when a writer has to apologize for or retract his words ..., at that moment he dies.'

We are also reluctantly recognizing that participatory democracy must be rediscovered and re-defended by every generation. The Left, once so noisily vociferous about the evils of bourgeois democracy and organized itself as a counter-elite, leading a vanguard of the proletariat keen to protect the younger generation from the seductive charms of liberal values, has suddenly woken up to face a majoritarian people's democracy squeezing out the last ounce of political advantage from a majority, a section of which seems to have lost self-confidence and begun to act like a cornered minority.

If you are no longer that impressed with the nineteenth-century social theories, still gloating over their iron laws of history, stages of growth, and the seventeenth-century Westphalian principles of state-formation and nation-building, you become an outsider in a populist, sloganeering psephocracy, living from election to election and mobilized for one artificially divisive political issue after another.

* * *

I was taught early in life that every book was a testament of its author, if only the reader knew how to read it as such, that some books can even be read as the last testament of their authors. This collection is only more openly so. I seek the reader's indulgence for the touch of narcissism that may have seeped into the following pages.

The only alibi I have is that I retail irreverence, doubt, and negation, not certitudes. But in some popular versions of a desirable society, that mix of irreverence, doubt, and negation is itself culpable. It plants doubt in the 'normal', sane citizen's mind that the cherished popular ideas of normality might not be that normal after all, and the direct link between a closed polity and an open society could even be a spontaneous lynch mob.

Yet, though politics has changed Indian society beyond recognition during the last hundred years, a civilization is a sturdier entity and usually outside the reach of transient rulers. No one can arrogantly talk of trying to save a civilization the way some talk of protecting a nation, religion, society, or community. Indeed, a civilization always retains the capacity to destroy a state or a political order that seeks to alter its core principles. The Indic civilization has always lived with fuzzy borders and its celebration of radical diversity and dissent, its distinctive ideas of enmity and tolerance, and its capacity to assimilate the seemingly unassimilable.

* * *

Many of these writings have come from a phase of my life when I was in close touch with a wide range of scholars, writers, and thinkers from South Asia, especially those from Bangladesh, Nepal, Pakistan, and Sri Lanka. These relationships have enriched not merely my work but also my life. I am not listing them here, afraid that I shall miss out a few names and feel guilty about that afterwards. I believe that the self-definition of each of these countries of South Asia is incomplete without the civilizational contributions of the others. Afghanistan does not figure in the list simply because it was out of bounds for us when we launched our major initiatives.

I hope that at least some of these writings will find resonance in the concerns of the South Asian intellectual community, and perhaps, at some rare moments, speak for them, too. It is to the future of that community that this book is dedicated.

Lastly, it will be unfair not to mention Vinay Lal who first suggested that I should bring out a volume titled *The Non-essential Ashis Nandy*. I am also grateful to K. Satchidanandan for writing the foreword to this volume. The poems out of which this foreword has been constructed can be found in *Not Only the Ocean: New Poems, 2015–18* (Mumbai: Poetrywala, 2018).

New Delhi
2020

BOOK I

THIS, OUR TIME

1

The Idea of South Asia

The Origins of Post-Bandung Blues*

The idea of South Asia is an artificial creation that is partly based on a denial of traditional ideas of peninsular India, and the attempts of the Indian nation-state to usurp the idea of Indic civilization without internalizing its complex confederating principles. It is only natural that while the officialdom of the region struggles with new-found, imported categories like nationalities and nation-states, and seeks to bludgeon the myriad cultures and community lifestyles into house-broken versions that would serve the purposes of the states, in the last three decades at the grassroots level, a separate set of principles is coming into operation—from the serious to the trivial to the comic—that subvert the bureaucratic concept of South Asia.

* This chapter is an extract from an unpublished keynote address at the 7th Sustainable Development Conference at Islamabad, organized by the Sustainable Development Policy Institute from 8 to 10 December 2004. It draws upon a paper published in *Inter-Asia Cultural Studies*, December 2005, 6(4): 541–5.

* * *

South Asia is the only region in the world where most states define themselves not by what they are, but by what they are not. Pakistan, Sri Lanka, and Nepal try desperately not to be India; Bangladesh has taken on the more onerous duty of avoiding being India, Pakistan, and the Bengalis in West Bengal. I once used to think that India was different, given its size. But Indian politicians have now begun to say, at the drop of a hat, that India is not Pakistan. The region can be called a collective of reluctant states, which are afraid that positive self-definition will not take them far. Sometimes, even historians, legal scholars, and public figures join the fray. Historian Ayesha Jalal and the distinguished jurist H.M. Seervai have both claimed that only the short-sighted leaders of the Indian National Congress during the last days of British rule virtually 'forced' the father of Pakistan, Mohammed Ali Jinnah, to reluctantly opt for an independent Pakistan.[1] Pakistan has even institutionalized this awareness in a somewhat touching fashion. Scholars have repeatedly shown cultivated bias and prejudices against Indians and the Hindus in Pakistani school texts but not noticed the disproportionate space given in the same texts to the history of the geographical region now called India, at the expense of the history of the region now called Pakistan. Pakistani children study biased history, all right, but it is mostly the history of India, not Pakistan, because Pakistan's past glory is tied up more with the Muslim rulers who ruled from Delhi and the civic culture centring on Delhi, Agra, Lucknow, and Hyderabad than with present-day Pakistan.

In this sense, the ideas of South Asia are partly mythic and partly artificial, and so are its nation-states. They are mainly products of political processes that are not synchronous with the cultural and sociological processes in the region. The two main political

---

[1] Ayesha Jalal, *The Sole Spokesman: Jinnah, the Muslim League and the Demand for Pakistan* (Cambridge: Cambridge University Press, 1985); H.M. Seervai, *Partition of India: Legend and Reality* (Bombay: Emmenem Publications, 1990).

developments that have apparently endorsed the imagination of the modern nation-state have been the anti-imperialist struggle, an ill-defined but powerful aspiration for what could be called an open society, and an aspiration that links the idea of a democratic order to an iniquitous caste society that nonetheless has the place for separation of powers. However, both these developments, while legitimizing the search for a democratic order, also created spaces for a robust scepticism towards the post-Westphalian, modern nation-state.

The freedom movement in British India, after it graduated from being an urban, middle-class movement to becoming a mass movement after the entry of Mohandas Karamchand Gandhi, brought into active politics sections less steeped in the lore of European-style constitutionalism and statecraft wedded to the emerging tetrad of nation, nationality, nationalism, and nation-state. Middle-class ideologues convinced of the centrality of the tetrad in modern times included liberals such as Gopalkrishna Gokhale and Muhammad Ali Jinnah in his earlier incarnation; Hindu and Muslim nationalists such as Vinayak Damodar Savarkar and Jinnah in his later incarnation; most Marxist and socialist thinkers, including Jawaharlal Nehru; and ideologically ecumenical nationalists like Subhas Chandra Bose. They all faced marginalization in Indian politics some time or other. (South Asians live with an extremely rich diversity of cultures and community lifestyles and have felt reasonably comfortable with the play such diversity offers. They also often live with plural selves. Even those who sing the glories of a more centralized state machinery cannot but unwittingly reveal their other selves less burdened by their statism. Indeed, there are indications that the statism in the region is partly powered by the seductive pulls of the philosophical anarchism they sense within them.)

That does not mean that these nation-states are automatically fragile or doomed to extinction. It means that, as individual entities, they will always act as if they were fragile and facing collapse. Indeed, they are probably fragile to the extent that they believe they are fragile, and act to remove their fragility in a determined, counter-phobic fashion by trying to be hard, tough-minded, national security states.

The idea of South Asia is also partly an imposed one, a response to other more successful regional groupings like Southeast Asia and the European Union. The idea was originally a by-product of the Cold War when the security community of the United States chose to divide many parts of the world into regional groupings in response to, and to plan for, America's security interests.[2] The result is that South Asia, as a regional entity, still does not make much sense to many South Asians; it just does not resonate with their imagination of a homeland. Nor does it fit the self-image and ambitions of the states in the region. South Asia's constituent nation-states are modelled on the pre–World War II nation-states of Europe, the kind that builders of nation-states in the region came to know during their formative years in colonial times. These states are poorly grounded in the everyday lives, cultural and political preferences, and moral frames of the ordinary citizens of the region. Hence the fear pervading the ruling culture in each of the countries that the state might not survive the carelessness of its citizens and the demonic conspiracy of its enemies, particularly its neighbours. The more scholars, artists, and writers talk of the common heritage of the region, the more the functionaries of the states in the region nervously eye their neighbours as enemies planning to wipe out their distinctive identities. Nation-states are supposed to have distinctive cultures, many well-educated South Asians feel, and anyone talking of two or more legitimate nation-states sharing a broader cultural frame must be either a romantic visionary or a person trying to undo one or more of the nation-states. Hence also the frequent, desperate attempts by each of the regimes to whip up nationalist frenzy, and the ruthlessness with which they treat anyone speaking of separation or even autonomy.

---

[2] Sanjay Joshi, 'Colonial Notion of South Asia', *South Asian Journal*, August–September 2003 (2), available at www.southasianmedia.net/Magazine/Journal/previousissues1.htm.

The idea of South Asia emerged in the 1970s, and acquired serious public status amongst journalists, writers, and academics in the 1980s because the medieval name of the region, Hindustan or Al Hind, and its ancient name, Bharatvarsha, or its less known variant, Jambudvip—as also their geographical approximation, what is still sometimes called the Indian peninsula or subcontinent—had become ideologically tainted. All had become associated with a brand new national state called India. Since India's relationship with most of its neighbours was not particularly happy, these neighbours were uncomfortable with geographical names that endorsed or invoked Indian dominance. They tried to create a space for South Asia by offsetting it not merely against other regions, such as Southeast Asia or Central Asia, but also against things past, like British India or Hindustan.

The effort has never quiet succeeded. Thus, while reading Rudyard Kipling's novel *Kim*, which some sensitive social scientists consider the best fictional ethnography of India, a young Pakistani is likely to be confused when, in the context of Lahore, Kipling brings in themes of Indianness and Indianisms. The traits he mentions cannot be re-read as either Pakistani or West Punjabi, and talking of them as British–Indian sounds silly. Nor have these cultural and psychological traits vanished with the disappearance of the Raj. Likewise, the works of Jibanananda Das, arguably independent India's greatest poet, invoke a Bengal that is primarily Bangladesh. He is an Indian poet only by his passport. Indeed, he could be called the unacknowledged national poet of Bangladesh. His creative imagination is linked more directly to what is now Bangladesh than that of Kazi Nazrul Islam, the official national poet of Bangladesh who came from West Bengal.

Everyone knows that something called India had entered the region's imagination by the time British India splintered into several nation-states, exactly as something like Hindustan had begun to make sense during the days of the Mughal Empire. South Asia is yet to enter our consciousness the same way. And it may or may not do so in the future, given that it is eventually an acultural, emotionally empty, territorial concept. Its real status is akin to that of Uttar Pradesh and Madhya Pradesh in India, two states that have, even after 70 years, failed to take off as viable cultural entities. You can meaningfully talk of Biharis, Tamilians, and Bengalis, but you cannot in the same breath talk of UttarPradeshis and MadhyaPradeshis, UPwallahs, and MPwallahs. If from Uttar Pradesh or the former United Provinces, you usually identify with a city—as a Lukhnavi or a Banarsi—or with a region, as an Avdhi or Purabaiya.

The term 'South Asia' remains a compromise, a neutral terrain. I have never been happy with the improvization, though I use it in deference to my friends and colleagues from the rest of the region. The usage has frozen a cultural region geographically (tearing asunder countries like Afghanistan, which has played a crucial role in the region from epic times, as anyone acquainted with the Mahabharata or classical North Indian music knows). It has also allowed the Indian state to hijack the right to the Indic civilization, forcing other states in the region to seek new bases for their political cultures, and disown crucial aspects of their traditional cultural repertoire; it has made grand civilizational strains look subservient to the needs of nation-states. (Many speak as if Islam was the responsibility of Pakistan, Hinduism that of India, and Buddhism of Sri Lanka: as if these faiths could not take care of themselves. As if a Hindu-majority country like Nepal and a Muslim-majority country like Bangladesh were destined to be only spectators in matters of faith.)

Painful though it may be to admit for many, the idea of South Asia stands for India in its older, broader sense, not for India the nation-state. This is the India the likes of A.L. Basham talk about and celebrate as the Indic civilization, which is of course another way of describing the region as only a partly territorial entity that has been a point of convergence of several civilizations and cultural areas. The writings of Rabindranath Tagore, Nazrul Islam, and Muhammad Iqbal endorse this formulation.

This other India and its inhabitants—known for more than a millennium as Hindustanis or Hindis—have subversive potentialities. Though some like historian Ravinder Kumar have tried to resolve the tension by talking of India as a civilizational state, Bharatvarsha, Hindustan, and Al Hind are in constant tension with the Indian nation-state. For the aim of the Indian nation-state is nothing less than to change the ground rules of the civilization according to the needs of a modern state and to engineer the cussed, change-resistant, everyday Indians into proper modern citizens of a state that, idea-wise, is only a pirated copy of a pre-war European nation-state, infiltrated by the idea of an imperial state internalized during colonial times. As it happens, that is also the official vision of a desirable future in all South Asian states. When they talk of the South Asian Association for Regional Cooperation (SAARC), they have in mind a compact among them to live or fight together within the format of the global nation-state system, not within the format of the cultural system within which they have survived for centuries. Hence their paranoiac fear of anything that might push the region towards what the Bangladeshi political scientist Imtiaz Ahmed calls a people's SAARC—involving free exchange of news, books, information, ideas, literature, art, films, and, above all, free circulation of free-thinking human beings.[3] Many refer to the size of India and its hegemonic ambitions as the main reasons for this fear. This is not entirely convincing. The relations between the other six members of SAARC are no less officious and frigid, and sometimes they are as bitter. It was as if all the states in the region were trying to become copybook examples of garrison states.

The Indic civilization inverts the process. An edifice built on layers of civilizations and a plethora of cultures, it is a confederation of lifestyles and life-support systems. The different strands within it are telescoped into each other, so that none can be described

---

[3] Imtiaz Ahmed, 'South Asia without SAARC: Between the Potency and the Existence', in Shaheen Afroze (ed.), *Regional Cooperation in South Asia: New Dimensions and Perspectives* (Dhaka: Bangladesh Institute of International and Strategic Studies, 2002).

adequately without reference to others. Islam in South Asia is unthinkable and incomprehensible without an understanding of Hinduism and Buddhism, which in turn are inconceivable without an understanding of South Asian Islam.

The South Asian nation-states, on the other hand, are exclusive of each other by design, perhaps because they are similar in too many respects and have to declare their autonomy by pretending to be radically different from each other. Sometimes one suspects that these states are built on the lowest common denominator of South Asia's cultural selves. These states are presumptuous enough to claim to be the guardians of the people who inhabit the SAARC countries, but would be happy to get rid of their peoples and populate the empty spaces with local versions of human beings that periodically catch their fancy. These versions have at various times included the rational, national-interest-minded English and the French in colonial times, the diligent Japanese and the disciplined Germans in the inter-war years, the progressive and egalitarian Russians and Chinese in the second half of the twentieth century, and the rich, powerful, consumption-driven, individualistic Americans now. Sri Lanka has, in fact, done even better. Just when it was being praised as South Asia's most successful state and a model for others, it decided to become a more monolithic Singapore-like entity, and in the process, invited a civil war that has set it back by at least 30 years.

When the states—and those trying to capture them—run out of secular role models, they begin to chisel their people into proper Muslims, Hindus, or Buddhists. As if, during their long tenure on earth, these people had not even learnt to be themselves and were waiting for their knowledgeable guides—the Taliban, the Jamaat, the Vishva Hindu Parishad, the Rashtriya Swayamsevak Sangh (RSS), or some of the fanatic, blood-thirsty Buddhist monks of Sri Lanka—to teach them to behave as respectable Muslims, Hindus, and Buddhists.

This dislike for one's own people, in those who most stridently proclaim their ethnic and religious nationalism, is coupled with a sneaking respect for one's declared enemies. India's policy elite suspects that, compared to the Indians, the Pakistanis are more aggressively nationalistic and driven by what in cricket parlance is called the killer instinct. Pakistanis return the compliment. Yet, both countries score high on nationalism, a recent 44-country, cross-national survey reveals. Indeed, the survey shows India to be the most nationalistic country in the world. Bangladesh occupies the second place.[4]

As against these games being played out by the regional elite, there is another kind of South Asia emerging in reaction to the mostly brain-dead, colonial, state bureaucracies of the region, the stodgily strident tones of the security community, and the region's totally bland, utterly manipulative political parties. This South Asia has begun to take shape at the ground level, based on a low-brow exchange of cultural artefacts. All cultures have high and low components; if high cultures cannot cross national boundaries, low cultures almost naturally do so.

The most important part in this emerging South Asia has been played by popular Bombay cinema. Indian and Pakistani TV, too, particularly their soap operas, have made important contributions. Popular cinema has, however been, usually the most aggressive, if unwitting, challenger of the demands of cultural insularity of the mimic states of the region. Once the Taliban regime fell in Afghanistan, two groups pushed underground for years by a harebrained idea of 'true' Islam emerged unfazed and full of confidence in themselves and in their own understanding of Islam: the barbers of Kabul, who knew that the population was not that keen to wear their beards as state-imposed markers of their piety, and some enterprising youth who quickly began to sell smuggled picture postcards of Indian film stars amidst the rubble

---

[4] Pramit Pal Chaudhuri, 'Poll Shows Indians are Most Nationalistic', *Hindustan Times*, 8 June 2003. The column is based on the results of the Pew Global Attitudes Project, which collected data from 44 countries, including Pakistan, the United States, Bangladesh, and the United Kingdom.

of Kabul. These defiant ones crossed borders to keep my idea of a low-key, slightly absurd concept of the South-Asian self, alive and open-ended.

Also, the smugglers—including arms suppliers and drug traffickers—have consistently tried to establish, over the last 50 years, a free-trade zone despite all official resistance. Older estimates claimed that the value of the unofficial trade between India and Pakistan was four times that of the official trade. I do not know if this estimate took into account the flourishing trade in drugs. To spite the paranoiac nation-states of the region, those involved in the game of smuggling seemed to operate on the basis of cross-national trust, the poor man's version of what some political analysts have begun to call, a post-nationalist awareness.

Finally, there are the NGOs or non-governmental organizations, as usual quarrelsome, flamboyant, self-certain, and totally immune to the rational arguments and realistic politics in which the national states reportedly specialize. They have bypassed the existing state system to establish links between young activists who have never lived in British India and are not burdened by ideas of historical guilt and culpability associated with the division of British India. When people complain to me about the biased text books of history in India, Pakistan, and Bangladesh or the hate propaganda mounted by ideologues of all hues, I always think of the young activist–scholars who so easily shed the knowledge they acquire in the schools and colleges of the region and the blinkers their states and political leaders expect them to wear as badges of nationalism. Obviously, the biased histories and strident advocacy of a whole range of nationalists coming out of the woodwork are not as effective as they are thought to be. The security community in South Asia has reasons to be nervous.

2

The Gift of Partition

*The Career of an Idea**

The longest lasting gift to Asia and Africa from the British Empire, the one on which the sun never set, has not been the railways, English education, or the eradication of social evils such as sati, child marriage, and genital mutilation. It is the set of four partitions that has divided four conflict-prone but functioning societies into warring nation-states, very neatly and very impartially. So much so that all four of them—Ireland, India, Cyprus, and Palestine—have, decades after the event, continued to bleed and stew in bitter, unforgiving hatred that the partitions were designed to lessen, not sharpen.

Years later, Kuldip Nayar—journalist, diplomat, and distinguished fighter for democratic rights in South Asia—met in England, Louis Mountbatten, the last British Viceroy in India. Nayar asked his lordship point blank whether he held himself culpable for the bloodbath of 1946–8 at the time of Partition.

* This essay was originally published as a foreword to Shail Mayaram, *Israel as a Gift of the Arabs: Letters from Tel Aviv* (New Delhi: Yoda Press, 2015).

Mountbatten was decent enough to admit that he did. He only added that he hoped to face his maker with the claim that, while on the debit side he was responsible for the 1,000,000 dead in the violence of Partition, he had saved 2,500,000 lives during the man-made Bengal famine in 1943 by disobeying Prime Minister Winston Churchill's orders to export even more rice from famine-stricken Bengal. So, he had to his credit 1,500,000 human lives. As it happened, only a few years after this interview, Irish nationalists killed Mountbatten, one of the last important victims of the oldest of the four partitions Britain had engineered.

The worldview and intellectual culture from which the idea of partitioning emerged—to turn complex, diverse, otherwise thriving societies into warring, often dysfunctional nation-states—is itself a fascinating story. The tremendous confidence brought by the new discoveries of science, the heroic exploits of the circumnavigators of the globe, and the massive social engineering project called industrialization had already changed the contours of the known world. The Americas had been discovered and the world's most successful genocide there completed; three brand-new, predominantly white continents too had been created; and a four-continent slave trade had marked the beginning of a new world order by taking a toll of at least 6,000,000 African lives. And breathless empire-building was promoting a new set of historical laws, with their civilizing and social–evolutionary messages. Those living in the civilized world seemed poised to break the monopoly of the gods on omniscience, omnipotence, and omnipresence.

In such an environment, human subjectivities had to have not only a secondary place but also look like so many annoying distractions, interfering with the predictability and manageability of the social universe. More so at a time when reason and rationality, backed by the positive sciences of nature and society, were looking perfectly capable of offering ideal solutions to human frailties and the apparently complex puzzles of culture. If Freud had shown that dream work could be decoded in the clinic, there was no reason why the work of culture could not be similarly decoded and re-engineered in the laboratories of political power.

Partition as a quick-fix for stubborn political problems could not but come at the end of this long, secular process of a growing mechanomorphic vision of society. As with the straight lines in the boundaries of countries in the maps of Africa and West Asia, it was a signature of arrogance, sense of omnipotence, and innocent faith in technocratic-managerial solutions. In this 'scientized' vision of public life, human feelings had already been distanced from scientific gaze. All that was left to do was to distance them from political 'science', redefined as the dispassionate, objective study of impersonal social and political forces. Agency and ethical responsibility could then be shifted from human actors to laws of history. Not only the perpetrators, but the victims too could then be reified, and statistics made the new measure of their suffering. Mega-deaths and mega-displacements were always a part of political ploys and gambits. Now they were finding new scientized justifications in smarter, modern, secular ideologies. The pathologies of human rationality were outstripping the pathologies of human irrationality.

* * *

It is fitting that Shail Mayaram—who has previously worked on the violence of Partition from the point of view of the Meos of Rajasthan, a community of Muslims who proudly trace their ancestry to the Pandava Kings of the Mahabharata, and used to, until recently, ritually celebrate that lineage—turns her attention to the long-term consequences of the partitioning of Palestine, not by design but by default. While a visiting professor in Israel, Mayaram kept a diary of her experiences in Israel by writing a series of letters to her friends, including the writer of this foreword. *Israel as a Gift of the Arabs* is a collection of these letters. It was while trying to capture the rhythm of everyday life in Israel that its author found the experience of Partition casting its dark shadow on contemporary Israel. Behind the easy, predictable routine of normality, she sensed, were more unpredictable, sinister forces outside the control of ordinary citizens.

The Palestinian partition, like ours, is not dead history. It is a painful, throbbing presence that has become a chronic illness. This Mayaram grasps, in the present instance, not through scholarly ethnography but by keeping her eyes and ears open when observing the flow of life around her, and from her encounters with Israelis of all hues. The diary only incidentally—though perhaps inescapably—becomes a glimpse at the social and cultural contours of the world's most intractable problem as seen through the eyes of an outsider visiting Israel.

In the case of Palestine, the task facing a serious political anthropologist, which is what the author is, can be tough. There are temptations to succumb to intellectual and ethical rabbit traps at every step. Scaffolding the Palestinian problem is the ideology of the Israeli state. Palestine was never some *terra nullius*, a term lovingly bequeathed to us by colonial knowledge systems, but the lively abode of a diverse set of communities, most of them Arab, including a sizeable number of nomads who were later redefined unofficially as a new kind of *untermensch*. Israel had to be built mainly through ethnic cleansing, probably not in its pristine form but certainly taking full advantage of the vulnerability of the resident non-Jewish Palestinians.

Today, the ideology of the Israeli state, modelled on colonial Europe's pre-war idea of the state, is constantly pushing Israel towards being a neat replication of South Africa's apartheid regime. Even Israel's often-repeated claim that Arabs living under Israeli rule have a better life than Arabs elsewhere, is a pathetic mimicry of a favourite slogan of South Africa's racist regime. Most people know this, including Israel's dissenting scholars, political activists, and even those who might be called the religious Left. And though the Israeli state has tried to silence its critics by using the European genocide of the 1940s, it is now a truism that as far as anti-Semitism goes, the record of the Arabs, over the centuries, has been consistently better than most European and North American states, including the ones that talk aggressively and self-righteously on issues such as human rights, terrorism, and democracy. In Palestine, Arabs had to pay for Europe's spectacular, public penance for racism. And the name of that conspicuous penance is today's Israel.

On this plane, the Israeli state is a compact between European civilization and the European and North American Jewish diaspora to declare the experiences of the rest of the Jewish diaspora and its dialogical relationships with other civilizations irrelevant to a modern, European-Jewish state. There can be no doubt that, in its present incarnation, Israel is a junior member of the Euro-American world, and an honorary member of an exclusive clutch of societies that were colonized, discriminated against, and marginalized but have now obediently chosen to believe that they have always been junior members of the exclusive club of the erstwhile colonizing societies. Theoretically, Israel's most significant other is perhaps Australia. Psychologically, both have opted out of the Asia-Pacific region, their natural habitat, to become extensions of the modern West.

* * *

Mayaram's book does not seek the demise of the Israeli state. But she will perhaps admit that most new states set up to protect the victims of history show an uncanny tendency to replicate the history of their oppressors. Those who have read Mahmood Mamdani's book, *When Victims Become Killers,* on the Rwandan bloodbath will find that parts of his argument apply to Israel even more than to Rwanda. One of my gurus, Sigmund Freud, has something to say about this tendency to 'live out' the past of your oppressors, but I shall spare the reader that part of the story for the moment.

Given my insufficient reverence for the Westphalian state and the Hegelian project, I do not trust a national state to correct the wrongs of history. I do believe that the only way to undo such wrongs is to actualize a state that can be trusted by those over whom it rules, and to bring into its politics some minimum degree of empathy and a touch of compassion, however unfashionable and clichéd these terms might sound.

Most people aspire for a state, a state that they can call their own. But that state need not be a national state. It is possible to imagine a modest but humane state that is more open, respectful towards cultures and at the same time especially caring towards those sections of its citizens who have lost trust in human goodness and the possibility of non-violent politics. If that sounds like too tall an order, at least the new state does not have to be a highly militarized, paranoiac, national-security state. Yet, that is what Israel has become—a standing monument to the way a victim community can be brutalized and can ultimately set up a system that, in the name of fighting racism, can itself become crypto-racist and colonial. One is tempted say that the Israeli state has become a disgrace to the Jewish people, Jewish culture and religion, and the Jewish victims of racism over the centuries.

Despite all its twenty-first century rhetoric, technological prowess, and democratic veneer, Israel remains a nineteenth-century enterprise, modelled on the colonial states that strutted around the globe fully convinced of their liberal–democratic credentials and civilizing mission. The subjugated peoples under them were part of the flora and fauna of the region, deserving benign neglect until they rebelled or questioned the authority of the state. Then they required firm handling, careful monitoring, and proper surveillance, so that they did not run amuck. This in turn required a hard-eyed, hyper-masculine, garrison state. Israel is now such a state, and it is no accident that it has played footsy with a whole range of states that share its self-definition—from the apartheid regime of South Africa to the citadel of Salafi and Wahhabi Islam, Saudi Arabia. It should now also get excellent support from India, where a very large section of the middle class and a succession of ruling regimes have come to adore Israel, and look wistfully at its many 'achievements' in the area of security, surveillance, and secrecy.

This is what the dominant canons of contemporary statecraft have done to a gifted people, who have lived through centuries of oppression and discrimination and, hence, must desperately deny that the state they have inherited is a brainchild of the colonial West, without which neither Europe's nor North America's self-definition can ever be complete. With that word of caution, I hand you over to Shail Mayaram's lively foray into present-day Israel, with the hope that you will also read it as a pointer to one possible future of India, Pakistan, Bangladesh, and Sri Lanka.

3

Is Australia a Victim of the Ethical Limits of the Enlightenment?

A Note on the Culture of a State[*]

For more than 200 years, the Enlightenment vision and the values it sanctions have provided the standard by which all cultures have been judged in the civilized world. It has shaped virtually every new imagination of a desirable society and every radical intervention in societies and states, even when during this same period, Enlightenment values have also often been used to justify some of the major projects of Satanism.

Everyone has the right to one's own cliches, C.P. Snow used to say. I, too, here reaffirm my belief that human beings, given

* This essay is a slightly revised version of Ashis Nandy, 'Is Australia a Victim of the Ethical Limits of the Enlightenment? A Modest Foreword for an Immodest Venture', in Baden Offord, Erika Kerruish, Rob Garbutt, Adele Wessell, and Kirsten Pavlovic, *Inside Australian Culture: Legacies of Enlightenment Values* (London: Anthem Press, 2014), pp. vii–xi. Reproduced with permission from Anthem Press.

enough time, opportunity, and a culture of impunity, can turn any theory of salvation—secular or non-secular—into its opposite. For instance, not only did the participants in the Atlantic slave trade find support in the idea of infrahuman Africans being brought into civilization, but some who penned the world's first democratic constitution did not find it anomalous that they themselves had large, private retinues of slaves. Nor did the colonial powers in Asia and Africa hesitate to borrow from newly fashionable theories of evolution to justify their colonial conquests, and to look at the colonized as newfound apprentices who would, in the long run, 'Europeanize' the globe. I, for one, find it impossible to trace the ethical, intellectual, and political trajectory of the nineteenth century and the first half of the twentieth century without referring to the Enlightenment and the age of reason.

The two World Wars finally broke the spell. The use of nineteenth-century biology and eugenics, particularly the idea of natural 'selection' and the principle of 'the right to destroy life unworthy of life', were already floating around in Germany since the 1920s, Robert J. Lifton says, and did not suddenly emerge fully formed in the Third Reich. Even in Europe and North America there are now murmurs that earlier popular explanations of the barbarism of the Third Reich as a betrayal of the Enlightenment cannot perhaps be gulped as the full story. The more innocent works of the likes of Erich Fromm, which saw Nazism as the pathological expression of an irrational fear of freedom and modernity, have given way to a more nuanced re-examination of the European heritage itself. After all, as early as the first decade of the twentieth century—when Enlightenment values were well in place—the genocide of the Hereros and the Namas had already occurred in a German colony in Southwest Africa, the concentration camp had been 'invented' and deployed by the British in South Africa, and famine had already been used as an instrument of state policy in Ireland. Among the later works on Nazi Germany, there has been, first, a vague, hesitant recognition, and then a more self-confident diagnosis of the role that was played by what one can only call pathologies of scientific rationality and of reason itself. That is the story of the European Holocaust as told by a whole series of scholars, from Hannah Arendt to Zygmunt Bauman.

Not that there were no earlier critics of Enlightenment modernity and Baconian science. William Blake (1757–1827), John Ruskin (1819–1900), Leo Tolstoy (1828–1910), Mohandas Karamchand Gandhi (1869–1948), and Ananda Coomaraswamy (1877–1947) are obvious, if random, examples. But they were mostly seen as romantic traditionalists, transcendentalists, or mystics driven by uncompromising pastoralist visions and a visceral hatred of modernity and its urban–industrial connection. And probably all of them except Gandhi, who was cussed enough to 'enter the slum of polities', could be shelved as lovable instances of literary or ethical excess, not fit to comment on or cope with the dirty world of politics and statecraft. Criticisms of modernity and challenges to the values of the Enlightenment acquired a political edge when voices from the South, such as Gandhi and Rabindranath Tagore, began to hint at the complicity of Enlightenment values in genocide and dehumanized exploitation customized for the lesser mortals in the tropics.

* * *

One would have thought that these arguments would make sense in Australia, a colonized society that was also a penal colony comprising not merely of criminals exported from industrializing England, but also dissenters of diverse background—Irish anti-imperialists and freedom fighters, Luddites, others who were on the wrong side of the Enclosure movement, and Scottish and Welsh nationalists.

Early Australians knew that their country was designed to host not merely pioneers trying to harness nature—the unknown flora and fauna of Australia that included a whole range of indigenous communities—but also those among the white immigrants who, according to officialdom, needed ideological discipline. This was to be done, if not through thought policing of the kind sometimes tried out in the case of the Aborigines, through 'proper' education and socialization. Such education and socialization were double-edged tools. They ensured that Australia would never see itself as a once-colonized society, the way large parts of Asia and Africa do; that there would always be a subterranean stream in Australian culture that would continue to see the country as a European colonial power—a subaltern colonial power perhaps, but a colonial power nonetheless. This explains many of the anomalies in its official worldview, its ambivalent perceptions of its geographically close but psychologically distant neighbours, and its distinctive style of self-negotiation.

That imposed discipline is now breaking down, and this book by Baden Offord, Erika Kerruish, Rob Garbutt, Adele Wessell, and Kirsten Pavlovic is another testimony to that. Years ago, I came across psychoanalyst Edmund Glover's formulation that even a wrong interpretation by a therapist has its uses. Presumably, learning to look within and acquiring the capacity to live with uncomfortable, even distressing interpretations of oneself, can itself be a learning experience and a therapeutic intervention. I believe that even those who disagree with the main thesis of *Is Australia a Victim of the Ethical Limits of Enlightenment* will also gain much from the effort. I certainly have.

During the last few years, I have read a number of self-exploratory works on Australia. They differ radically in their approach and conclusions, and cannot all be correct simultaneously. But even if most of them are flawed empirically and even politically, I like to believe that they are different parts of the same story. They are all products of a new awareness that is moving from the periphery towards the centre in that lonely continent. Obviously, something is happening there that cannot be easily reconciled with the global stereotype of Australia as an easy-going, sports-loving, beer-swilling, developed welfare society. There are cracks in the mirror in which Australians used to see themselves.

Other countries have gone through similar phases of self-examination. Post–World-War-II Germany and its anguished self-negotiation is an obvious example, and the long, often-strident debate on India's self-definition is a crucial part of its political culture. In the United States, another immigrant society, such attempts to look within have had a mixed reception. They usually come in clusters, and once the fashion ebbs, fade into glorious obscurity. The Americans have the gift of containing all dissent within small intellectual ghettos and sealing it off from the rest of the society, particularly from its mainstream media and its policy elite. Dissent flourishes in the United States as popular courses in famous universities and as respected cults that are politically irrelevant but are crucial components in the self-definition of the American elite and of the society's ethical ballast. They are 'rediscovered' for the general public on special occasions, and then the mainstream returns to its commitment to the time-tested algorithm of its life. Will Australia's self-examination go the same way?

I doubt it. Australia is a small country that does not have much scope for containing dissent within pockets of sanitized, fashionable, academic islands as self-contained intellectual communities. The country's intellectual landscape seems, to me, close to being a face-to-face one that spills over the boundaries of universities, newspaper columns, and party lines, and, ultimately, even begins to divide families. The public culture seems to me, an outsider, to be closer to that of South Africa than to that of 'the mother country', as some Australians may like to call England. I am inclined to believe that the number of books that have come out on the underside of Australia's self-definition and the darker side of its past—during the colonial period, and later, during the years it pursued the White Australia Policy—are a more radical intervention into the myth of origin with which every country lives, and on which every culture of state is built.

This self-negotiation, however, is built on a mixture of denial and pained recognition of changing realities. For nearly two centuries, Australia was officially a phalanx of Europe in the Asia-Pacific region, geopolitically *and* culturally. Indeed, in the high noon of colonialism, there seemed to be some cultivated forgetfulness in the country's policy elite that it was a colonized society. They looked at themselves as the junior partners of those who colonized, and aspired to one day be equal participants in the venture. Of course, there were dissenters who did not fit into this frame. In recent years, I have read about some of them and have come to admire their lonely, often doomed battles. But, as I have already proposed, mainstream Australia did not feel it was colonized in the way, say, the Irish felt they were. Australians considered themselves soldiers of the empire—foot soldiers undoubtedly, but soldiers nonetheless.

Strangely, it is this past that the country has begun to fight today with an apparatus that, in its case, is mostly inherited from the Enlightenment. Perhaps the Enlightenment also had as its underside strands of thought that could not be entirely wiped out by the triumphal march of what could be called unalloyed, uncompromising reason. There is, thus, a built-in double bind in this self-excavation.

If I can hazard a guess as to one of the sources of discomfort with the Enlightenment in the savage world for the sake of the authors of this book on Australia, I shall say the following: a system of values that unconditionally prioritizes reason cannot ultimately serve the purposes of any civilized society. Such values also have to be backed by compassion and empathy, however anti-climactic and Puritanical this may sound. When Offord, Kerruish, Garbutt, Wessell, and Pavlovic discuss the limitations of the Enlightenment vision through three real-life problems that have at different times stumped public policy in Australia, it becomes more obvious that those who have questioned the official line—from the academy, media, judiciary, and politics, including the authors of this volume—have mostly done so from outside the conventions of mainstream intellectual debate, whether they admit it or not. This has not impoverished Australia's political culture or maimed the intellectual exercise undertaken in the following pages, but has instead enriched and deepened them.

4

Living and Dying in Kashmir*

Kashmir overwrites almost everything that is written about it. Not because of its unique culture, its geopolitical significance, or its breath-taking natural beauty, but because of its pain. Like Palestine and Northern Ireland, Kashmir is a typically twentieth-century problem that has gatecrashed into the twenty-first century. All three places are beneficiaries of partitions mindlessly implemented by a tired imperial power, and all are associated with gory, repetitious, gratuitous violence that wears out outside observers and analysts, but not those who participate in the violence.

State-formation and nation-building have an ugly record the world over. The subsequent humanization of many states and nations cannot wipe off that record, for the earlier memories are immortalized as part of a myth of origin that includes the idea of an unavoidable birth trauma. The sufferings experienced and the sufferings inflicted blend in that myth. Under the lofty rhetoric of today lie the persistent fears, bitterness, and anxieties of the past,

* Originally published as 'Negotiating Necrophilia: A Postscript', in Nyla Ali Khan, *Islam, Women and Violence in Kashmir: Between India and Pakistan* (New Delhi: Tulika, 2009), pp. 149–54.

even when the past has become distant. Every nation-state, thus, is permanently on guard. So are its detractors, enemies, and critics. That is because the myth of origin never fades or dates. Each generation rediscovers it, sometimes with even more passion than the earlier generations did.

Sadly, Kashmir has been captive, during the past 60 years, in the making of the myths of origin of India and Pakistan. Even more sadly, it now seems unable to resist the birth of a new creation myth of its own, which promises to replicate the efforts of its tormentors faithfully. Once a community experiences the trauma of state formation at its expense, its capacity to envision a different kind of political arrangement weakens. Happily, the myth may not have yet gelled in Kashmir. This is where Nyla Ali Khan comes in.

* * *

The main issues in Kashmir, as officialdom would have it, centre on national interest, strategic significance, territorial contest, and security implications. Only ordinary Kashmiris trying to live ordinary lives in extraordinary times—Muslims, Hindus, and Buddhists—sense that the problem of Kashmir has to do with survival, the clash of death machines, and the collapse of social ethics; that the pain of communities and families, however unfashionable and outdated the idea may sound in the security community and policy elite, is the central reality in the land. To the experts and professionals who man the higher rungs of a state apparatus, and increasingly to the mainstream media, things like trauma and suffering are artefacts that have little to do with realpolitik, diplomacy, and public policy. They want to solve the problem of Kashmir the way such problems are usually sought to be solved—very scientifically, dispassionately, and professionally—backed by the coercive machineries and censorship regimes of the states concerned. They would rather not solve the problem if the solution involves straying beyond their known world.

In the meanwhile, Kashmir is becoming a haunted land where tens of thousands dead question the living on the meaning and purpose of their death. The living cannot answer, because their melancholia has no place left any more for lofty ideas and ideologies. At some level they know that the dead have died in vain, whether they have died resisting the Indian army or fighting militant Islam or Pakistan's territorial ambitions. Because Kashmir's own creation myth is not yet fully formed and functional, the rhetoric of martyrdom fails to compensate for the sense of loss. Kashmiris know that the death machines have done their job; that both sides can now only hope to say, if they win, in the language of Yudhisthira in the Shanti Parva of the Mahabharata, 'This, our victory is twined with defeat.'

The high casualties of violence in a small community only 3 million strong leave no one untouched. Neither the official figures nor the non-official estimates of human rights groups include the permanently maimed, those whose lives have been cut short by the trauma of uprooting, bereavement, or psychosomatic ailments. Everyone is bereaved and everyone is a mourner. The casualties include not merely the official and unofficial dead and the incapacitated, but also those who have disappeared without a trace. Family and kinship ties are strong in South Asia, and the death of a distant cousin or an aunt can be a shattering personal tragedy. There is in Kashmir a miasma of depression that touches everyone except the ubiquitous tourist determined to consume Kashmir's unearthly beauty. For decades, I am told, Srinagar's only medical college has had two beds for psychiatric patients. Sometimes they seemed insufficient but usually they sufficed. Now some psychiatrists and psychotherapists estimate that the college requires facilities to treat at least 1,500 at a time.

There are also the invisible victims of Kashmir, in Kashmir and outside. Thousands have died fighting for Kashmir; others have died in Kashmir, fighting for India or Pakistan. But there are even more humble victims, invisible and inaudible. I once met a few Kashmiri Muslim families, staying on the banks of the Yamuna at Delhi in an impromptu slum. Someone took me to meet them because no one even wanted to listen to them. I listened to them but could not find out why they were there; they gave contradictory, often incoherent reasons for their plight. Were they simply looking for jobs in the plains pretending to be uprooted? Were they the victims of militants for real or imaginary collaboration with security forces? Were they victims of suspicious security forces for their connections with the militants? I still do not know, but it seemed to me at the time that the political upheavals in the valley had created new kinds of refugees who had fallen through the black holes of the history of South Asia. To mix metaphors, they constitute parts of the flotsam and jetsam of our times.

One tragic instance of such uprooting is that of the Kashmiri Pandits. Ancient inhabitants of the Kashmir valley, almost all of them have been driven out of the valley to become invisible refugees. Even human rights groups look at their uprooting either as a case of minor collateral damage or an instance of foolish, self-induced trauma. Was the community really seduced by Governor Jagmohan's advice to them to leave their ancestral home? Do people leave a place where they have lived for centuries just because one bureaucrat, however important and powerful, single-handedly goads or invites them to implement the world's only known case of self-induced ethnic cleansing? Were there no genuine reasons at all for them to fear for their security? After their ouster from the valley, some of the Pandits in their bitterness have organized themselves into a cacophonous, Hindu nationalist political group, further arousing the disdain of most human rights activists trying to be politically correct. Indeed, militant Kashmiri leaders have spoken to me about the Pandits with more compassion than have most scions of progressivism and radicalism.

During the last 60 years, Kashmir has emerged as the ultimate litmus test for the two largest South Asian states, of their commitment to the ideas of a humane, democratic state and political imagination. Nyla Ali Khan's book spends much time in detailing the dishonesty, chicanery, inhumanity, and sheer cruelty that have characterized the behaviour of the Indian and Pakistani states, the former claiming to be the world's largest democracy committed to global peace, disarmament, and Gandhian values, and the latter continuously and noisily claiming to be an upholder of Islamic virtues. However well-intentioned Khan's efforts, she has probably wasted her time. For this part of the story is, by now, well known to all except rabid nationalists and the cocooned bureaucracies and foreign policy elite of the two countries. What is less known is how, in the process, the problem of Kashmir has strengthened some of the worst trends in the political cultures of the two countries that comprise nearly three-fourths of South Asia.

The most noticeable of these trends is the growing culture of impunity around the two states. As they have intermittently unleashed their army, police, and paramilitary forces against the local populations in Kashmir, Nagaland, Baluchistan, and Manipur in the name of territorial nationalism or Islamic solidarity, strangely, they have succeeded in debasing both the languages of nationalism and political Islam, and discrediting the armies and the police. Indeed, many of the technologies South Asian states have deployed to fight secession and armed dissent are now being routinely deployed to crush dissent and abridge freedom, even in normal situations and normal times—such as state-sanctioned, fake, encounter deaths, sometimes for reasons as trivial as bravery medals or businessmen facing threats from local thugs; large-scale use of third-degree methods during interrogation, an official euphemism for torture; and proliferating cults of violence. People have been subjected to aerial bombing in South Asia for aggressively articulating their grievances against the state. Entire villages have been burnt down and women raped in the wake of army operations against secessionist movements. The large-scale degeneration and dehumanization in the state sector in the region finds expression not merely in normal pathologies of the security sector such as multi-million-dollar scams in defence deals and the emergence of the region's own arms dealers with vested interests in war and conflict, but also in the triumph of the culture of nuclearization (which encourages the Left in India, backed by the silence of the First-World Left, to demand not the de-nuclearization of the country, but full sovereignty for India's nuclear weapons programme) and the growing culture of secrecy, censorship, and surveillance.

But nowhere have the two most populous states of South Asia faced such stubborn, recalcitrant people unwilling to turn docile, obedient citizens, safely integrated into either the world's largest democracy or the world's only nuclear-armed Islamic country. And the resistance has been more exasperating because of the passive-aggressive style that has often characterized it. A clue to this unequal battle lies probably in Kashmir's unique version of Shi-ism, with its distinctive touch of the androgynous. The Kashmiris were officially seen by the British—Indian state—and, following it, by the court of the erstwhile Maharaja and the successor regimes—as a non-martial race, mired in passive, life-denying *sufiana*, ever unwilling to aggressively confront political authorities. They were underrated by the rulers of India and Pakistan, the way the latter had underrated the non-martial, poetry-chopping Bengalis in East Pakistan in 1971. No one believed that the worm would turn one day, that Kashmiri teenagers would react to and defy popular stereotypes to pick up guns and give the Indian army a run for its money. They were out to assert their masculinity the hard way.

Yet, remarkably, as in Bangladesh in 1971, while Kashmiri men were trying to erase the feminine within themselves, Kashmiri women showed a resilient capacity to meet head-on the violence let loose in Kashmir, the violence that saw Kashmiri suffering and pain as nothing more than necessary blood sacrifice at the altar of nation-building and state-formation. The Kashmiri women, Nyla's book suggests, have mostly been a defiant yet healing presence, signalling restitution and reconciliation—in a battle-ravaged, terrorized society mediating between yesterday and tomorrow to keep hope alive today. Lall-Ded, who can be considered the protagonist of the following narrative, directly in some ways and indirectly in others, is significant by virtue of being a surviving symbol of what Kashmir was and still could be. Nyla Ali Khan uses her as a possible key to a future that contemporary politics chooses to see as only a red-ribboned fantasy produced by a fevered imagination.

The memory and imagination of that singular woman seem to emerge out of the pages of her book to acquire an autonomous existence that mocks the merchants of war. She waits to become the presiding deity and moral pivot of another Kashmir that lives in the hearts of the Kashmiris—and perhaps also in those of the rest of South Asia—as a political possibility that has not yet been erased by the war dogs of our times.

* * *

Nyla Ali Khan's passionate, affectionate portrait of Kashmir looks to the future with hope because her reading of Lall-Ded and the Kashmiri women's struggle for survival is the story of the possibilities that may not have been crushed by the combined efforts of fanatic militants and the Indian army. Kashmir can still be, under an imaginative visionary arrangement, a culture mediating between South Asia and Central Asia, between India and Pakistan, and perhaps even between Islam, Hinduism, and Buddhism.

A few suspicious of the format of contemporary nation-states speak of Tibet not as a cat's-paw that may help break China, but as a country that might someday help us resume a number of vital dialogues, some ancient and some new—such as those between the Sinic and the Indic civilizations; between Confucianism, Buddhism, and Hinduism; between a rigid, copybook version of a nation-state and a loosely territorial, proudly soft state; and perhaps even between the secular, the non-secular, and the post-secular. Like Tibet, Kashmir can also become a location of our experiments with our selves, outside the apparently inescapable frame of the European-style, nineteenth-century idea of progress.

In any case, most Kashmiris, like most Tibetans, carry three invisible, imaginary passports, and spiting the rules of well-defined citizenship, they may in future want to be simultaneously citizens of Kashmir, India, and Pakistan. That imagination has nothing to do with the nation-states in the region; it will have something to do with the conversations among cultures and civilizations going on for centuries in this part of the world.

5

Despair, the Missing *Rasa*[*]

The classical theories of creativity and philosophy of arts in India
do not have any obvious space for three states of consciousness:
despair, banality, and absurdity. Perhaps it has no space for irony
either, if you separate irony from sarcasm. Indian classicism has
place for sorrow, cynicism, pessimism, and even self-alienation.
It has also a place for—as anyone who has read Bhasa will
know—the trivial, the lowbrow, and the comic. But till now it has
shown no sign of formally registering the despair that afflicts
some works of Vincent Van Gogh or Franz Kafka, involving
a sense of the futility of it all and meaninglessness backed by
melancholia or total hopelessness. Nor has anyone created space
for the cultivated or stylized pop that celebrates the banal the way
Andy Warhol does or for the unashamedly surreal. Of the four

* This is a revised version of a foreword to Harsha V. Dehejia, Prem
Shankar Jha, and Ranjit Hoskote, *Despair and Modernity: Reflections
from Modern Indian Paintings* (Delhi: Motilal Banarsidass, 2000). Every
effort has been made to trace the copyrightholders of the essay. The publisher would be pleased to hear from the copyright owner so that proper
acknowledgement can be made in future editions.

states, we are concerned here with the first, as it affects aesthetic philosophy and awareness.

The absence of a proper philosophical and aesthetic status for despair is not unique to Indian traditions. Despair is alien to most traditional cultures, including premodern Europe. True, some have mentioned the personification of despair in Judas Iscariot in Late Antiquity Europe. His betrayal of Christ and subsequent suicide, it has been argued, have left their mark on the European consciousness. Surely, one sees the shadow of that Biblical instance of desperation and self-destruction in modern times on the likes of Friedrich Nietzsche, when he takes the voice of a madman to proclaim that God is dead and that we are the ones to have killed him. However, it is doubtful if that premodern model of despair has any close philosophical links with the full-blown recognition of radical despair in our times that Nietzsche himself comes close to admitting. One is tempted to say that, in the premodern West, despair as a *rasa* in the philosophy of art or of literature was not known. The most one can say is that some works of art and some characters in literature—Sophocles' Oedipus and Shakespeare's King Lear, for instance—can be read as pointers to an ontology of despair. Perhaps, despair in earlier times was not so much an unknown state of mind as a rare analytic category. It has acquired a serious social, ethical, and aesthetic status only in modern times.

Especially in South Asian traditions, one guesses that even when confronted with total existential hopelessness, in a world imbued with sacredness and alive with transcendental possibilities, existential hopelessness does not easily translate into utter hopelessness of the heart and the soul. Despair remains a psychosocial response rather than a philosophical position. I use the term 'transcendental' broadly here, not necessarily in the sense in which it has been used elsewhere in *Despair and Modernity*. In the Mahabharata, after Krishna reveals to Karna the secret of his birth, Karna has every reason to give in to despair, but he does not. He now knows that he is not fighting distant enemies but his own brothers, and behind all his humiliations in life lies his mother's decision to abandon him at birth. Yet, life and death continue to make sense to him, as does the difference between them. Even in contemporary Europe, the open-ended transcendentalism in the worldview of Albert Einstein and Arthur Schrödinger tries to offer a unified or integrated philosophy to act as a psychological defence against the utter hopelessness that imbues the creative efforts of many like Samuel Beckett. Even when his worldview comes close to the idea of despair, Albert Camus remains somewhere in touch with hope, unlike Van Gogh. In his novel *The Plague*, Camus foists a framework on an existential experience that recognizes the primordial question to be: why should I not commit suicide? He answers it by imposing a meaning on his world almost by a sheer act of will.

Perhaps a philosophy of despair has more immediate relevance and appeal in secularized societies where the individual has been atomized and cut off from most community ties, and where impersonal, contractual relationships have come to dominate social life. All said, for despair to be something more than an artistic posture, the gods have to die. Harsha Dehejia's term for despair, *nastik nairashya*, makes that clear. Even existential despair can be primarily the disease of a society that offers its inhabitants not merely the option of a nihilistic worldview but also the promise of ways of negotiating it.

However, it is doubtful if even the term *nastik nairashya* captures, for the older South Asian philosophies of art, the range of meanings associated with the concept of despair. (I feel that the expression *nastik nairashya* might have covered the domain of despair better.) *Despair and Modernity* recognizes that atheism enjoys a certain legitimacy in the Indian spiritual domain that Nietzsche could not have dreamt of. In Buddhism, Jainism, and in the philosophical schools represented by the likes of Shankara and Charvaka, for instance, atheism, godlessness, or the denial of the authority of the Vedas does not convey the feeling of total abandonment and hopelessness, tinged with a touch of rebelliousness, that it does in European Judeo-Christian traditions. South Asian atheism certainly does not convey any impassioned acknowledgement of utter loneliness in a godless universe that forces one to define one's own fate, ethics, and meaning of life.

* * *

Things, though, have been changing in South Asia during the last 150 years. The reasonably stable psycho-ecological balance, which large sections of people lived with in the region for centuries, is now under severe stress. Earlier the region had seen plenty of oppression, violence, famines, and pestilences, but never hopelessness spreading like wildfire in some sections of society.

To start with, the introduction of modern political economy under a callous colonial regime and the gradual spread of values and systems of knowledge inadequately sensitive to the cultural, environmental, and community-based concerns of the region have been traumatic. The breakdown of embedded theories of life that once mediated between the sacred and the profane, and above all, the introduction of a ruthless theory of progress and its cannibalistic progeny, developmentalism, have released cultural forces that threaten to destroy that balance. Not so much by subverting a pan-Indian, integrated *way* of life, as Prem Shankar Jha in this book seems to suggest, as by subverting and desacralizing the diverse, cross-talking, interlocked *ideas* of a good life.

Jha's argument has, however, a hidden dimension of which he seems unaware. Many of the communities now facing despair are exactly the ones that have lived with worldviews that are more integrated and do not allow the 'controlled splits' with which the Brahminic worldview is more at ease. What was once a source of strength *has*, thus, become a source of vulnerability. Between them, the breakdown of the earlier psycho-ecological balance and uncritical progressivism have turned despair into a recognizable state of mind in the landscape of Indian creativity. Despair is not unimaginable in Indian arts and letters anymore; it hounds many Indian painters, writers, and thinkers. It has

become an unwelcome house guest that shows no sign of cutting short its stay.

Understandably, as an end-of-the-century art critic and classicist,
Dahejia has tried to create a legitimate place within the mainframe
culture and philosophy of Indian art for an analytic category called
despair. Till recently, art criticism in India kept double ledgers. It
had one set of aesthetic theories for the non-modern and the folk,
and another for the modern. As late as in 2009, Roma Chatterji
could attempt an ethnography of traditional picture story tellers,
Patuas or *patachitrakars*, who depict the 9/11 event as a clash
between George Bush and Osama bin Laden, two estranged brothers in touch with each other through the telephone. Despair has
still not entered their world. One can only marvel at their innocent
interpretation of a desperate act of extravagant cruelty.

Dehejia's initiative expands the space for the modern within
Indian classicism by negotiating the philosophy of despair in classical terms. As a result, the basic schism that has grown during the
last 100 years between the philosophy and history of modern art,
on the one hand, and the philosophy and history of traditional arts,
is today closer to being breached. This is no mean achievement.

* * *

Perhaps because of the emphasis on individual artists in *Despair
and Modernity*, in Dehejia's overarching scheme of things, there is
no place for the despair of communities. Indeed, he openly admits
that this book takes the approach of an antiquarian to reconstruct a
civilization by concentrating on its arts. Such an approach bypasses
the 'verbal testimony' of those living in or with the civilization.
Yet, life has ways of gatecrashing into art that exasperate aesthetic
theories in every age. This is mainly because the translation from
the passions of life to the passions of art is neither perfect nor
entirely transparent. One might even argue, using some of the
same sources that Dahejia uses in this book, that art in any society
can be a double-edged weapon. It can be both a creatively 'distorted'

reflection and a defensive shield against changing civilizational realities. This double-edged nature of art is patent in contemporary South Asia, where commentaries on arts have become more distant from many carriers of art and their cosmological crises.

I, for one, foresee a time when the entire Indian tradition of artisan crafts—and the communities that have come to represent these traditions—will begin to head quickly towards a massive epidemic of despair. Probably they are already doing so. This epidemic cannot be interpreted as only a matter of individual choice or individual psychopathology. It is patterned by larger social choices and larger political pathologies. Nor can an epidemiology of this looming despair wait for creative responses to emerge from the artistic products of the victim communities, for these forms of artistic self-expression are themselves threatened by the new social and cultural forces unleashed in the region. The sudden spurt of suicides among the farmers of some of most prosperous states of India in the last three decades is a grim pointer to the way things may move in the future.

The most important point to remember in this connection is that the desperation of the farmers was not an individual character trait that afflicted lonely, isolated individuals as in classical instances of despair in the modern West. The Indian farmers did not commit suicide the way some businessmen did in the 1930s, during the Great Depression in the United States. Even in their desperation, the farmers retained some tenuous grip on life-affirmative forces. Many of them hoped that, after their death, the paltry compensation the survivors would get would itself mitigate the suffering of their families. Their self-destruction often came packaged as calculated self-sacrifice. To that extent, they remained, even in their death, just outside the rim of true despair and its amalgam of utter hopelessness and total meaninglessness of life. Their suicide was not merely a response to the existential question: 'Why should I not commit suicide?' It was often a response to a question that had a very different philosophical ring: 'Am I not more useful to the world dead than alive?'

The fate of the Indian farmers should have made us aware that despair in India might now stalk entire communities, the way it has done in the case of some American Indian communities Kai Erikson describes in his book, *A New Species of Trouble* (1994). Of about 250 tribes in India, reportedly one-third have already been uprooted from their traditional habitats by the process of development. They have become parts of the flotsam and jetsam that have surfaced in India's urban slums, in the wake of South Asia's march towards development and globalized capitalism.

The four crucial, if tacit, concepts that frame the South Asian culture of public life today are obsolescence, dispensability, exile, and invisibility of large parts of the population. We have unilaterally declared—according to the latest available textbooks of social change, progress, history, and development—hundreds of communities, lifestyles, and the artisan skills and systems of knowledge associated with them redundant. When we talk of them or their cultural assets and traditional knowledge pool, we usually do so in the past tense. Indeed, we talk of them as if they lived in some distant past, romanticized by impractical false visionaries such as Mohandas Karamchand Gandhi, Rabindranath Tagore, J.C. Kumarappa, and Ananda Coomaraswamy or politicized by rowdy, self-serving activists, such as Sundarlal Bahuguna, Medha Patkar, Vandana Shiva, and Claude Alvares.

Even much of the rhetoric of population control in the region is a response to the shared anxiety in middle-class India that the obsolete and the redundant continue to be a drain on the resources of the country. There is a growing consensus that enlightened democratic regimes should facilitate, if not actually do what some of the colonial regimes did to the native populations in Africa, Asia, and the Americas—allow them to gracefully slide into oblivion in glorified reservations or sanctuaries. There is of course the other 'exit policy' that wishes that communities and persons unable to adjust to the current ideas of the new and the progressive should no longer strain the resources of a poor country and should gracefully quit the stage and enter the pages of history for the sake of their compatriots.

Most of the time, the persons and communities that are targets of such benevolence know that they are not even audible to us, that they have become mere statistics, open for public inspection and subject to academic debate. The resulting sense of desperation in them threatens to make the despair in many urbane Indian artists, writers, and thinkers look feigned or artificial even when perfectly genuine.

Organized social knowledge might have avoided them, but the four tacit concepts—obsolescence, dispensability, exile, and invisibility—will have to explicitly constitute, one suspects, the core of any future social knowledge system that hopes to meet the ethical test of our times. Dehejia's openness to the idea of despair, backed by the openness of the classical Indian philosophy of art, I hope, will also mean a new sensitivity to the sources of despair in the contemporary world. These sources are usually man-made, though it remains an open question whether the processes of social change that have brought them about are themselves reversible.

This is doubly important because creativity, both as an activity and as a technology of desire, must deploy a new chemistry of emotions, motives, and fantasies. Neither can it start from scratch nor can it use the available chemistry as a given. An encumbered mind is rarely creative. If some creative artists and writers feel that they have a right to despair and give vent to their despair, we shall have to take that urge seriously. For, artists and writers, toying with or playfully exploring the idea of despair, are often authentic by default. They can be highly creative even when experimenting with or mimicking a new, trendy mood called despair. We must take seriously their creativity, whether we like its sources or not, whether it looks to us reasonable or not. This also means that if Indian traditions do not have categories that describe contemporary feelings of despair even in India, such categories will have to be produced from within the Indian aesthetic practice and experience and the theoretical stances implicit in them. For that is the only way one can link the experience of many to the creativity of a few.

* * *

This, then, is the story that Harsha Dehejia and his associates trying to tell in their book. They do not bypass philosophy of art, to concentrate on only art history and aesthetic theory when facing despair, either as a motivating force or as an ontological posture. This is only appropriate, and they have a precedent to draw upon. When, centuries ago, Indian aesthetics internalized the concept of *shantarasa*, in the wake of the aesthetic–moral challenge Buddhism posed, it only enriched our inner world. No dedicated researcher, no Bhandarkar Institute can expel it as an interpolation or *prakshipta*.

One last word. This book seems to argue that there are two major sources of despair in contemporary Indian creativity: the subversion of earlier self-definitions by colonialism in various spheres of life and the wholesale substitution of the non-rational and the mythic by the rational and the real. (If you are one of those brought up on slogans of scientific rationality and realism, please remember that we are talking here of the creative arts in which there has to be the freedom to play with not only time and place but also with the magical and the impossible.) The two processes are not independent of each other. The subversion of self-definitions was undertaken in response to the needs of a changing political economy and an urban–industrial vision of India's future. And the deification of rationality and realism came as a justification of the colonial theory of civilizing mission.

Both these sources of despair might have also opened up new possibilities in Indian art and literature, even if by underwriting the spread of despair as a psychosocial and philosophical state. Existing works on despair in the West are not very familiar with either of the two sources, though they should be able to host the former—loss of self under colonialism—within their framework more easily than the latter. Self-alienation is known in the West, though self-alienation as a by-product of cultural engineering of the kind in which colonialism specialized may not be.

More difficult to reconcile with contemporary aesthetic theory and art criticism could be the second source of despair in Indian arts—the displacement of the irrational by the rational and the mythic by the historical. Even those uncomfortable with the presumptions of social evolutionism will consider the displacement a 'natural' and necessary correction in Indian society, and part of an inevitable process of global change. Indeed, contemporary common sense seems to assume that the movement from the irrational and the mythic to the rational and the historical is *the* clue to the emergence of philosophy itself. Few are willing to waste time bemoaning the loss of the mythic or empathizing with those mired in the magical or the supernatural. Even fewer will admit that no collective choice becomes ethical by virtue of being collective or because there is no other alternative.

The end result is that, along with homelessness, breakdown of some of the central social institutions, cynicism, and pessimism, a form of philosophical pessimism hitched to an increasingly nihilistic world image has grown. It is in response to this that contemporary Indian creativity has begun to represent what to a growing number of Indians looks like the utter hopelessness of the human condition itself. For this, at least there was no precedence in the older worldviews of India—classical or folk, urban or rural, Brahminic or non-Brahminic, Hindu or non-Hindu.

As it happens, this new status of despair in Indian theories of art links up in a strange way with the melancholia of what could be called post-Enlightenment modernity. When gods die, they leave behind the ruins of a moral order and a fragile and transient set of aesthetic and ethical values that defy all existing hierarchies and priorities. As a result, the high culture of modernity is now partly defined by its inverse—a sustained radical critique of modernity. The overall tone of our times now can be summed up in that overworked expression, 'modernity as a loss'. Yet, in the operative philosophy of modernity, there is now a new cleavage and a new hierarchy of cultures. Those living in 'advanced' modernity live with its more nuanced, slightly self-deprecating form. Postmodernism is basically a derivation from that. The apprentice societies trying to catch up—whether in Asia, Africa, South America, or in East Europe—are expected to act as the drummer boys of modernity's nineteenth-century, colonial version.

Locating the experience of despair within the Indian philosophy of art makes more accessible the anguish that is an inescapable but voiceless part of Indian modernity. Scholars, activists, and observers of Indian life and contemporary arts will be grateful to Harsha Dehejia, Prem Shankar Jha, and Ranjit Hoskote for the scope and imaginativeness of their venture.

6

From the Age of Anxiety to the Age of Fear*

When the likes of W.H. Auden and Erich Fromm announced the arrival of the age of anxiety a few years after World War II, it was obvious that their point of reference was the modern West, with its full-blown middle-class culture, increasingly unfettered individualism, and its triumphant vision of an urban-industrial future for humankind. In that world, there was place for fears, but

* Sections of this essay draw upon presentations made at the World Social Summit in Rome on 'Fearless: Discussion on How to Combat Global Anguish', 24–26 September 2008; Forum 2000 at Prague on 'Openness and Fundamentalism in the 21st Century', 12–14 October 2008; and the Jaipur Literature Festival, 22–25 January 2009. Work on this essay was done when the author was an Open Society Fellow at the Central European University in Budapest during September–December 2008. The essay was first published in *Seminar*, and was re-written for a festschrift for Swami Agnivesh edited by Rajesh Chakrabarti, *The Other India: Realities of an Emerging Power* (New Delhi: Sage, 2009), pp. 94–100. © Rajesh Chakrabarty. All rights reserved. Reproduced with the permission of the copyright holders and publishers. SAGE Publications India Private Limited, New Delhi.

for only those fears that were adjuncts to modern society and its anxieties—the fears of loneliness, anomie, alienation, and other such lofty states of mind. Anxiety, after all, was a modern disease. Even psychoanalytic theory seemed to endorse that modern connection; it proclaimed that anxiety did not usually have a fantasy behind it but fear, being a more primitive emotional state, often did. Particularly if the fear was unrealistic.

Hence, many who wrote on such issues knew, but did not take seriously, the less respectable fears that stalked the Southern Hemisphere—the fears of starvation, loss of livelihood and vocation, humiliation, the fears of loss of self and loss of agency, and above all, insecurity about personal and collective survival. These were seen as correlates of underdevelopment, and thus, by-products of an earlier stage of history, anachronistically surviving in the contemporary world due to the irrationality and the cussedness of ignorant, change-resistant societies at the peripheries of the world. Implicitly, progress was redefined as the journey from the age of fear to the age of anxiety.

It took time for small groups of intellectuals to recognize that, even in the modern West, in the interstices of anxiety lurked more primitive fears—fears of annihilation that some of the great discoveries of science such as nuclear weaponry and biological warfare had triggered, fears of totalitarianism and machine violence that had outlived Auschwitz but not the Gulags, and the fear of dissent that made censorship and surveillance a matter of life and death in a large number of polities that still constituted the other West. Fears about survival, freedom, self-expression, and identity were not the monopoly of the southern world. American psychiatrist John Mack and Italian sociologist and futurist Eleonora Masini's work, for example, showed that the fear of nuclear annihilation, banished from the public sphere, *did* enter the psychological world of North American and European children.

Now, just when some intellectuals have begun to assure us of the end of history, and the idea of democracy has become triumphant enough to force even recalcitrant police states to claim that they are moving towards liberal-democratic ideals, just when there seems to be a global consensus on the beauties of capitalism, mass culture, and knowledge society, a new age of fear has begun to unfold before our unbelieving eyes, this time at the very centre of the globalizing world. The coming decades may belong to a form of terror that threatens to change our public life by setting the pace of all debates on individual and collective security.

Yet, terror was always there, though often invisible and unacknowledged, in the political cultures of liberal democracy and capitalism. Terror has always constituted the underside of Western modernity and prosperity, especially in the formative stages of industrialization and urbanization. Even its most serious critics could not break away from its culture of violence, especially if they belonged to the culture's Jacobin variations. It is the terror without which, Maximillian Robespierre believed, virtue was impotent. Indeed, all ideas of progress that have dominated the world since the middle of the nineteenth century, including the ideas and ideologies that legitimized the two early attempts at globalization—the four-continent Atlantic slave trade and modern colonialism—have believed in the emancipatory potentials of terror. The concept of the revolutionary role of vanguards in radical theory and the use of the idea of revolutionary violence to transubstantiate cruelty and mass violence, as S.N. Balagangadhara might put it, are merely extensions of the same tradition. When, in the first half of the twentieth century, the socialist countries made an effort to work on an alternative pathway to globalization, the first thing each one of them did, whatever else they did or did not do, was to set up a terror machine to serve the causes of 'liberation' and 'progress'.

That European belief in the socially creative role of terror has now come home to roost. There is some poetic justice in the efforts of others, who have often been at the receiving end of a world system, to dismantle the system using the same technology. Terror as a means of actualizing values such as justice, liberty, and equality now faces terror that invokes the same values and defines itself as counter-terror.

* * *

For some reason, anguish, the third constituent of the triad that includes anxiety and fear, seems to be in short supply today, despite the growing belief that we must combat anguish the way we fight anxiety and fear. As I grow old, I notice lesser anguish and decreasing sensitivity to anguish around me. I also see, in the media and in public discourse, consistent and systematic efforts to marginalize intellectuals and thinkers who think that there are reasons to be anguished about things such as the environment, the growing violence in everyday life acquiring nihilistic tones, threats to life support systems of smaller cultures and communities at the peripheries of modern political economy, the impunity with which genocidal projects are implemented, the way cruelty and torture have made their way into the reigning culture of politics, and the pockets of utter destitution within a culture of consumerism that is obscene in the way it flaunts itself.

Anguish *is* in short supply today. Yet, the anguished are seen as spoilsports, impractical romantics, or doomsday prophets, not in tune with the contemporary liberal–capitalist vision of a good society. The tacit assumption is that technology and managerial expertise will take care of every problem we face today, including the ethical ones.

Thus, the happiness industry is thriving. So are the instant vendors of bliss—from the agony aunts in Sunday newspaper columns to the gurus that India now routinely exports to the world, from the expanding domain of virtual reality to the flourishing guidebooks on how to conquer happiness. Happiness is now something like a medal in an athletic meet, to be won after arduous work under expert guidance. And one of the hurdles you must learn to cross while reaching the goal of happiness is anguish. Anguish is no longer the prerogative of the socially sensitive and the ontologically alert, confronting the human predicament. It is part of the excess baggage called unhappiness. The new stage of capitalism we have entered has a cultivated festive style. It has proscribed unhappiness by making it unfashionable. Unhappiness is now seen as an intermediate state between mental health and ill-health. And like the poor, who are held responsible for their poverty in the mainstream culture of capitalism, the unhappy are held culpable for their unhappiness.

Unhappiness is now permissible only in literature, art, and cinema, in controlled, time-bound doses. At one time, in some police states, psychiatrists diagnosed the unhappy and the anguished as mentally ill, for daring to be unhappy in a utopia. Now anguish has been included in the syndrome of unhappiness. Only its suppression has become subtler; anguish on the state of the world is called 'return to a bucolic past', for we have now reportedly arrived at the end of history. Anguish is now defined as a form of self-indulgence, nostalgia, and Puritan self-mortification.

It is sporadically said, with a dramatic flourish, that we have nothing to fear except fear itself. Does that tired aphorism admit a concept of courage that includes the courage to be anguished about the state of the world? Does that courage acknowledge the despair that lies behind the psychopathic, nihilistic terror that haunts a large part of the globe today? Where does fear end and anguish begin? Towards the end of Mahabharata, after the ungodly have been defeated in a fratricidal war, after the five brothers who fought for justice and virtue have won and the eldest of them has been crowned king, the new king, Yudhisthira, instead of being elated, is anguished. He says, 'Alas, having defeated the enemy, we ourselves have been defeated.... The defeated have become victorious.... This, our victory is twined with defeat.' This anguish is not something Oriental, esoteric, or defeatist. Nor is it a by-product of a tragic vision of life. It is an admission that there is a continuity between the self and its others that is only briefly interrupted by the responsibility to confront evil. It is at the same time a courageous defiance of the conventional idea of victory and defeat as a zero-sum game.

Elsewhere, I have told the story of how the ominous date 9/11 marks two beginnings bridged by a strange coincidence. On that day in 2001, the power and the presence of terror captured the imagination of the ordinary citizens of the world and initiated a new age of fear. And the Pathans, the main ethnic community in Afghanistan and Northwest Pakistan, soon became associated with the tragedy as the ultimate symbols of Islamic terror for having produced the Taliban and hosting Osama bin Laden.

However, another 9/11 took place, unheralded and unsung, in 1906 at Johannesburg in South Africa, at the time a proudly authoritarian, racist police state. That day *Satyagraha* or militant non-violence was born. Though the theory and the strategy was Mohandas Karamchand Gandhi's, the first person to proclaim the principle from a public platform at Johannesburg was Abdul Ghani, a Muslim merchant, and their closest associate who first published the statement was Haji Habib, another Muslim. It has been said that one source of Gandhi's non-violence was his mother's religious beliefs. She belonged to a small Hindu sect, the Pranamis, known for their uncompromising pacifism and the significant impress of Islam on their religious life.

Do the coincidence of dates and the Islamic connection have something to tell us? One clue to an answer is that, later, when Satyagraha became a major movement in colonial India, the Pathans led by Abdul Gaffar Khan played a stellar role in it. Gandhi himself called them the finest practitioners of the art of militant non-violence, and he traced this to the valorous, martial past of the Pathans. At the height of their movement, there were 100,000 participants called *Khudai Khidmatgars*, God's servants, and they faced every form of police atrocity from a colonial regime that had fought four bitter, unrewarding wars in Afghanistan against the Pathans. But there was not one instance when a Pathan in the freedom movement faltered in his or her commitment to non-violence.

Does this odd attempt to flout global common sense by blending religion and politics have something to tell us today? One answer is that the two models of self-sacrificial intervention, one violent and the other non-violent, struggle for dominance as traits or potentialities in each Pathan, or for that matter, in every person in every community. Global forces outside the control of a person and the geopolitics of national interests converging on a community determine which potentiality is unleashed. If Gandhi helped unleash one kind of potentiality, Soviet occupation, American intervention, and Pakistan's politically ambitious army generals released potentialities of another kind.

It is essential in the latter form of thought engineering to create large-scale meaninglessness and despondency, and then, offer an emulsion of a closed mind and a closed ideology as a cure-all. Physicist and human rights activist Pervez Hoodbhoy of Pakistan may be correct in his diagnosis of drone-like killing machines that the suicide bombers produced by fanatics become, but the focus, I insist, must be on the assembly line, not the product. In some ways, the polities of South Asia have failed to capture the imagination of their youth; sizeable sections of them are in search of a cause and are willing to be shot for it like rabid dogs in at least five of the seven countries in South Asia. I shamefully admit being anguished that we have not seriously explored how the powerful of the world may have helped set up their feared private and public ghosts in Afghanistan and Pakistan.

* * *

This essay is not an invitation to anguish. Its goals are mundane and less than heroic; it reiterates what we mostly know but try hard not to know. It suggests that the fears that now stalk the upper rungs of global politics are the fears with which large parts of the world, including sections of Indian society, have lived for decades, and in some cases, centuries. Unable to take control of their lives, increasingly victimized by forces that they do not understand and sometimes cannot even identify, if they in their desperation have flayed their hands and struck out at random, even normal political pragmatism demands that we scan the sources of their desperation and spot the reasons that have prompted some of them to knowingly sacrifice their lives for causes that give meaning in an otherwise meaningless life. But it has now become fashionable to denigrate every reference to 'root causes' as an attempt to derail serious discussion of the new face of terror. If realism and self-interest mean something more than petty profiteering and bureaucratic quibbling, they should push us to admit that we can survive the new age of fear only by lifting the siege on communities caught in the hinges of time for the sake of causes that make little sense to them and enter their lives as natural calamities—national security, development, progress, state-building, and nation-formation.

I am not trying to complicate a simple act of terror that targets ordinary citizens living ordinary lives. I know that a growing proportion of the victims of modern terrorism are children, women, and the elderly. But we also battle terrorism at a time when the continuities between victims and perpetrators are becoming clearer, and all efforts to design neat solutions to human problems are turning out to be inhuman and self-defeating. To use Tarun Tejpal's evocative metaphor, the untold story of our assassins is gradually turning out to be a story about us. For their fears and ours are not so radically different.

This indivisibility of terror we have learnt to deny. Worse, the more blatant the indivisibility, the more aggressive and strident our denial becomes. We love to talk of *Jihadi* terrorism without mentioning Kashmir and Gujarat 2002, and we love to believe that the militancy in Punjab in the late 1980s and 1990s had nothing to do with the anti-Sikh pogrom at Delhi in 1984. The furious arguments on the menace of Maoist violence in India never mention how shabbily we have treated our tribal communities, the mainstay of Indian Maoism today. Nor have official histories and historians documented our gory record at Nagaland and Manipur. We love to mention Pakistan's use of air power against their Baloch separatists, not India's use of its air force in the Northeast against our tribal separatists.

The culture of the Indian state is what it is today because of our dedicated efforts to ignore its criminalization. One of the great paradoxes of Indian politics is that the police, the bureaucrats, and the politicians enjoy the least respect and trust of the Indian citizens according to virtually every opinion poll, but they seem to become more trustworthy the moment they open their mouths on terrorism, national security, and international relations. Fortunately, even that trust seems to be wearing off as we regularly come across cases of false accusations of terror and deliberate attempts to concoct cases against political opponents.

At the centre of that process of criminalization is the use of ruthless, often extra-legal force in the name of counter-insurgency and counter-terrorism, applauded by much of the media and the intelligentsia, in turn backed by the much-heralded Indian middle class. We fear sections of our citizens because we know what we have done to them. And we see all around, our neighbours embroiled in similar exercises. The Sri Lankan state tries hard to dissociate the problem of Tamil terrorism from the consistent record of discrimination against the Tamils, and the Colombo riots of 1983; Pakistan's civil establishment hopes to resist army rule without confronting the army's role in the Bangladesh genocide. Bangladesh in turn grudges Chakmas the rights that it claimed from Pakistan.

Security in any polity is indivisible; unlike wealth, memories are not that easy to lock up. Terror today is the fear that defines the age of fear, and each day it is becoming more anomic. However woolly-headed and impractical I may sound, I insist that such terror cannot be fought only through efficient use of arms. After combatting terrorism inspired by Irish nationalism and its counter-players for about 90 years, Britain has learnt that lesson the hard way; they have fallen back on politics. In Palestine, after fighting terror so ruthlessly for more than 70 years, Israel is as insecure as it was at birth. Indeed, known all over the world for its brutal ethnic cleansing and anti-terrorist measures, the Israeli state itself has become, in the words of a retired officer of its own army, 'a gangster state'. If I may revert to my own cliché, you can afford to choose your friends carelessly but be careful when choosing an enemy because, in long run, you cannot but come to resemble your enemy.

7

Idealism, Ideology, and Total Politics*

Idealism and ideology come to us naturally when we are young. Most of us do not have to struggle to acquire them; we are eased into them by our early life experiences and our 'significant others'. As we pass through childhood and adolescence, we reconfigure the moral sensitivity that comes from identification with parents, peer groups, religious, and political leaders, and from heroic figures we have read or heard about. Out of that emerge forms of idealism and ideology that we can call our own.

Obviously, I am not talking here of the idealism associated with philosophical schools such as Neoplatonism or perennial philosophy in the West or Buddhism and Vedanta in the East, nor of ideology as defined by Karl Marx and Karl Mannheim. I am using the two concepts as they are used in everyday life, and in political sociology and political psychology.

* This is a revised version of an essay ('Hibernating Idealism') published in *Outlook* (August, 2017). Every effort has been made to trace the copyrightholders of the essay. The publisher would be pleased to hear from the copyright owner so that proper acknowledgement can be made in future editions.

* * *

The base of idealism is laid once the child crosses the stage of conventional morality, and is able to make increasingly complex, socially sensitive, moral choices. That change takes place mostly outside the range of the child's awareness. It is part of normal child development that falls under the regime of what psychoanalysts call the superego, and is part of what child psychologists Jean Piaget and Lawrence Kohlberg call normal moral development.

Attempts to find an ideology that demands long-term, personal commitment come later, during adolescence. It can be a more self-conscious, intellectual search. One usually knows when one is looking for an appropriate ideology for personal use and can give reasons for one's choice. But such reasons can be misleading. For, the choice can be shaped by deeper forces within one, to which one has no clue. An ideology can be a defensive manoeuvre to find certitudes to keep at bay deeper uncertainties and insecurities; it can be constrained by the moral sensitivity and idealism one has grown up with. It can even be something as predictable as a disempowered, marginalized man opting for a hyper-masculine ideology to feel vicariously powerful and potent.

Being a more self-conscious process, one can control one's allegiance to an ideology. One can embrace an ideology with unbending passion or with some detachment, so as to use it to access political power, social status, academic respectability, or even as a handy, post-facto self-justification for all kinds of Satanism—from organizing or presiding over a full-fledged genocide to running a free-for-all kleptocracy.

Ideology is also a handy tool to discredit idealism as an irresponsible, naïve, romantic response to real-life political and social issues. This is often so effective that many learn to package their idealism in the language of ideology to deflect damaging criticisms. If that does not work, you can deploy an ideology to discredit a troublesome idealism, however impressive or lofty, by calling it a hidden counter-ideology with a built-in political strategy. No wonder, many insist that as adults, we should be able to rise above idealism and ideology, and to use both in public life as political technologies at opportune moments.

However, there is also something in these two concepts that is deeply seductive, if not fatally attractive. Even those who lead an obscenely successful, high-cholesterol, calorie-counting life, love to talk of fits of idealism and ideology through which they have passed. I have heard veteran politicians and successful business tycoons proudly saying how naïve and idealistic they once were, till experience taught them to be tough, shrewd, and cynical. Perhaps they want to convey that they too had an innocent, lovable, moral self, till they were forced to disown it to pursue a more realistic dream. Had he been young, G.D. Birla once said, he too would have joined the Maoists.

Fortunately, those were not the days of the United Progressive Alliance (UPA) II or the Bharatiya Janata Party (BJP). Otherwise, Birla would have kept the company of the 6,000 villagers in Tamil Nadu fighting cases of sedition slapped on them for opposing the building of a nuclear reactor in their village. Their leader Udayakumar, a peace researcher, has 101 cases against him. The villagers are still trying to find out what sedition is and why, if the reactor is such a safe and beautiful thing, it cannot be built in places where the powerful and the rich stay.

* * *

Idealism and ideology are cousins. In normal times, they check each other's excesses. But, these are not normal times in India. As in the Mahabharata, these cousins live in a dysfunctional family. They work together only when under attack from politics. The job of politics is to dissolve idealism, often in the name of ideology, and to subvert ideology, usually in the name of political realism. I can find no better example of this than a statement of Deng Xiaoping who, I am told, once claimed, 'The West builds capitalism, for the sake of building capitalism. We build capitalism, so as to build socialism.' Faced with a clash between ideology and idealism on the one side, and the politics of survival on the other, Deng was merely revealing his priorities as a practising politician.

In Indian public life, 'doing politics' has become a term of abuse. Yet, the ability and the freedom to do politics is the ultimate sign of life in a democracy. Democratic politics is not only the right to vote but also to organize and seek votes in the name of a party or movement of one's choice. North Korea regularly holds elections and its dynastic rulers regularly win these elections, getting more than 90 per cent of the votes. Nobody has accused the country of being a democracy.

Democracies begin to die when normal, open interplay between idealism, ideology, and open politics stops, and 'total politics' takes over. Such politics seems to have three features. First, everything is reduced to politics and politics intrudes into everything. Once, caste- and religion-based politics and dynastic politics were seen as cases of primordial ties trespassing into democratic politics. Now they are part of normal politics. If you think they are parts of an unavoidable phase in a highly diverse, unequal society where political ideologies do not have much play, there is for your edification, university politics (subsuming student politics, politics of college admissions, appointment of teachers and vice-chancellors, and political interference with curricula); politics of science and science-bureaucracy; politics of sports, cinema, and other forms of entertainment; and cutting across some of these domains, politics of awards and state honours (which was always there as part of normal politics till it produced an unworthy progeny called politics of returning awards, seen officially as anti-national, conspiratorial politics). Now to this long list you could add new, colourful entrants—the politics of post-retirement benefits and that hoary presence called politics of censorship and surveillance.

In almost all such forms of politics, the key player has been the Indian state. Yet, no one has affirmed that the Indian state is getting overloaded. Not even the ones who spend sleepless nights on India's overloaded judiciary; nor the ones who wonder why our terribly busy prime minister did not find any time in two years to comment on the country's newly popular national sport—lynching.

Second, the technology of political warfare and political mobilization has been changing dramatically in India in recent times. As populist rhetoric, clever use of media, especially social media, and smart sloganeering have acquired salience in political campaigns, we have failed to notice that our politicians have rediscovered an important truth, which clever demagogues and propaganda chiefs have always known: hatred goes much farther than positive sentiments in politics, particularly when you are trying to mobilize people or when the state faces a crisis of governance.

Hatred defines our enemies. And that definition is always sharper than that of our allies. That is why all nationalisms, especially if they are state-centric, tend to be hate-based. The only exceptions are those nationalisms that defy the conventional meaning of nationalism and use it as a synonym of patriotism, a much older word that refers to a natural human sentiment called territoriality. Unlike nationalism, it is not an ideology but a sentiment, and is more manageable politically. Built into nationalism, on the other hand, is the awareness that it is easier to mobilize people *against* enemies than *for* friends; people usually know better what they hate than what they love. A dystopia can quickly produce a monolithic wall of public opinion deaf to all isolated voices of sanity.

Third, statist nationalism invariably seeks to establish a monopolistic, one-way relationship with the individual citizen. It suspects all communities, and has an instrumental view of all religions, sects, castes, as well as other non-state actors—trade unions, nongovernmental organizations (NGOs), students' unions, citizens' movements, and professional bodies—that can become an alternative means of mobilization and an alternative source of power. Such social divisions and organizations may be used during election campaigns and when the ruling elite want to put up spectacular rallies, but such uses are almost entirely instrumental. At least on this issue there now seems to be a perfect consensus among all political parties in an otherwise chaotic, bitterly divided polity.

The individual citizens, thus, increasingly face the state alone—with very few autonomous institutions, community leaders, or movements left to intervene between the two. The judiciary, one of the few checks on the state, is inaccessible to ordinary citizens due to its costly, time-consuming ways. And the various commissions supposed to protect the human rights of different sections—minorities, women, scheduled castes and scheduled tribes, the press—are often ineffective or, as in the case of vigilance in India, not in place. Over time, (1) the plurality of voices itself becomes a casualty of high-pitched, divisive politics; (2) the very existence of opposition in the polity is made to look like a conspiracy against the ruling regime and the nation-state; and (3) the reigning cabal of decision-makers, small to begin with, shrinks further.

* * *

In India, the fall-outs of these changes are gradually becoming visible. And they go far beyond the simple 'developmental authoritarianism' Herb Feith talked about in the 1980s, and from which many East and Southeast Asian countries have been suffering from the 1950s, and for which many naïve Indians, blinded by the 'success' of China and other Asian Tigers, have been pining for the last five decades.

In the meanwhile, the waves of what Ziauddin Sardar, philosopher and historian of science and Islamic thought, calls post-normal times have reached the shores of India and are showing no signs of receding. If I read Sardar correctly, post-normal times are defined by the collapse of our shared moral universe, fragmentation of communities, and pathetic dependence on managerial skills in situations that call for empathy and compassion. To confront such times, Sardar believes, we require a different set of beliefs, which even many well-meaning Indians will find difficult to gulp:

> Post-normal times demand...that we abandon the ideas of 'control and management', and rethink the cherished notions of progress, modernization and efficiency. The way forward must be based on

virtues of humility, modesty and accountability, the indispensable requirement of living with uncertainty, complexity and ignorance. We will have to imagine ourselves out of post-normal times and into a new age of normalcy—with an ethical compass and a broad spectrum of imaginations from the rich diversity of human cultures.[1]

If I may add a post-script to this challenging statement, we are talking of a post-normal culture of public life in which the idea of normality no longer applies to the present; it is exiled to the past, the often distant past, or to the future, often an undefined future, or a refurbished past-as-the-future. (This is not Gandhi's *Ramarajya*, which is a powerful critique of the present; it is a version of Ramarajya that is complicit with the present and endorses it uncritically.)

The present has to be renegotiated through this dark reality and read as a transitory, doomed state of affairs waiting for a decent burial. In the meanwhile, ordinary decency, idealism of any kind, political sagacity and vision, even the distinctive spiritual contents of the various religious faiths will have to survive in small oases-like locales.

As for the larger public sphere, unlike in the last days of the Roman Empire, which reportedly survived by ensuring its citizens a steady supply of 'bread and circus', Indians will have to be satisfied with an endless supply of 'circus and circus'.

---

[1] Ziauddin Sardar. 2010. 'Welcome to Postnormal Times'. *Futures*, 42(5):435–44.

8

Uprooting and the Landscape of Clandestine Selves*

The idea of the nation-state, when wedded to visions of urban-industrial life and development, is a potent concoction. It almost invariably goes with uprooting, breakdown of communities, and an inner sense of exile. The combination is turning India, too, into a country of the psychologically uprooted.

Most old-societies-turned-young-nation-states have learnt to live with this inner state of exile, which is 'real' to the person who feels exiled but looks unreal to onlookers. The twentieth century has been a century of refugees. Some like Hannah Arendt identify them as virtually a new species of human beings symbolizing the violence of our times. Refugees represent a form of psychosocial displacement that has become endemic to modernizing societies. One no longer has to cross national frontiers to become a refugee, and one can be as easily seduced by the 'pull' of a supposed El Dorado as by the 'push' of an oppressive system at home.

---

* This note was written in 1997 for a conference at Locarno, and was published in Italian.

Many seem to be comfortable with this state of affairs. Some philosophers have already begun to argue that human beings need not have a 'home', that the idea of home is itself a red herring. One must, they argue, get reconciled to living with a transient sense of self. To others not so philosophically minded, displacement and the psychology of exile look like fashionable diseases of the rich and the powerful. For those not infected by these diseases, cultural continuities and settled communities carry a touch of tiredness and *ennui*, and look terribly antiquated.

Adjustment to the culture of exile is more disorienting and unnerving in India, because many of us are accustomed to viewing India as stable and unchanging. We have not cared to notice that the psychology of displacement is becoming a serious presence in South Asia, and our public life is quickly adjusting to this presence. However, politicians everywhere are a superbly alert lot. They never wait for the political scientist or psychologist to guide their action. The politicians of South Asia have grasped the power and the reach of the culture of psychological lability. They have sensed that, though it probably is still the culture of a minority, it offers immense political opportunities, especially for quick, media-driven, large-scale mobilization. Anticipating the future, many populist politicians have refurbished their platforms and campaigns to cater to the passions of the banished and the uprooted.

This has given a strange new status in India to the idea of continuity, turning it into a potent political myth. The more Indians feel uprooted and live with a culture of flux, the more they seek small, symbolic areas of a turbulence-free life of predictability and continuity. They demand psychological security and cultural constancy of an order that even a highly stable, isolated society cannot supply.

In this respect, what the Partition riots in 1946–8, which uprooted nearly 20 million people, could not do, massive urbanization backed by development, and now, globalization have promised to do. The toll of development in India, conservative estimates tell us, has been more than 55 million. Many communities in

India are already predominantly communities of the displaced. For instance, one-third of the country's 250 different tribes have been displaced. Some tribes are now entirely tribes of refugees, and their deculturation and disintegration as communities seems complete.

Some other communities are being been pushed into urban–industrial life by the loss of their traditional vocations, social discrimination, or sheer exploitation. When India became independent, its urban population was less than 70 million. Today, though the population of urban Indians has risen by only 5 per cent, it is already around 250 million, larger than all except three countries in the world. Demographers expect the figure to double in a few decades. We do not have comparable figures for Indians who have moved from one language area to another, from villages to urban slums, from family vocations to blue-collar jobs. These urban Indians show the characteristic psychology of the uprooted, and they too have begun to bend the Indian political culture to their needs. Many communities of traditional artisans, especially the Muslims and the Dalits among them, fall in this category. They are increasingly migrating to cities and assembling in slums, the down-market yards of the culture of exile.

There is a growing mass of environmental refugees, too. Prosperity acquired through large-scale cultivation of cash crops and through industrialization of agriculture has led to mega-dams, increasing corporatization of and limits on direct access to water, deforestation, and rising salinity.[1] These in turn are leading to further uprooting and a deepening sense of dislocation. Thus, the Farakka barrage and the destruction of the Ganges has not only led to emigration from Southwest Bangladesh to India, but also from Bihar, and to a lesser extent, from some districts in West Bengal

[1] Very few in South Asia would have believed, even 30 years ago, that one could become a millionaire by selling drinkable water, or that the state of the environment would become an object of professional study and spawn a whole series of new disciplines from eco-philosophy to environmental engineering.

to other parts of India. And the Ganges being the Ganges, this has also led to a sense of disjunction with the past. Such psychological discontinuities are only going to grow in frequency and scope.

* * *

This is, however, an age of exile in more than one sense. When we nowadays talk of a global order dominated by one super-power, that power represents, among other things, the power of immigrants and the culture of the displaced. For the surviving superpower is the ultimate prototype of a culture of displacement, transience, and exile, and a symbol of the best possible use of these states of mind. American culture upholds public values that can survive mainly in a society of refugees. But then, while few will disagree that America is primarily a culture of the uprooted, fewer have noticed that it is a culture that denies that it is atypical. Indeed, it prefers to see itself as a model for the rest of the world—a haven where the poor, the powerless, and the discarded of other lands come and remake their lives. That self-confident culture of exile now seeks to reorder the world in its own image. The entire second half of the twentieth century can be read as an unfolding of that effort.

The self that uprooting spawns has a few specific features. In its more healthy form, it takes the shape of what Robert Lifton calls a protean self. It is flexible, adaptable, and seems particularly suited to a situation of flux. But there is another part of the story that is unravelling at a rapid pace in India. The obverse of the pro-tean self is a clandestine self that confronts India's over-stretched modernity mainly through religious and ethnic chauvinism and ultra-nationalism. Few recognize the promise of psychological security and 'therapeutic' solace that fundamentalism and nation-alism have begun to offer in this part of the world. Violence can sometimes bind together a fractured self and give a false sense of community. Those living with a dislocated cultural self-definition, precariously perched on a fluid sense of the self can, for that very reason, continually seek a grand national, religious, or ethnic community to restore a sense of cultural—and through it, personal—continuity. They may not be open to serious political appeals or to deep analysis of public life, but they are always open to populist slogans and demagoguery, especially of the kind that promises new brands of easy 'pseudo-solidarity'.

Predictably, South Asian slums, like the South American and East Asian ones, are becoming the ultimate targets of mobilization by every kind of extremists—from ethno-religious chauvinists to crime syndicates that, like the *cosa nostra*, promise the individual a smaller, close-knit, intimate community, and a chance to escape loneliness and massification. The 'anti-social elements' of whom political analysts and journalists in South Asia talk incessantly as the main actors in communal or caste violence, are the fringe of a larger social sector that is contiguous with the Indian middle class, a fact that the latter loves to forget.

This sector is going to be particularly susceptible to the appeals of a destructive, uncritical nationalism that depends on centralized, mass-media-based communications and mobilization. India may not yet be a mass society, but the process of massification has created spaces for ideologies that promise to fill the void that the breakdown of communities has produced. The promise is based on packaged versions of faiths that cannot otherwise survive under globalized capitalism, and give vent to the simmering violence of the uprooted urban Indians constantly seeking new targets.

The psychology of exile underwrites a number of personality traits that have been much adored in the folklore of development: greater individual initiative, enterprise, competitiveness, and a desperate attempt to achieve as a technology of survival. Studies also show that immigrants are more pushy, risk-taking, and less burdened by principles of sociality and shared cultural norms in their professional and business deals. They are also often overly aggressive within the family and outside, and their trust in others is low. The aggressiveness and distrust acquire a dangerous edge because the uprooted also usually have a stronger sense of invulnerability. One of the unnoticed findings of the once-popular studies of achievement motive was the links between mobility, uprooting, and high achievement motivation. Indeed, to complete the picture of the contemporary ideal of the achieving person, David McClelland borrowed the imagery of Hermes, the Hellenic god who started travelling from the day he was born.

Hermes presumably had a place to come back to, and that place of return must have been for many immigrants a living reality for centuries. Today, the idea of a place to return to has primarily a mythic status and is available mainly as a consumable fantasy. Vladimir Nabokov's Russia and Salman Rushdie's India are obvious examples. When, by a happy conjunction of events, that place of return becomes a geographical and political reality, as in the case of Israel, the memories of past victimhood push the previously exiled to build a violent, dehumanized, garrison state. That state too has to perpetually look for new targets who could be exiled the way most citizens of Israel were over the centuries.

9

The Peasant*

The peasant is a multivalent idea in our times. It arouses strange passions and often brings out the worst and the best in human nature—from genocidal rage to cultivated apathy to dissenting moral visions. The idea is often autonomous with the social sector or vocation it is supposed to describe. As a result, while the proportion of peasants in the world population has dwindled dramatically in the last 200 years, their importance as a cultural–psychological category has not. Indeed, the social sector or the occupational group it represents has often been forced to bear the brunt of our tortuous, love–hate relationship with the idea of the peasant.

The peasants have been the target of virtually every form of radical social engineering during the last two centuries. They have defined most utopias and visions of desirable societies that continue to shape our lives—directly or indirectly, or as the constituents of a dystopia that we have to learn to fear. Indeed, only in recent decades have we tried to break out of the nineteenth-century visions of

* An earlier version of this essay was first published in Vinay Lal and Ashis Nandy (eds.), *The Future of Knowledge and Culture: A Dictionary for the 21st Century* (New Delhi: Penguin [now Penguin Random House India], 2005) pp. 211–17.

desirable societies that almost invariably defined progress and social evolution by the movement from a peasant lifestyle to an urban–industrial culture. At least some of the new works on the shape of things to come do not seem to get embroiled in a debate on the sustainability or moral stature of a peasant lifestyle. However, that is a recent trend, and none of these new intellectual exercises have yet caught public fancy or become influential among the policy elite.

All urban-industrial societies—modern or partly modern—have emerged by explicitly repudiating peasant lifestyles and the state of mind reportedly associated with the peasantry, whether the association is true or false, real or imaginary, 'natural' or 'unnatural'. Industrialization began in Europe with the Enclosure Movement, which, whatever might have been its stated goals, was basically an attempt to re-engineer the peasants into an industrial proletariat. And, one of the last states in the world to complete its industrialization, Singapore, saw its peasants, along with their pigs and poultry, being huddled into apartment buildings as part of an attempt to convert them into a developmental resource, that is, a prospective industrial working force.

Such projects have often acquired a murderous look in despotic, self-righteous regimes. During the twentieth century, in the Soviet Union and Maoist China, peasants were victims of state-mentored genocides—in Russia in the name of equity through collectivization, and in both Russia and China in the name of a state-designed, non-exploitative society through man-made, avoidable famines. According to the relatively conservative estimates of R.J. Rummell, in 1932–3, about 5 million Ukrainian peasants were deliberately starved to death, and during 1930–37, 6.5 million better-off peasants or peasants resisting collectivization were slaughtered. In 1943, in the man-made Bengal famine, the 3 million victims were all peasants and their dependents. They died for the sake of the British war effort in the eastern sector, when there was enough food in Bengal. For the moment, I am ignoring the case of the horrendous, man-made, Irish famines, mainly because they targeted not so much the Irish peasants as the Irish people.

Such exterminations were not widely condemned—indeed, they were often condoned or whitewashed by well-meaning, thinking people, partly because the idea of transformative politics, which demands blood sacrifices, satisfies some deep-seated, primitive, human need, and helps us to grapple with some of our core fantasies. The fantasy of fighting for a just cause or bringing about radical social change, by meting out death to hundreds of thousands, has had a peculiar appeal for social engineers. It seems to bestow omnipotence upon insecure rulers and millennial political movements.

However, these organized exterminations were often not condemned also because, during the last two centuries, most progressive thinkers have thought poorly of peasants. Peasants have been seen not only as irrational and traditional, but as specifically steeped in stereotypes and prejudices, superstitions and magic. Politically, peasants have looked irredeemable, perhaps because they have been notoriously tough to organize along modern lines.

Not surprisingly, during the nineteenth century, a century that saw a certain innocent, uncritical commitment to modernity and social evolutionism as the final indices of progress, there were systematic efforts to redefine all peasants as redundant and disposable—as useless drags on societies, who should be ideally supplanted by a new agricultural working class given to industrialized farming and driven by technological innovations—a theme that has recently staged a comeback under a new guise, as part of the package called globalization. Till Mohandas Karamchand Gandhi and Mao Tse-tung began to sing a different tune, the peasant was popularly perceived as an impossible target of social engineering and transformative politics. Karl Marx called the peasant a sack of potatoes, and spoke of the idiocy of village life. The great eastern civilizations that he held in contempt, as ahistorical, static entities, were predictably agrarian societies. He accepted colonialism as an agent of history, despite recognizing the oppression and violence it unleashed, because it opened such societies to historical changes.

That idea of the peasant lasted a very long time. In poor societies—now euphemistically called developing countries—that constitute the so-called third world after World War II—peasants appeared to be the main stumbling block to social change and agricultural innovations. Literally hundreds of papers in journals of social sciences and dozens of books were written on the subject, and on strategies to change the peasant attitudes to time, leisure, money, occupation, family, and above all, agricultural practices in general and agricultural innovations in particular.

Strangely, when new seeds and pesticides and irrigation systems were introduced in these societies, the peasants took to them rather quickly, though often with a clear touch of scepticism. Indeed, today, in retrospect, it seems that they sometimes accepted the innovations a bit too eagerly. Often living at the margins of survival, oppressed and exploited by unjust land-ownership patterns and land relations, and targeted by the rulers and local tyrants eager to extract surplus from them, the peasantry perhaps saw in the new agronomy an escape from poverty and drudgery. In some societies, they were already softened up by famines, wars, and other major social and political upheavals. Yet, few states were impressed by that adaptability. The peasants still looked to them incapable of handling modern agronomy, cash crops meant for the global market, and scientific farm management. Convinced that development had to be defined as the means of siphoning off resources from the agrarian sectors to the cities, many third-world regimes particularly resented, what looked to them like peasant obstinacy and peasant cunningness in matters of social change, subverting major state projects in, what some psychoanalysts might call, a passive–aggressive manner.

However, just when the image of the peasant began to look less recalcitrant and more change-prone, just when the Green Revolution began to spread in South and East Asia and in parts of Latin America, and the re-imaging of the peasant as a major tool of history initiated by Gandhi and Mao began to seep into popular consciousness, the Soviet Union collapsed. And an astonished world found the famous Russian peasant of Leo Tolstoy and the Narodniks pathetically waiting, without a clue, for instructions from the now-extinct Soviet policy-makers—the agricultural bureaucrats and the laboratory-driven agronomists—who had come to set the pace of Russian agriculture after asserting their dominance through a series of particularly cruel, genocidal interventions. Evidently, progressivism had done its job. The Russian peasants had obviously lost some of their traditional, crafty, robust scepticism and their self-confidence in their own lifestyle, practices, and beliefs.

The Chinese peasantry met a similar fate in the second half of the twentieth century. Even the formidable Indian peasants today seem to be caught in the same rat trap. They have modernized themselves enthusiastically and at break-neck speed. In the process, they have become more, not less dependent on forces outside their world. During the last three decades, an epidemic of suicides has broken out among farmers in three of the most prosperous states in India, where modern agricultural practices are triumphant. And to spike our ideas of what constitutes progress and healthy development, the poorest states in the country, still ill-governed and mired in exploitative land relations, have seen virtually no instance of suicide. According to some estimates, more than 300,000 farmers have killed themselves already in what could be called an invisible genocide. Indeed, the number of suicides has long exceeded the total number of those killed by what India's power elite calls cross-border terrorism and all the wars independent India has fought put together. Only the news of the self-destruction of farmers is usually reported in the inside pages of newspapers as minor misfortunes, and as a sad but accidental by-product of the process of modernization.

The epidemic of suicides, in exactly those parts of India that are the most progressive and are globalizing themselves most efficiently, could turn out to be the final denouement of the fate of the traditional peasantry in Asia. Agri-business and industrialized farming by multinational corporations have arrived. A lifestyle and a vocation at least 4,000 years old is at last facing extinction.

10

The Final Obituary

Death, Responsibility, and Sanjay Gandhi[*]

Ashis Nandy: Good evening, Mrs Gandhi.

Indira Gandhi: Good evening. I don't understand this. You want to have an imaginary dialogue with me?

AN: Yes. Sometimes an imaginary dialogue becomes the only real one.

IG: (confused) Well!

AN: I want to speak to you about Sanjay. His second death anniversary, as you know, was on 23 June. What do you have to say on the occasion, now that two years have passed?

IG: (heaves a sigh of relief and reels out mechanically) Sanjay was a young man who stood for political performance. He had courage and fought against his dedicated enemies single-handedly. As a youth leader he was one of the first to take action on demographic, ecological, and urban development programmes. He even dared to be unpopular for the sake of the nation....

* First published in *Debonair* (August 1982): 40–1, 68.

Young intellectuals will not acknowledge his contributions to Indian public life; you will in fact denigrate him because he was a doer. But the people who voted us back to power knew his strengths. They made a clear choice between Sanjay and his enemies. No talk about the flaws of Indian democracy can wipe away that fact.

AN: I agree with your assessment of your son. I am here not to attack Sanjay but to mourn a young man who did not have to die so early. And to grieve with a mother so captive to her public image that she could not even fully mourn her son.

IG: (suspicious) But I am told you were against him.

AN: I was against him as long as he lived. In this culture the rules of history apply, if at all, only to the living. For the dead, there are the rules of mythography. Instead of becoming the subjects of life history, they become subject matters of life stories.

IG: (defensively) Are you suggesting that anything good said about Sanjay is a myth?

AN: I am suggesting that the memories of public figures are useful in this culture mainly as a means of reaffirming the right values. In a culture that has to uphold such values against tremendous odds, each life story is a text on ethics. The modern West is concerned with the truthfulness of a biography; traditional India is concerned with using a biography as an example of a good life, serving as a guide for the living. The former seeks a critical view of a person and his time; the latter seeks standards by which the present can be criticized. The so-called truthful life histories with their amoral, impersonal, empirical sweep are considered worthless by most Indians, at least by those outside the modern sector.

IG: I don't understand what you are saying. Have you or have you not changed your mind about Sanjay?

AN: Sanjay has changed my mind by dying. He has brought different rules into play. They are the rules of life story.

IG: You are playing with words.

AN: Such play is allowed by a life story; only life histories are supposed to resemble a scientific discourse.

IG: (knits her brows) Why have you come to me? What can I say about the strange issues you are raising?

AN: You are not dead and you are in power; the rules of life history may apply to you. In any case, you are one of the few who may have to live with Sanjay's life history for the rest of your life.

IG: What does it mean?

AN: The reality of Sanjay may haunt you.

IG: (more suspicious) How?

AN: By reminding you of the choices that were available to you in life, not in myths.

IG: (now curious but half-convinced that the interview will proceed on the plane of the absurd) For instance?

AN: To start with the trivial, if the Janata regime had managed to put Sanjay in jail for his Emergency antics, he would have been still living.

IG: (with a touch of sarcasm) You mean to say we should not have contested the cases? You don't think that would have been cowardly and a step towards political suicide?

AN: Politics is not the end of life, and Sanjay has shown that there are other forms of suicide too...(apologetically) Frankly, I suspect that our dreams always come home to roost. You dreamt of unlimited, total politics. You lived in a world of instruments and instrumentalities. Your son shared that worldview. To him, the Maruti car company was politics and the anti-Maruti opinion was politics; the Janata government's cases against him were politics; his fight against them was politics. And his final successes were political. This confirmed his faith that everything was politics, even decisions such as who flies which aeroplanes when, who gives the permission to fly, and what decides flight safety. Ultimately, he died of politics.

IG: But all these *were* politics.

AN: Of course they were, but sanity demanded that some attempts be made to identify the non-political, moral components in these decisions or situations. The wise postulate such a moral order even when none seems to exist.... Nothing is purely political; nothing is entirely apolitical. In the long run, it is better politics—mind you, not only better morality—to remember this ground rule. Like good theoreticians who know the limits of their theories, good politicians know where to draw the line. After all, politics is about self-interest, and one's own death is the very negation of one's self-interest. By dying mindlessly, a politician proves the failure of his politics.

IG: (obstinately) You do not know what you are talking about. Sanjay was an excellent politician. He entered politics when pushed to the wall and made a good job of it. Certainly, he did better than the sons of Morarji Desai and Jagjivan Ram in India, and those of Sirimavo Bandaranaike, Chiang Kai-shek, and Kim Il-Sung outside. In 1980, it was his organizational skills which brought me back to power, not the other way round. People seem to forget that when they criticize me for pushing him to the forefront.

AN: He brought you to power. But he himself succumbed to an acute case of politics.

IG: Why do you repeat that peculiar statement?

AN: Remember Air Vice Marshal Jafar Zaheer? When he, as the director of civil aviation, objected to Sanjay's flying habits, he lost his job. His objections could be seen as an expression of aviation norms; Sanjay and you chose to see them only as political ploys. Sanjay later proved that Zaheer's warnings were not purely political—by dying, of course.

IG: Zaheer was against Sanjay, wasn't he? At least that is what many of us suspected.

AN: Depends on how you look at things. In the very long run, we might all be dead, but in the not-so-long run, only some are needlessly dead. On that plane, Zaheer was *with* Sanjay. So were on another plane, the Janata chaps. Even Rajiv was with him; he often told Sanjay not to try mock heroics in the air. Dhirendra Brahmachari was never with him; to him, as to your other factotums, Sanjay was an instrument. They did not have the courage of true family friends to stop Sanjay from being careless about norms. They were not their brother's keepers. They egged him on and facilitated his self-destruction. That is why Brahmachari had to glorify Sanjay's death as that of a tiger cub.

IG: (wistfully) In the final analysis, Sanjay and I could only depend on each other.

AN: You *think* you were with your son always. You were not. In fact, if you had refused to be with him on some issues, you could be with him today.

IG: You are speaking as if I wished Sanjay's death.

AN: I am speaking as if responsibility must always be shared.

IG: (bitterly but also with a touch of pain) Doesn't this apply also to Sanjay's actions which you criticized? Wasn't Sanjay a scapegoat for people like you? Are *you* not responsible?

AN: Of course. We in this society produced Sanjay, nurtured him, and then, when society's tolerance limits were crossed, destroyed him. We destroyed him the way we have traditionally destroyed our enemies—by overtly giving in and doing nothing. Sanjay's rootlessness, his simple-minded solutions to India's problems, his ruthless interventions when these solutions were resisted, his faith in pure politics, his ideology of a hard state—all these were derived from the political culture of India's Westernized middle classes and the middle-class intelligentsia. And when things went wrong, they turned against Sanjay the way we always turn bitterly against a part of ourselves which we want to disown. In another context, that is called exorcism.

You, too, Mrs Gandhi, were often an indirect instrument of these classes. You depended on pure politics and were left only with Sanjay. You wanted around you fully loyal pure politicians—which is a contradiction in terms for anyone except a close relative. You too played up to Sanjay's simple, conventional 'wisdom' and his crude activism. You, I, everybody collaborated in producing the Sanjay phenomenon.... All suffering is interrelated; so is all responsibility. I, for one, plead guilty. More so for often using overly impersonal social forces as political explanations. That has been my way of disowning responsibility.

IG: (distant, cautious, and yet vaguely curious) You are a strange person. What do you do for a living?

AN: Some call me a psychologist, others a political sociologist. At the moment, I am a mythographer, trying to find out the minimum ethical frame with which this polity can survive—unheroically. A healthy, well-functioning democracy not only tends to be unheroic, it avoids hosting dramatic spectacles.

IG: (mildly apprehensive still, but also at last having 'read' the interviewer as one of those anti-political, dim-witted moralists, who provide grist to the Gandhian mill, she is now trying to make political use of this reading) If you are so interested in morals, I hope you will be truthful when you write up this interview on Sanjay.

AN: I am not interested in truth; I am interested in constructions of truth.

IG: That is another kind of politics.

AN: Certainly. But not in the sense you imply.

BOOK II

NEGOTIATING NECROPHILIA

11

Breakfast with Evil

Vijay Tendulkar as a Social Theorist of Violence*

To most of those who will read this note, the chronicle of the first five decades of independent India is a history of modernization, industrialization, and the emergence of a democratic polity. Less frequently, it is the story of myriad communities turning reluctantly into a nation, with growing pockets of mass culture and atomized individuals. Few seem aware that that there are people in India who read the five decades as a story of gradual but consistent increase in violence—manifest and covert, active and passive, outer- and inner-directed.

Dramatic or spectacular social changes extract a heavy toll on any society. After a point, many begin to feel uprooted, deracinated, and buffeted by forces that strike like natural calamities,

* This essay was written as a foreword to Vijay Tendulkar, *The Last Days of Sardar Patel and the Mime Players: Two Screenplays* (Delhi: Permanent Black, 2001). Also published in *The Hindu*, 2 September 2001.

without notice, without scope for appeal or remedial action. The uprooted then come to see the new world unfolding before their eyes as one running on principles and conventions that are clearly disjunctive with the older moral order, ways of life, and familiar gods and goddesses. It is not easy to live with such an experience, and the result, often, is vague, unfocussed anger, anomie, and anxiety that become nagging, integral parts of the self. The blend can be deadly. Violence—wide-ranging, unpredictable, seemingly unprovoked—is almost always a natural outcome of it.

Few want to study such violence. For our political sensitivities, visions of a desirable society, systems of knowledge, and techniques of social interpretation are all enmeshed with the dislocation we see around us. We suspect that we may be culpable, and we do not want to know more about that part of the story. In this sense, the violence unfolding before us is doubly orphaned: it has neither self-exploring parents nor willing observers.

Vijay Tendulkar is an exception. His consistent, prolonged engagement with human aggression has made him one of the most distinguished social theorists of violence in the country. He will be surprised by this compliment and may find it difficult to gulp. He considers himself a writer of plays and film scripts on a wide variety of subjects, not a closet philosopher or a sociologist who has missed his vocation. Like all prolific writers, he has other incarnations; it is a trifle unjust to read his entire work as a commentary on human violence. However, those caught in the hinges of post-Independence intellectual life and public affairs in India cannot but recognize the way Tendulkar has, over the last few decades, scanned the life-world of contemporary Indians to identify the sources and nature of the violence that has come to pattern it. Even when violence is not ostensibly his theme, it casts its shadow on his characters—their cultivated or panicky reactions to it, their numbing fear of their own selves, and above all, their desperate attempt to recover agency through pointless violence. By bringing their world close to ours through his creative powers, he has shaped the way we look at ourselves.

* * *

Tendulkar's perspective on violence is bifocal. In works like *Giddh* (staged in 1971; written in 1961) and, less directly, in *Shantata, Court Chalu Ahe* (1968), *Sakharam Binder* (1972), *Ghasiram Kotwal* (1973), and *Kanyadan* (1983), violence tends to become an end in itself. It is the easiest way left for many ordinary citizens to cope with their fractured selves and problems of living. No longer does violence come from ideology, faith, or even self-interest. On the contrary, it seeks outlet through ideology, faith, and perceived self-interest, and latches on to these 'causes' to find public expression and legitimacy. In this paradoxical world, violence is prior to its causes.

Tendulkar's violence, therefore, is sometimes tinged with— as psychiatrists might diagnose it—the psychopathic. It carries the impress of an empty interpersonal world and a maimed conscience. *The Mime Players* in this volume is an example. It is a film script that has grown out of a powerful Bengali story by Dibyendu Palit. However, the original story does not possess the disturbing ambience of the sinister, psychopathic, narcissistic violence and the uncanny, stylized, surreal counter-violence that confronts the reader. That ambience is almost entirely Tendulkar's.

However, while such violence may not have clear causes, it has sources. It is free-floating mainly because these sources are inaccessible to the conscious selves of the violent and their victims. In many of Tendulkar's works, you stumble inadvertently upon these sources. He often invokes a milieu where the individual is caught in a crosscurrent of social forces that he or she does not understand. Buffeted by these forces, the individual finds the traditional concept of evil diffused, fragmented, or invalidated at every step. Evil lurks everywhere, yet it rarely takes tangible form, and when it is tangible, the victim's survival frequently demands his or her silence. In such a milieu, violence—unprovoked and gratuitous—becomes a way of fighting unknown demons outside, and more crucially, within. It becomes a means of grappling with a world shot through with an unpredictable, dangerous, undefined evil that threatens to destroy you unless you strike out at it pre-emptively, through your version of violence.

Violence can also come from attempts to exorcize parts of one's own self that have been violated, and to fight other parts that have made unacceptable compromises with a ruthless, cruel world. One hates oneself for being a victim and tamely giving in to aggressors. One blames oneself even for being a passive, impotent witness of someone else's victimization. But that self-hatred can also lead to self-destruction, and the fear of self-destruction helps the person to project the hatred outwards into the interpersonal world. One sets up demons, as targets of hate, so that they symbolize disowned parts of one's own self. The anomic violence that finds expression in religious and ethnic riots in the lonely streets of urban India is an example of that self-hatred.

There is a third, related, but less obvious coordinate in this anthropology of violence: Victims of violence turn out to be excellent tools of violence. Being at the receiving end of a system of dominance, being a helpless witness to oppression or corruption—as happens to the protagonist of *Ardhasatya* (1983)— produces a psychology of vulnerability. Such victims hate themselves for allowing others to objectify them, for turning them into something akin to merchandize—saleable and purchasable by the highest bidder. Victims of this kind hold themselves culpable. The resulting self-denigration and vague search for mastery over fate propels them to do to someone else what has been done to them. The heroine of *Nishant* (1975) is only apparently a passive witness; a part of her identifies with the killers of her husband and his family. This is not simple revenge or scapegoating. For she is not even aware of her own vicarious violence, so close is the target of violence to her. In the domestic space, such violence could be the prerogative of women and children; in workplaces, subordinates or colleagues who cannot strike back. In *Giddh*, it is an infirm father.

Such displaced violence is not always a matter of volition or controlled choice. The personality of the passive witness is often so distorted—violence, humiliation, and exploitation in daily life can be so overwhelming—that the traumatized begin to seek voice and audibility through their violence: as does the protagonist in *Akrosh* (1980). Violence speaks, and through it speak the secret histories of hatred, humiliation, and oppression. Even outwardly extraverted victims, through their episodic engagements with violence, acquire a new, hidden depth in personality, as does the anti-hero in *Kamala* (1982). A rich, extravagant underworld of violent fantasies crystallizes and constitutes a substratum of the victim–aggressor's personality. Years ago, in the wake of World War II, some psychoanalysts identified the forms of sadomasochism that underlie mass violence and authoritarianism. Tendulkar's diagnosis parallels that discovery, and has ominous implications for the long-term well-being of Indian public life.

The three coordinates of violence are silently at work even when Tendulkar deals with issues and situations involving little overt violence, as for instance in *The Last Days of Sardar Patel*. For violence can be latent not merely in statecraft and organized politics, it can also power the most trivial forms of everyday politics. For an ordinary citizen, living life as a silent victim of silent violence or fighting inner demons in a situation of flux, ordinary social exchanges sometimes become a means of coping with violence. In this respect, Tendulkar is close to the other great, time-transcending chronicler of violence that South Asia has produced in recent decades, Sadaat Hasan Manto. Neither gives any respite to the reader. As you read them, you read yourself. And it is not a pleasant experience.

Readers should be warned that Tendulkar never guarantees a good bedtime read, not even when dealing with 'dead' history. He never fails to make you feel that you have entered a dentist's chamber with an undiagnosed abscess in the molars. The two scripts within these covers give you ample scope to dislike his world. You should be well prepared to put the book down as a perverse, ill-motivated intrusion into your private life.

12

How to Live Happily with Torture[*]

It is said we live in modern times
In the civilized year of seventy-nine
But when I look around, all I see
Is modern torture, pain and hypocrisy...

As the bureaucrats, speculators and presidents alike
Pin on their dirty, stinking, happy smiles tonight
The lonely prisoner will cry out from within his tomb
And tomorrow's wretch will leave its mother's womb.
                                —Bobby Sands in 'Modern Times'

The human body is a site where power has been negotiated since time immemorial. From attempts to establish dominance through physical strength in collective combat to self-inflicted suffering to acquire spiritual or temporal power through divine intervention,

* This essay is based on a presentation made at a meeting of Amnesty International in New Delhi in 2009, and a column written in *The Telegraph*, 25 June 2014, on the eve of the United Nations International Day in Support of Victims of Torture. A later version was published in Mercy Kappen, M. Sudhir Selvaraj, and S. Theodore Baskaran (eds), *Re-visioning Paradigms* (Bangalore: Visthar Publications, 2015), pp. 91–9.

from spectator sports to rape, the use of the body has been an inalienable part of power play in both everyday reality and fantasy life. However, this power is negotiated power, and frequently a contested one.

These negotiations shape not merely the nature of the power but also the persons negotiating, willingly or unwillingly, and the outcome or aftermath of the negotiations. These can be life-altering, though not often in predictable ways. The unpredictability increases when one of the parties is an unwilling participant. In both rape and torture, the dominant ones often begin as defeated participants. For they know their persuasive powers have failed and they have to get what they want through naked force. This knowledge makes them doubly determined, cruel, and ruthless. But the story does not end there either.

* * *

More than 30 years ago, in 1988, an agitated Turkish scholar in the United States brought to me a handbook on torture.[1] It was a handbook meant not for victims, physicians, or human rights activists, but for torturers. The one who showed me the book was outraged by it; she thought it to be a weird instance of America's cultural decadence induced by its global dominance. Shoddily printed, published from a small town in the southern United States, and sprinkled with ghoulish humour and some line drawings to help its readers and prospective users, it was a mail-order book reportedly circulating widely and quite openly. When reading the text, one could not miss the writer's sadomasochistic glee in detailing the actual process and technology of torture.

For all I know, the entire enterprise might have been a tongue-in-cheek effort to tap the secret fantasies of readers the way pornographic books or movies try to do, and to make some quick money. Esoteric business ventures and professions are not unknown in

---

[1] Richard W. Krousher, *Physical Interrogation Techniques* (Port Townsend, P.O. Box 197, WA: Loompanics Unlimited, no date).

the United States. Yet, strangely enough, despite all attempts of the author or authors to banish all thought, ethics, and compassion from the text, the book also made it obvious that torture was a form of human relationship. It was a dark, pathological, extreme form of relationship, but it was relationship nonetheless. The unintended message of the book was that no torture was possible outside human relationship.

This relationship is always triangular. It involves the victim, the torturer, and the onlookers or—it comes to the same thing—the ones who come to know of organized torture in their society and either order and condone it, or remain silent. Let us call them, following novelist Bernhard Schlink, 'accommodators' or 'accepters'.[2] They usually justify their passive complicity or the silence of their conscience in the name of 'higher values' that may range from public order and the nation's territorial integrity to abolition of terrorism and defence of the constitution. Paradoxically, democratic constitutions usually do not sanction torture, and the practice of torture in democratic societies becomes, invariably, a game of fighting one attack on the constitution with another. The only difference is that, while the secessionists or terrorists are usually from parties or movements outside the ken of 'normal' politics, torture by state agencies quickly becomes part of the institutional fabric of the state, and over time, a durable part of the culture of politics.

There is a fourth possible participant in the politics of torture—the citizens or the organizations that reject torture and seek to eliminate it from society. They are frequently weak or invisible in a polity, and their focus is naturally on the victim. This is as it should be. But if one's aim is to prevent society from being drawn into a culture of torture, one must never forget the torturers and the audience that sees or comes to know of instances of torture and then continues to live, comfortably or otherwise, with that memory and knowledge. This is because there has emerged in many societies an over-concern with what happens in the high streets of politics

[2] Bernhard Schlink, *The Reader* (New York: Random House, 1997), p. 104.

and cultivated forgetfulness about the happenings in the alleys or backstreets of power. I shall highlight here the second part of the story. I remember that a very useful handbook on torture edited by Metin Basoglu began with an epigraph from a survivor's testimony: 'I didn't mind the pain so much. It was the cries next door I couldn't bear.'[3] In large parts of the world, people are learning to live a normal life by cultivating a form of deafness to such cries. In the South Asian region, in at least five countries—Afghanistan, Pakistan, India, Sri Lanka, and Bangladesh—such deafness has taken an epidemic form.

In my youth, I read Franz Fanon's remarks on torture during the Algerian freedom struggle. At the time Fanon was not a popular figure in India's knowledge industry. Brainwashed by bloodthirsty, ultra-positivist versions of Marxism, the Indian Left ignored him as an esoteric, Francophone psychiatrist who had nothing to say to them. But my disciplinary interest at the time, psychoanalytic sociology, brought me close to him. This paid me handsome dividends. Fanon was the first to tear through my innocence and describe vividly the psychosocial consequences of torture.[4] His theory of colonialism included a sharp awareness of what happened to the torturer outside his 'work'. The torturer carried the violence with him into his family and personal life, and—this was tacit, given that Fanon's theory of oppression neatly separated the oppressor from the oppressed and did talk of violence as a legitimate means of breaking with the past—could not protect his personality from the ravages of his profession. As in the case of the soldier, the torturer, too, is vulnerable to various forms of psychogenic and psychosomatic ailments and the consequences of trauma. He, too, carries the scars of his noble duty.

It is probable that a small proportion of torturers have clear-cut sadistic streaks in them. This minority—even when they come to torture inadvertently through posting, transfer, or promotion—may

---

[3] Metin Basoglu (ed.), *Torture and Its Consequences: Current Treatment and Approaches* (Cambridge: Cambridge University Press, 1992), p. viii.

[4] Franz Fanon, *Black Skin, White Masks* (New York: Grove Press, 1967).

come to enjoy their occupation. It may click with something deep within them of which they themselves have not been aware till then. They are like ordinary, law-abiding citizens who come across accounts of torture and cruelty in newspapers, on television, and in official reports, and develop a taste for them and begin to justify them as a political or strategic necessity.

It is also possible that when there are, in a team of torturers, some who have eroticized their violent predispositions, the cultural psychology of the team begins to change, and what was previously ethically reprehensible, illegal, instrumental violence becomes a passionate, pleasurable, psychopathic, or pornographic venture, serving similar needs of the invisible power-wielders who hold the torturers in leash and of a section of the onlookers or acceptors. Torture then begins to become an end in itself. We all know of powerful rulers, sophisticated and cultivated in other ways, who opened unintended, transient affairs with torture and found themselves driven by these affairs deeper and deeper into the world of sadomasochism.

As in the case of a soldier, it is not easy to produce a torturer. At the end of World War II, it was found that only 15 per cent of the soldiers fired their guns in the battlefield to kill.[5] These soldiers were well-trained and courageous; they did not run away or flinch from battle. But it was easier to be brave than to master the art of

---

[5] Gwynne Dyer, *War* (London: Bodley Head, 1986), pp. 118–19. Dyer's data come from a study of S.L.A. Marshall, a United States Army colonel. Though Marshall's research later became controversial, it led to radical changes in the training of soldiers in the 1950s; they were now trained not to shoot but to kill. Dyer traces the enormous rise in the incidence of Post-traumatic Stress Disorder or PTSD to this change. The moral inhibitions that are bypassed in contemporary military training methods seem to return to take their revenge later on. War veterans earlier mostly showed a pronounced tendency towards alcoholism, depression, and less frequently, suicide. Now there are more instances of psychotic or quasi-psychotic episodes, and crimes of gratuitous, meaningless, or sick violence and cruelty.

killing. Of course, the army establishments, when they saw the data, were not amused. They did not consider bravery as an end; they wanted soldiers to be efficient killing machines. They recognized that it would take more intense training, including symbolic rituals of rebirth and rites of passage, to make killing a more impersonal act, and to acquire the required levels of 'soldierly conduct'. The American Marine Corps is now well known for taking its recruits through a process that turns them into hardened combatants and killers. Becoming a marine is now a matter of psychological rebirth too. The Foreign Legion of France has a similar tradition.

All modern armies now must have a system that can produce killers, and some armies also make sure that they have a steady supply of torturers to meet exigencies. To train efficient torturers, a regime must also set up institutions which, officially or unofficially, would share a culture that condones torture and accepts it as necessary and legitimate. Those who have read Dave Grossman's revealing and often-disturbing book, *On Killing*, will know what I mean.[6] Grossman, who has taught in military academies for years and knows his job, shows that killing is a difficult art to master. For resistance to killing is part of our biological inheritance, virtually a species characteristic. To train a person to torture in a face-to-face situation, the trainer faces even tougher hurdles.

However, that resistance can be weakened. Following political psychologist Herbert Kelman, Zygmunt Bauman has specified three conditions under which inner resistance to killing, and by implication, torture, weakens or breaks down: when torture can be inflicted as part of a role; when legitimate authorities, such as political leaders and trained scientists, sanction it; and when, through propaganda or education, target groups are successfully demonized.[7] The first two of these conditions are of course derived from Stanley Milgram's well-known, though controversial studies,

---

[6] Dave Grossman, *On Killing: The Psychological Cost of Learning to Kill in War and Society* (Boston: Little, Brown, 1995); see particularly chapters 1–2.

[7] Zygmunt Bauman, *Modernity and the Holocaust* (Cambridge: Polity Press, 1989).

which show that role-playing and obedience to authority do help transform ordinary law-abiding citizens into killers and torturers.[8]

Once torture is 'normalized' and is made to look like an unavoidable part of statecraft, governance, and day-to-day policing and a necessary adjunct of a national security apparatus, the culture of torture survives the goal or the task for which it might have been used in the first place—to inculcate fear or an extreme sense of humiliation, to extract information to ensure security, or to intimidate dissenters or prospective rebels.[9] Once torture is introduced into a polity, the culture of torture does not die when the original reasons for torture end or the victim dies or the torturer disappears from the scene. The culture of torture has the capacity to become autonomous of its victims and their political causes, for it links up with the institutional frame of a polity and the dominant culture of politics. And it can sometimes do so as easily in a democratic polity as under an authoritarian regime.[10]

[8] Stanley Milgram, *Obedience to Authority: An Experimental View* (New York: Harper and Row, 1974).

[9] Getting vital information through torture from an enemy agent or combatant is always given as an important reason for the persistence of torture, more so if the enemy is as uncompromisingly ruthless, and invisible. Eduardo Galeano has something to say about it. 'The confessions of the tortured are worth little or nothing. Since the days of the Inquisition it has been clear that the information obtained through torture is not credible, or barely so, for the simple reason that pain transforms anyone into a prolific author of fiction. The powers that use torture, on the other hand, reveal their true identity through this grim practice: in the chambers of torment, the commanders take off their masks.' Eduardo Galeano, 'Confessions of the Torturer', *New Internationalist*, November 2004 (373): 5.

[10] For a recent discussion of this linkage, though from another angle, see Philip N.S. Rumney, *Torturing Terrorists: Exploring the Limits of Law, Human Rights and Academic Freedom* (London: Routledge, 2015). For an example of how for this purpose expert opinion and the authority of modern science can be mobilized, see 'Psychologists Shielded US Torture Programme Post-26/11: Report', *The New York Times News Service*, 2015, reproduced at http://www.business-standard.com/ article/

Without the benefit of expert knowledge and access to the right kind of books, we all know this in India but pretend that we do not. We know that when militancy in Punjab ended in the 1990s, it did not mean that the culture of torture, secret killings, and disappearances ended. In fighting the secessionists through extrajudicial killings and use of torture, the Punjab police acquired many of the features of the enemy they were fighting. So when the insurgency ended, the corruption and criminalization of the Punjab police turned them virtually into the state's largest terrorist group. They were available for settling property disputes, abducting unwanted bridegrooms on behalf of choosy or conservative parents, and arbitrating between quarrelling businessmen, all for a fee of course. In Kashmir too, the police and the army have come to resemble the terrorists in many respects, with the ordinary citizens sometimes caught between two sets of terrorists and torturers. Likewise, there is no reason to believe that the killing of delinquent street children in metropolitan Brazil was unrelated to the previous record of the Brazilian army and police under earlier authoritarian regimes (military juntas), and that the easy acceptance of violence in everyday life in Cambodia today bears no relationship with the cruelties of the Khmer Rouge in the 1970s.

Torture chambers, once built, do not collapse on their own, nor are they easily dismantled. Once the torturers die or retire from 'public service', new recruits take their place. Like hangmen, they come from the margins of society or from low-status communities or families with limited life chances. I have heard earnest feminists shrilly demanding the death sentence for all rapists and

---

international/psychologists-shielded-us-torture-programme-post-26-11-report-115071100765_1.html (accessed 27 April 2016). For an excellent, early, investigative report by a journalist, see Gordon Thomas, *Journey into Madness: Medical Torture and the Mind Controllers* (London: Corgi, 1989).

molesters;[11] aggrieved family members seeking death sentences for all murderers; and flamboyant nationalists asking for the death penalty for all terrorists and spies. If one accepts all such pleas, the number of hangings in India will surely be in tens of thousands a year, and will require a large contingent of hangmen. Yet, none of the lobbyists have ever offered to train themselves or their children as full-time executioners. Nor have they pleaded for job reservations for specific castes and communities, or for a corps of women executioners to ensure gender equity when executioners are selected. Such delightful, high-status jobs are left permanently reserved for other people's children. In the whole of South Asia, executions are usually the prerogative of Dalits and other low-castes. This is so even in the officially caste-less, Islamic republic of Pakistan.[12]

After all the brutalization and de-civilizing effects of institutionalized torture, does a regime get what it seeks to get through torture? According to all available data, the answer, alas, is 'no'. Philip N.S. Rumney, in a recent assessment, summarizes the picture on the basis of a number of cases, amongst them the French use of torture in Algeria in the 1950s, the long flirtation with torture when dealing with IRA terrorism, and the more recent

---

[11] See for example, Priyanko Sarkar, 'Even Molesters Should Get the Death Penalty', *The Times of India*, 13 July 2008, p. 20. Those who may consider columns as purveying odd individual opinions might like to remember how every television channel showed, during the demonstrations against the Delhi gang rape, young girls insisting that rapists should not only be hanged to death, but must first be tortured and then put to death.

[12] Two powerful, fictional explorations of the culture that crystallizes around capital punishment in South Asia are Shashi Warrier, *Hangman's Journal* (New Delhi: Penguin, 2003) and K.R. Meera, *Hangwoman: Everyone Loves a Good Hanging*, trans. J. Devika (New Delhi: Penguin, 2014). For an excellent documentary on the subject, see Vani Subramanian, *The Death of Us All* (Producer, Rajiv Meherotra and Public Service Broadcasting Trust, New Delhi, 2018).

experiment with institutionalized torture by the United States in the wake of 9/11.[13] The Senate Select Committee on Intelligence Report, though not officially released, has reportedly concluded that torture or enhanced interrogation techniques by the CIA:

> [d]id not produce significant intelligence disclosures and that the CIA misled the Congress and the White House on a number of matters, including the effectiveness of these techniques. The report took three years to complete and involved six million pages of internal CIA memos and other records. The controversy has continued with the chairwoman of the Senate Intelligence Committee, Dianne Feinstein, accusing the CIA of spying on the committee's work and intimidating the investigators.[14]

As for the Algerian case, Rumney quotes a review of several books in the following words: 'Torture failed not only to repress the yearning for independence among Algerians, it increased popular support for the FLN (the targeted terrorist group), contributing to the transformation of a small vanguard into a revolutionary party with mass support.... Indeed, France's tactics helped FLN to win over Algerian moderates.'[15]

The long-term victims of torture are the general citizenry. Public awareness of the very existence of torture chambers within a country's law-enforcement or defence establishment, outside the reach of the country's judiciary, brutalizes a population, a section of which even begins to derive some unhealthy pleasure from the stories of what happens, say, at the torture chamber at the Red Fort or at the headquarters of the Research and Analysis Wing in Delhi. Public opinion polls should soon be able to tell us proudly, as they have already done in the United States, that a majority of the country favours the use of torture if it yields information about the future plans of terrorists.[16]

---

[13] Rumney, *Torturing Terrorists*, esp. chapters 2 and 3.

[14] Rumney, *Torturing Terrorists*, p. 102.

[15] Rumney, *Torturing Terrorists*, p. 103.

[16] See 'New Poll Finds Majority of Americans Think Torture was Justified after 9/11 Attacks', *The Washington Post*, 14 December 2014.

There are also the professionals and specialists who think themselves to be passive onlookers but are fully complicit with torture. Torture is not possible in rule-bound, law-governed, democratic societies unless official doctors give false medical reports that whitewash torture injuries, or dishonest death certificates when the tortured die. Higher rungs of the police and the bureaucracy and their political handlers, too, have to be a part of the torture system. That is why in countries like India, there is such reluctance to make an international commitment to abolish torture as part of normal police work or as an instrument of the state's security agencies. India's convoluted strategies to avoid signing the international convention on torture have been a direct product of the awareness of the implications of that convention for our political leaders, higher echelons of the bureaucracy, and the law-and-order machinery. They are signs of the deep inroads the practice of torture has made into India's state apparatus. Actually, the Indian state has never dismantled the glorious Imperial tradition in this area. Occasional lip service is paid to the memories of freedom fighters who were the victims of torture in colonial times, and the memories of notorious torture sites such as the Cellular Jail at Port Blair in the Andamans have become popular themes of public speeches on national holidays, but few have spoken about the need to question the system that broke the body and the spirit of the freedom fighters, sometimes driving them to lunacy or suicide.[17]

---

[17] On the concentration-camp-like ambience of the Cellular jail in the Andamans, see the recent account by two British journalists, Cathy Scott-Clark and Adrian Levy, 'Survivors of Our Hell', *Guardian Unlimited*, 23 June 2001, http://www.guardian.co.uk/Archive/Article/0,4273,4207876,00.html. Scott-Clark and Levy depend not only on survivors' testimony but also on official records. See also S.N. Aggarwal, *The Heroes of Cellular Jail* (New Delhi: Rupa, 2006). There is also the well-known account of Vinayak Damodar Savarkar, *My Transportation for Life*, trans. V.N. Naik (Bombay: Veer Savarkar Prakashan, 1984).

* * *

In the end, we are forced to conclude that torture in the long run does what no militancy or terrorism can ever hope to do. It changes the people of a country to accept cruelty as a way of life, and as a normal means of settling political differences, ideological debates, and even personal scores. At that point, a country can as well give up fighting its dedicated enemies outside its borders, for it has become, psychologically and ethically, a mirror image of its enemies. There is nothing left to fight for or protect.

13

Nuclearism

An Epidemiology*

Nuclearism is the ideology of nuclear weaponry and nuclear-arms-based security. It is the most depraved, shameless, and costly pornography of our times. Such an ideology cannot be judged only by the canons of international relations, geopolitics, political sociology, or ethics. It is also a well-known, identifiable, psycho-pathological syndrome, as recognized by a series of studies done by psychologists, psychoanalysts, and psychiatrists, of genocidal mentality in general, and nuclearism in particular. What follows is a summary of its clinical picture, epidemiology, and prognosis, as they emerge from these studies.

Nuclearism does not reside in institutions, though it may set up, symbolize, or find distinctive expression in social, political, and scientific institutions. It is an individual pathology and has clear identifiers. Many years ago, Brian Easlea argued in his

* This essay was previously published as 'Nuclearism, Genocidal Mentality and Psychic Numbing: On the Psychopathology of the Nuclear-Arms Race' in *Himal South Asian*, July, 1998.

book, *Fathering the Unthinkable*, that nuclearism went with strong masculinity strivings. Easlea was no psychologist, but the works of Carol Cohn and others have endorsed the broad contours of Easlea's analysis. They show that not only the language and ideology, but the entire culture of nuclear weaponry is infiltrated by hard, masculine imageries, and those participating in that culture usually suffer from deep fears of emasculation or impotency. Indeed, that is the reason they participate in that culture with enthusiasm.

Such strivings for hyper-masculinity usually go with various forms of authoritarianism. Even people ideologically committed to democratic governance may vicariously participate in subtler forms of authoritarianism associated with nuclearism. Robert Jungk's work on the nuclear state shows that secrecy, security, surveillance, and police-state methods invariably accompany the nuclear establishment in every country. In that sense, the culture of nuclearism is one of the true 'universals' of our time. Like Coca-Cola and blue jeans, it does not permit much cultural adaptation or many edited versions. It is the same in Paris and Pokhran, Lahore and Los Alamos. The meaning of the product may vary, and the producers and advertisers may try to give it a fashionable ethnic touch, but the product has to be, ultimately, true to only itself.

Nuclearism is framed by a specific personality type, the spread of which at some points of time may acquire epidemic proportions in a society. Eric Markusen and Robert J. Lifton have systematically studied the links. In their book, *The Genocidal Mentality* (1990), they make a comparative study of the psychology of mass murderers—in Nazi Germany, in Hiroshima and Nagasaki, and among the ideologues of nuclearism today—and find remarkable continuities. In the genocidal person there is, first of all, a state of mind called 'psychic numbing'—a 'diminished capacity or inclination to feel' and 'a general sense of meaninglessness'. One so numbs one's sensitivities that normal emotions and moral considerations cannot penetrate one any more. Numbing 'closes off' a person and leads to a 'constriction of self process'.

To him or her, the death or the possibility of the death of millions begins to look like an abstract, bureaucratic detail, involving the calculation of military gains or losses, geopolitics, or mere statistics. Markusen and Lifton may not agree, but such numbing can be considered to be the final culmination of the separation of affect and cognition—that is, feelings and thinking—that the European Enlightenment sanctioned and celebrated as the first step towards greater objectivity and scientific rationality.

The genocidal mentality also tends to create an area protected from public responsibility or democratic accountability. Usually such responsibility is avoided by re-conceptualizing oneself as only a cog in the wheel, advancing one's own bureaucratic or scientific career like everybody else, by taking and obeying orders from superior authorities faithfully, mechanically, and without thinking about the moral implications of the orders. The Nazi war criminals tried at Nuremberg at the end of World War II all ventured the defence that they were under orders to kill innocent people, including women, children, and the elderly, and could do nothing about it. Hannah Arendt's *Eichmann in Jerusalem* (1963) is a classic study of the evil that masquerades as banal, harmless, everyday conformity to bureaucratic norms.

The other way of avoiding accountability is to remove it from individuals and vest it in institutions and aggregates. As if institutions by themselves could run a death machine without the intervention of individuals! After a while, even terms like the military–industrial complex, fascism, imperialism, Stalinism, ruling class, or American hegemony become ways of freeing actual, real-life persons from their culpability for recommending, ordering, or committing mass murders. In a society where a genocidal mentality spreads, intellectuals also find such impersonal analyses soothing; they contribute to the creation of a business-as-usual ambience, in which institutions are ritually blamed and the psychopathic scientists, bureaucrats, and politicians who work towards genocides move around scot-free, and are even celebrated as national heroes.

This is not surprising in a world where the persons responsible for the genocides in Rwanda, Cambodia, and Bangladesh—to give only recent examples—face no serious threat of prosecution today. Sometimes they are protected by the lethargy of and loopholes in the operative regime of international criminal law, sometimes by the fact that the killers enjoy the protection or patronage of the powerful and the wealthy. The Indonesian massacres of 1965 and the Bangladesh massacres of 1971 are two of the least studied genocides of our times, and have not attracted the attention of too many activists. Their perpetrators also look perfectly safe, perhaps because both the genocides were made possible by the political establishment of the United States of America, including Henry Kissinger, a Nobel Laureate for peace.

In acute cases, the genocidal mentality turns into necrophilia, a clinical state in which the patient is in love with death. Indeed, he or she wants to sleep with the dead, in fantasy, and in some cases, in real life. Saadat Hasan Manto's famous story, 'Cold Meat' or 'Thanda Gosht' is, unknown to the author, the story of an 'ordinary' murderer and rapist who, while trying to satiate his sexual greed during a communal conflict, confronts his own necrophilia and is devastated by that. Those interested in more authoritative case studies can look up Erich Fromm's once-popular *The Anatomy of Human Destructiveness* (1973).

Nuclearism does not remain confined to the nuclear establishment or the nuclear community. It introduces other psychopathologies in a society. For instance, as it seeps into public consciousness, it creates a new awareness of the transience of life. It forces people to live with the constant fear that, one day, a sudden war or accident might kill not only them, but also their children and grandchildren, and everybody they love. This awareness gradually creates a sense of the hollowness of life. For many, life is denuded of substantive meaning. The psychological numbing I have mentioned completes the picture. While the ordinary citizen leads an apparently normal life, he or she is constantly aware of the transience of such life and the risk of mega-death for the entire society. Often this finds expression in unnecessary or inexplicable violence in social life, or in a more general, high state of anxiety and a variety of psychosomatic ailments. In other words, nuclearism begins to brutalize ordinary people and vitiates everyday life. Studies by the likes of William Beardslee, John E. Mack, and Eleonora Masini show that these traits express themselves even in adolescents and children. Even children barely eight or ten years old begin to live in what they consider to be a world without a future; they are fearful and anxious about their life but unable to express that fear and anxiety directly because in a nuclearized society, the fear of nuclear death is made to look like an abnormal psychoneurotic state.

The situation could become worse in countries or societies where despair stalks the landscape, where life and the future have already lost much of their meaning. A good example is the chilling description by Peter Landesman, in the *Atlantic* monthly, of his conversation with a politically influential Pakistani army officer casually talking of a nuclear war with India:

'We should fire at them and take out a few of their cities—Delhi, Bombay, Calcutta,' he said. 'They should fire back and take Karachi and Lahore. Kill off a hundred or two hundred million people. They should fire at us and it would all be over. They have acted so badly toward us; they have been so mean. We should teach them a lesson. It would teach all of us a lesson. There is no future here, and we need to start over. So many people think this. Have you been to the villages of Pakistan, the interior? There is nothing but dire poverty and pain. The children have no education; there is nothing to look forward to. Go into the villages, see the poverty. There is no drinking water. Small children without shoes walk miles for a drink of water. I go to the villages and I want to cry. My children have no future. None of the children of Pakistan have a future. We are surrounded by nothing but war and suffering...'

...He told me he was willing to see his children be killed. He repeated that they didn't have any future—his children or any other children.

Many neurotics and psychotics at first look like charming eccentrics. To start with, nuclearism may appear a smart game, and the partisans of nuclear weaponry may look like normal politicians, scholars, or defence experts. Many psychopaths, too, have attractive, almost seductive personalities. Apart from that, in many societies, there is ample scope for keeping double ledgers. As we all know, the Nazis killers, too, were usually loving fathers, connoisseurs of good music, and honest, tax-paying citizens. However, beneath such facades lies a complex set of insecurities—anxiety about one's masculinity, fears of the interpersonal world, and the inability to love. The mindless violence such a personality anticipates or plans is a pathetic attempt to fight these inner feelings of emptiness, and the suspicion and the fear that one's moral self might already be dead within. You father the unthinkable because you have already psychologically orphaned yourself. Like the Pakistani army officer, you make contingency plans to kill millions because you fear that your innermost core has already been cauterized against all normal feelings and human relations. Acquiring the power to inflict death on millions, and living with the fantasy of that power, you pathetically try to get some confirmation that you are still alive. However, that confirmation never comes. For in the process of acquiring that power, you may not be dead physically, but you are already dead morally, socially, and psychologically.

14

The Fear and the Allure of Self-Destruction*

The introduction by the editors of *Anthropology in Bombay, 1886–1936* has within it all the ingredients for an excellent foreword. The editors did not need me to write it. Especially so because all I can do here is to supply, for those who want it, a brief reflection on the larger cultural and psychological awareness within which such studies of suicide in India might be located.

Suicide in South Asia does not have the same associations that it has in the European civilization, from within which most theoretical and empirical works on suicide have been done, not only in Europe and North America, but also in India and other Afro-Asian societies. The early sociological explorations assembled in this book are no exception. In Europe, the idea of suicide has an unacknowledged moral metaphysics undergirding it. That metaphysics draws power from Europe's Christianity, for which the prototypical case of suicide

---

* The chapter was previously published as a foreword to Arvind Shah and Lancy Lobo (eds), *Anthropology in Bombay, 1886–1936: Contribution of a Learned Society and Its Journal*, Volume 1: *Suicides in Bombay, 1886–1907 and Other Essays*. (New Delhi: Primus Books, 2018).

remains that of Judas Iscariot, the disciple of Jesus Christ who betrayed Christ and then hung himself. Guilt, betrayal, atonement for a sin of deicide that cannot be atoned, and doomed attempts to avoid facing the enormity of one's transgression are themes inextricably linked to suicide in European Christianity. Suicide itself is sinful, even when one chooses it not for some real or imagined moral lapse but for escaping unbearable suffering or injustice. The expression 'moral statistics' used in some of the papers in *Anthropology in Bombay, 1886–1936* hints at that cultural connection.

In South Asia, on the other hand, suicide is not located in a dark world of sin, repentance, and attempts to evade self-confrontation through self-erasure. Suicide might be a sin in all cultures, as classics scholar Surabhi Sheth argues, but it does not mean that all communities have the same idea of sin or make the same emotional investment in the sinfulness attributed to suicide.[1] Evil in Christianity is a more concrete and darker reality than it is in even other Abrahamic faiths that are close to Christianity. And we know of other cultures where suicide seems to carry very different emotional loads. For instance, some Mesoamerican cultures had a notorious tradition of human sacrifice, but few know that they also had a venerated tradition of auto-sacrifice, seen as a legitimate offering to the gods. Some Europeans were surprised that when they offered to free 'victims' waiting to be sacrificed, the victims refused to be freed.[2]

In South Asia, suicide seems to carry more than one set of associations and is framed by a diverse set of moral demands. And all of them certainly do not carry intimations of sin. First, suicide in South Asia may imply voluntary renunciation of the body for reasons that

---

[1] Surabhi Sheth, 'Suicide and the Indian Tradition', in R.I. Nanavaty (ed.), *Professor H.G. Kantawala Felicitation Volume* (Delhi: Bharatiya Vidya Prakashan, 1998), pp. 60–72.

[2] For a brief introduction to the complexity of human sacrifice in a Mesoamerican culture, and the treatment of the sacrificial victim as divine, and death in sacrifice as one of the two highest forms of good death among the Aztecs, see Mark Cartwright, 'Aztec Sacrifice', in *Ancient History Encyclopaedia*, www.ancient.eu (accessed 11 June 2016).

could be personal or collective, religious, or secular. There is neither any pronounced sense of guilt nor, unlike in Japan, an explicit aesthetics of suicide. In many Indian traditions, including Indian versions of the Semitic creeds, suicide is often a less intense affair. It has more to do with serene courage, the ability to face death as a natural ending of life, and a belief that perfect, self-chosen modes of death, in which one retains one's agency—including complete mastery over one's body and mind to the very end—enhance the overall quality of one's life. A good life should end with a good death, and though there may not be an aesthetics of death, there can be a touch of gentle grace in the way one exits life.

Icchamrutyu, the ability to choose one's moment of death even when one is otherwise a mortal, is a boon given to a chosen few, but lesser mortals can approximate the feat by calmly inviting death, as in the traditional rites of *santhara* and *prayopovesana*. There is another variation on this way of exiting life that draws upon traditions, though perhaps not self-consciously. I remember that years ago, while working on the assassination of Gandhi by Nathuram Vinayak Godse, I was often tempted to read that instance of murder as an ill-disguised case of suicide scripted by Gandhi, in which his naïve, young assassin dutifully and obediently played his assigned role. If Rabindranath Tagore's reply to the earlier forms of Hindu nationalism was the novel *Gora*, which uncannily anticipates the arrival of Gandhi and supplies the first serious critique of Hindu nationalism, Gandhi's response to Vinayak Damodar Savarkar was his own superbly crafted death. Sarojini Naidu's response to women grieving over Gandhi's dead body is a clue to the larger meaning of that self-chosen death. Reminding the women that it was appropriate for him to die in Delhi, the city of kings, Naidu said, 'What is all this snivelling about? Would you rather he died of old age or indigestion? This was the only death great enough for him.'[3]

---

[3] Sarojini Naidu, quoted in Robert Payne, *The Life and Death of Mahatma Gandhi* (London: Bodley Head, 1969), p. 647.

Second, there *is* also a place in the Indic civilization for suicidal courage and heroic death. *Atmabali* is not unknown to the world of epics. And a warrior's self-sacrifice can be read as part of his *swadharma, kuladharma, or jatidharma*. By stretching the meaning of *jatidharma*, this model can also be made to include the practices of communities that traditionally used to stand guarantee against powerful borrowers who refused to honour their obligations to lenders. The community was then expected go and sit on *dharna* in front of the defaulter's home threatening suicide. Dharampal sees such practices as precursors of Gandhi's Satyagraha.[4] Suicidal heroism, such as that of Abhimanyu in the Mahabharata, too, can be fitted within this normative frame, even though Vyasa's Mahabharata does not see it that way.

Third, it will be dangerous to ignore the growing instrumental use and secularization of suicide. The nature of that growth can be gauged from the career path of the three well-known epidemics of sati in India. The first two epidemics—one in the declining years of the Vijayanagara Empire and the other during the period when the Rajput principalities were under attack from the Delhi Sultanate and the Mughal Empire—were more like collateral damage at times of crisis. Like the cases of sati in mythic times, they derived strength from the scriptures and community or caste traditions, and were confined to only small sections of the elite. The third outbreak of sati in an epidemic form was in late-eighteenth-century urban Bengal—undergoing massive socio-political changes under its new colonial rulers, coping with the collapse of the traditional moral universe and brutalized by the loss of about one-third of its population in the famine of 1772—where sati became a *pratha*, a well-institutionalized system, literally what the term 'widow burning' implied. Given the distinctive Hindu law of inheritance in Bengal, which gave the widow control over her deceased husband's share of the property till her sons grew up, the

---

[4] Dharampal, 'Civil Disobedience in Indian Tradition', in Dharampal, *Collected Writings*, Vol. 2 (Goa: Other India Press, 2000).

widow's exit from the scene became an attractive proposition to many in the family.[5]

That process of secularization has now gone farther. The political use of suicide bombing has been one of South Asia's proudest contributions to the present global culture. The Liberation Tigers of Tamil Elam's (LTTE) ideologically motivated, instrumental use of teenaged suicide bombers has been improved upon by the suicide-squads in Kashmir and Pakistan. Death here derives meaning and sanctity from a thin cover of religious justification that to outsiders may look like brainwashing. S.N. Balagangadhara calls it, perhaps more appropriately, transubstantiation of violence, cruelty, and, if Surabhi Sheth is right, suicide itself.[6]

Fourth, in recent decades, suicide has emerged as a response to unbearable suffering, injustice, or despair. This has made suicide front-page news and a politically live issue. Indeed, the domain of despair is expanding rather fast in South Asia. Among Indian farmers, increasingly feeling caught in a collapsing lifestyle and a dying vocation, suicide has become a serious temptation and a popular option in their fight against despair. P. Sainath says, using National Crime Records Bureau data, that as many as 296,438 farmers have committed suicide in India between 1995 and 2013.[7] An entire social sector, it seems, is being ruthlessly pushed to the wall, so as to shrink the two-thirds of India that depends directly or indirectly on farming, to a size befitting a modern, urban–industrial nation-state. This is probably our version of the Enclosure

---

[5] Ashis Nandy, 'Sati: A Nineteenth Century Tale of Women, Violence and Protest', in *At the Edge of Psychology: Essays in Politics and Culture* (New Delhi: Oxford University Press), 1980, pp. 1–31.

[6] S.N. Balagangadhara, 'What Do Indians Need, a History or the Past? A Challenge or Two to Indian Historians', Seventh Maulana Abul Kalam Azad Lecture, delivered at the India International Centre on 14 November 2014, under the auspices of the Indian Council for Cultural Relations, unpublished MS.

[7] P. Sainath, 'How States Fudge the Data on Declining Farmer Suicide', *India News*, 1 August 2014, www.rediff.com (accessed 2 July 2016).

Movement in Britain. We already have the smog and the slums of Victorian Britain; we are now waiting for the gin alleys.

* * *

Anthropology in Bombay, 1886–1936 is not only a sociological book on suicide but also a book on the sociology of sociology. The focus is on the concern of early sociologists with suicide and what they at the time called moral statistics. Today's sociologists will readily admit that the data their elders used do not leave much scope for more sophisticated statistical analysis. Nor have the data—and sources from which they came filtered—left much scope for any reclassification.

Yet, this book *does* invite us to build upon its empiricism, and engage with an issue that, at the time the study was done, was not a major social problem. Times have changed. Suicide in its various incarnations has become a prime concern in the global public culture. Suicide bombers are tearing apart communities, which have lived together peacefully for centuries, to create a new culture of terror—Jews or Hindus versus Muslims, Buddhists versus Hindus, Sunnis versus Shias, Muslims versus Christians. In some of these transmutations, South Asia has played a major role. Yet, research on the subject has been, till now, scanty and half-hearted. Why?

One answer is that human beings have never been comfortable with suicide. Social scientists and political commentators are no exception to the rule. Suicide defies the biological instinct of self-preservation that crosses species boundaries. It is not surprising that it arouses primeval fears and anxieties and a counter-phobic attempt to 'normalize' it through intellectualization or denial. (An example is the long-surviving myth about the mass suicide of lemmings, a variety of rodents, despite all evidence to the contrary.) Just when we are witnessing spectacular public anguish over the Paris tragedy and India is furiously debating the tragic suicide of a sensitive young student, pushed by an insensitive system and its heartless functionaries, we also grapple with the cold-blooded indifference towards the suicide of tens of thousands of farmers in the country. Suicide prompts mourning, empathy, and guilt; it also triggers fear, awe, and in a defensive manoeuvre, apathy and denial. Suicide induces contradictory emotions that can become a strange amalgam of guilty admiration and angry silence. Witnesses to a suicide are simultaneously seduced and repelled by the act, sometimes more than the one who opts for self-destruction.

This then is the fifth frame from within which suicide in South Asia can be studied. But, while recognizing its importance, we also have to admit that despair did not have any noticeable presence as an acknowledged state of mind in premodern India. In the co-authored book *Despair and Modernity*, art historian Harsha Dehejia has even pleaded that despair should be acknowledged as an additional *rasa* to make the rasa theory comprehensive enough for modern Indian art.[8] Even the not easily reusable data in *Anthropology in Bombay, 1886–1936* will reveal that a century ago despair-driven suicide was already carving out for itself a place, albeit small, in Indian society.

[8] Harsha V. Dehejia, 'Introduction', in Harsha V. Dehejia with Prem Shankar Jha and Ranjit Hoskote, *Despair and Modernity: Reflections from Modern Indian Painting* (New Delhi: Motilal Banarsidass, 2000), pp. 1–7.

15

Who Won the World Cup in 1994?[*]

Who should have won the World Cup in 1994? Columbia, as Pele had predicted at the beginning of the tournament, only to be proved wrong in less than two weeks? Brazil, as Diego Maradona predicted, after being thrown out of the competition for drug offences, crippling the Argentinian team? Or Italy with its band of elegant, gifted players? I have no answer to these questions. But I think I know who has already won the World Cup, establishing total dominance over world soccer. And my answer will please neither Pele nor Maradona nor the devotees of football the world over. I am afraid it may not even make sense to many of my readers.

I think the cup has already been won by the global market which we Indians are trying so hard to enter now. The final proof of this lies in the assassination of Andres Escobar, the gifted defender in the Columbian World Cup team. Escobar, in trying to save a goal during Columbia's first-round match against the unfancied United States, accidentally scored what in my childhood used to be

[*] Revised and expanded version of a column first published as 'Sudden Death', *The Times of India*, 10 July 1994, p. 14.

called 'a same-side goal', and which the South Americans in their wisdom call an 'auto-goal'.

In response to the killing, editorials have already come out in the Indian and international press about the Latin American passion for football. This passion, it is being said, has led to serious violence in the past, and not surprisingly, has burst into the open at the first opportunity during the 1994 World Cup.

Many have chosen to remember in this connection the four-day war that took place over a series of three football matches between Honduras and El Salvador in Central America more than two decades earlier in 1969, to the great amusement of the rest of the world. The war was less amusing for the citizens of the two countries. It, along with the two days of rioting that preceded it, killed 5,700 persons, injured another 15,000, and displaced 100,000.

Much of that part of the world was then under military rulers whose sole source of legitimacy was their manifest hatred of communism and their subservience to American economic and political interests. These rulers would have been a comical presence in global politics but for their unending bloodthirst and avarice. Nobody took them seriously, not even their American patrons. What the press called a Football War only confirmed the worst stereotypes of Latin temper, particularly those centring on the immature, excitable Latin personality that allegedly required firm, patriarchal rulers who might not have been paragons of decency but immaculately fitted the political cultures of their societies.

It is now obvious that Escobar's death does not fit in with that hoary stereotype. Contrary to the impression created by the first reports on the shooting of the footballer, this was not, by any stretch of imagination, a typical Latin crime of passion. The killers *did* say 'Thanks for the auto-goal' while pumping into Escobar 12 bullets, and that *does* give the impression that it was another case of irrational rage and loss of self-control in South America's volatile football fans.

However, later news reports have not allowed us to stick to that easy reading. Passion might have been involved in the killing, but it was obviously packaged in self-interest and greed. It now transpires that the anger against Escobar was triggered not so much by nationalism as by financial losses and hard calculations about what the auto-goal cost in terms of wagers won or lost. Football is no longer principally a popular game played in the lanes and backstreets of cities and on village greens. It is now, before everything else, a consumable spectacle that the global entertainment industry and media produce for the market.

It seems millions of dollars are involved in the transactions that take place over the course and results of football matches in South America and Europe. In Columbia, these wagers often involve the easy fortunes amassed through drug trafficking and laundered by tainted financial, bureaucratic, and political institutions, and increasingly, through corporatized football.

Escobar was from the city of Medellin, Columbia's drug capital, and the gamblers who staked their fortune on Columbia's easy success against the United States were some of the most ruthless drug barons in the world. Escobar's very success in the game of soccer made him an important player in the big league of financial transactions. Unwittingly, he had acquired the ability to affect the economic fortunes of thousands but could not share that unwanted responsibility with anyone except the other players in his team.

Escobar's death is only a dramatic portrayal of what is fundamentally wrong with organized, international sports today. It shows that, increasingly, it is not the quality of football or national self-respect or pride that determines the fate of footballers; it is their location in the alternative liminal world of high finance. The World Cup, like most other sports events today, has been taken over by these financial interests. Sponsorships, contracts, endorsements, advertisements, transfer fees—these are the things that determine a player's status and worth today. And in this world have now entered many shadowy investors.

My daughter, when she heard of the killing of Escobar, felt that the World Cup contest this year should be cancelled as a protest against such mindless brutal violence. The organizers of the event would have found such an idea silly, if not funny. The World Cup is no longer a human-scale affair, a lovable self-expression of *homo ludens*, as Johan Huizinga might have said. It is a mega-event involving the investment of millions of dollars, long-term planning, and detailed calculation of financial gains and losses. The nature or quality of the game and the personal fate of the players are, after a point, incidental to such an arrangement.

Perhaps it is this sense of being caught in a soulless grid that makes players like Maradona so self-destructive. They come to sense that, after a point, despite all their talent and all the adulation they get, they are no better than gladiators in a Roman amphitheatre. Their sporting skills, their bodies, in fact their entire careers, have been commodified and controlled by the methods and technology of the global market. Drugs probably give them a sense of having a choice and mastery over self, however false or fleeting.

I hope it will not sound heartless 'if I say that Escobar's death has no intrinsic dignity to it. He might have looked upon himself as a simple footballer playing according to the rules to the best of his ability. But he was only an old-fashioned cog-in-the-wheel, a lifeless factor of production for others. The World Cup will go on, not as a defiance of the forces that brought about his death, but as an abject surrender to the first principles of industrial civilization and consumer society.

16

Invitation to a Beheading

Political Assassinations in the Third World*

The relationship between an assassin and his victim is deep and enduring. Death only openly and finally brings them together. Of course, there are tyrants who turn virtually everyone in a country into a prospective assassin, and leaders who build bastions against their assassination in the minds of the ruled, thereby reducing the circle of prospective assassins to a microscopic group of hired sociopaths and the mentally ill. Emperor Nero belonged to the first category and Martin Luther King to the second. There is also the

* First published in *New Quest* (November–December 1975), 98: 69–72. Every effort has been made to trace the copyrightholders of the essay. The publisher would be pleased to hear from the copyright owner so that proper acknowledgement can be made in future editions.

I remind readers overly sensitive to gender-specific pronouns used in this chapter that it was published in the high noon of the Emergency and censorship imposed in India by Indira Gandhi during 1975–7. The message contained herein was, however, obvious to readers less obtuse than the Indian censors.

special case of totalitarian rulers who, by the consent of a manufactured majority of the ruled, are tyrannical within the country, and to the extent they get the chance, in the world outside. Their pathology often leads to collective suicide rather than individual assassinations. The rulers of the Third Reich have remained cliched but glaring example of the species.

But such leaders are hardly typical. There is a much broader range of situations where the ruler is popular and charismatic, but propelled by his inner drives, prepares the ground for his assassination. In such cases, there is a close fit between the motivational imperatives of such a ruler, his attempts to remould the polity after his own psychological needs, and the type of invitation he extends to his potential assassins.

The first characteristic of such a ruler is an inability to trust deeply and wholly. Though his flamboyant style may hide it for a long time, he lives in an inner world peopled by untrustworthy followers. Even when he trusts some, it is transient. A chain of lieutenants come in and go out of his favour in a fashion reminiscent of people getting in and out of a railway compartment. The ruler suspends this suspiciousness only in the case of his family members, those recruited from outside politics to act as 'commissars', depoliticized bureaucrats, and politicians who have no independent base and are fully dependent on the charismatic pull of the leader.

Now, politics is a game of modulated trust. The politician deploys a mix of the basic trust and distrust in his or her personality—to use one of the well-known conceptual polarities Erik Erikson used in his work on the human life cycle—and operates within a system of interpersonal coalition-building, negotiations, and competition. If this inner balance of trust and distrust is disturbed, he becomes either a paranoiac or a 'sucker'. In either case, he goes out of high politics. However, there is also the politician who retains this balance till he enters a critical power position and then begins to falter, and the politician whose paranoid predispositions match the political culture and institutions of his country (such a man may perform exceedingly well when it comes to cut-throat political competitions and bitter struggles for political succession). In both cases, once in power, the distrust gradually forces the ruler to circumscribe the area within which policies are made, to strangle or ruthlessly contain those who generate alternative models and fundamental criticisms of the polity, and to pack the decision-making system with loyal lieutenants, whatever be their competence.

Power, thus, continues to be concentrated in the ruler's hand. Worse, he is seen as all powerful. Thus, not merely all credit for the achievements, but also all grievances gradually begin to be directed at him. After a while, there remain no intervening shock absorbers whom he can fob off as subversive reactionaries within the ruling circle. Unlike Jawaharlal Nehru, who was simultaneously the head of the government and the leader of the opposition, and thus survived even disaster such as the India–China border war, such a ruler personally becomes the focus of all the anger and frustration of which a poor country is capable. And remember, in polities with large proportions of dispossessed and deprived citizens, the successes of a regime are invariably less obvious than its failures. To say that a Third World leader is deeply identified with his nation is to say that he is primarily identified with its failures.

Moreover, no decision-making structure is monolithic. Even in the smallest of polities, there are bound to be piques and hostilities against petty officials, against the ruler's relatives who actually may have nothing much to do with him, and against men who use his name or pretend to act under his orders but in reality are time-servers and petty tyrants operating independently. These hostilities cumulate against the ruler himself. Increasingly, it seems to a growing number of people that the regime can be changed by merely changing one individual. Traditional monarchies fall in this category, and the American presidency, depending upon its incumbent, is sometimes not very different. The regime that Richard Nixon ran must have nurtured many political assassins and those who hooted him out might have, for all we know, saved his life. Some might say that, during the last few years of his life, Sheikh Mujib's Bangladesh, too, was moving towards becoming such a polity.

Sometimes, not merely does the ruler get too deeply identified with the regime, the regime may seem closed to internal competition to a large number of people. Yet, psychologically, no regime is entirely closed. It could be so only normatively. Even the most rigidly closed regime is open to one whose values permit him to include in the available means of political competition revolution, rebellion, coup, and assassination. Of these, revolutions require immense planning, massive organization, first-rate skills in mobilization, and a developed ability to feel the pulse of a large section of the population. Naturally, in the Third World, in some of the less organized, more apolitical societies, revolutions are at a discount. Of course, every petty rebel or tyrant may call himself a revolutionary, but Lenins and Maos can hardly be mass-produced. To some extent, the preconditions of revolutions apply to rebellions and coups, too. Coups require lesser organization but immense secrecy, and are not easy to sustain in South Asia. Pakistan, which presently holds the South Asian record for army rule, has seen four army regimes toppled by nearly non-violent street demonstrations, which in turn is a world record. At the same time, failed coups are not a rarity in the country. Army rules are not as impregnable as they look in the region.

On the other hand, assassination is the cheapest of the four means mentioned, requires the least planning and organization, and does not need the assent of any section of the population. Understandably, it is at a premium in the Third World. In some parts of it, such killings have, in fact, become a standard means of deciding political succession. In Latin America, for instance, the popularity of political assassinations at one time was exceeded only by football and bullfights.

It is through this linkage that the average assassin and his average victim ultimately find each other. The few studies of assassins done elsewhere in the world show them to be unhappy marginal men having low conformity to social norms and deep feelings of inferiority and impotency. The portrait which Irving Horowitz draws of the terrorist applies to the assassin, too. He is likely to be young, male, middle-class, economically marginal, relatively well-educated but without high achievements, and cut off from the peasants and the working class by his origins. Such men are produced in many traditional societies by urbanization, expanding communications, collapsing traditional hierarchies and norms, technological changes, and occupational insecurities.

When living under an authoritarian regime, these marginal citizens sense that their society is open on one plane. Most of their compatriots, conforming to the existing political norms, may remain convinced that it is closed. But these norms are not applicable to the sector from which the assassin comes. Having low self-esteem and trying to redeem themselves in their own eyes, these potential assassins are always seeking situations in which they can do something dramatic and, in one move, counter their own poor self-image and passivity and, through an act of desperate violence, get a new heroic self-image endorsed by a sizeable section of the citizens.

The assassin is not a murderer. A murder is too personal, too mundane, and has less dramatic and exhibitionistic potentialities. As Arthur Danto points out, you and I are safe from the assassin's bullet because we are only prospective victims of collateral damage, and do not enjoy the 'privilege of assassinability'. Even if we are accidentally killed in an assassination attempt, the event remains only a failed assassination attempt with inadvertent lethal consequences for others. The reason for this is obvious. We can only relieve the immense tension of the undischarged aggressive needs of the murderer, but cannot satisfy the assassin's search for grandiose self-validation and protection against self-abnegating oblivion. Nor can our murder provide the assassin with the ideological rationalization he needs to express openly his deepest aggressive feelings, directed against a symbol of parental authority.

The assassin badly needs this rationalization. The major political philosophies of our times provide excellent justifications for political violence but not for political assassinations. Hatred

towards a person is difficult to rationalize in an age which prefers to speak in terms of aggregates such as class, race, religion,
caste, and social stratum. Thus, like Horowitz's terrorists, most
assassins must operate on the basis of poorly defined, home-made
ideologies. In this respect, too, the assassin is a lonely man.

No one can kill himself, some psychologists say, unless he feels
like killing somebody. Suicide always is, symbolically, an attempt
to murder an unacceptable part of one's own self modelled after
a figure outside. Perhaps the reverse is true for the assassin. His
attempt is to kill a figure in the external world who represents an
alien self. If he succeeds, the result may turn out to be popular, and
there may be a widely shared discharge of psychic tension, a justification of the assassin's way of handling his private problems. It
may also be unpopular, arousing guilt of patricide in the onlookers
to the extent they identify with the assassin. This guilt can hardly
be bound by the small symbolic expiation which the assassin-
turned-ruler often makes—like burying the assassinated ruler
with full military honours as happened in the cases of Gandhi and
Mujib—or by the *post facto* rationalization of the patricide through
improved statecraft, more popular policies, and a more democratic
style. Unconsciously the assassin fears his 'guilt' and the possibility that it may turn the citizens against him. In response and as
an atonement, he resorts to a behaviour pattern which invites his
own assassination. He begins to protect himself through authoritarianism and blind terror. He dangles before the other little men
in society the opportunity to not only self-advertise but also to transcend their vague feelings of alienation by assassinating the assassin and satisfying the free-floating feelings of revenge which the
first assassination let loose. Psychologically, this revenge promises
to undo the first patricide magically, through a second. It is often
thus that a culture of assassination emerges in a country.

The tragedy of the assassin is that the symbolic killing of only
a part of himself never ends the story. Only his own assassination
can do so. After all, he seeks to acquire through assassination the
public prominence his victim had but he lacked. The ultimate vali-
dation of this acquired renown is his own assassinability.

The tragedy of the assassinated ruler is that though he can avoid the fate towards which he often moves blindly and inexorably, he is in effect a driven man. Like his killer, he rebels against a part of himself which seeks self-preservation, acceptance, and contact with the real world of people.

What can such a ruler do to grapple with his own self-destructive tendencies? Danto believes that two courses are open to him. He can seek total protection, which means an impregnable shield of bodyguards. But who can protect the ruler against a treacherous guard? And who will guard the guards or guard the guards who guard the guards? Total security is a situation of infinite regression. The alternative strategy is to treat all subjects as if they were loyal. Benign policies by themselves are not enough; the modern prince must widen political participation so much that everybody has a stake in the system. In other words, he must make true citizens out of his subjects. Only then can he hope to abridge their alienation and marginality and exorcize the ghost of assassination.

17

Laughter in a Mortuary

O.V. Vijayan[*]

Good cartoonists may or may not need a foreword; the great
ones never do. Not merely because their appeal is direct, but also
because they constantly subvert interpretations of their own work.
Cartooning at its best is an irreverent, de-ideologized venture; it
cannot but snipe at the ideological straitjacket into which viewers
often try to push it. A foreword to the work of a cartoonist, on the
other hand, even when a modest introduction or an inane commendation, helps the viewers to push the cartoonist even more
self-confidently into a straightjacket. A foreword to the work of a
cartoonist is never politically innocent.

I must confess at the beginning that I write these words not to
help introduce or decode O.V. Vijayan's work, but to celebrate his
decision to choose cartoons as a vehicle of his thought, when he
was already deploying literature brilliantly for that purpose. Also,
this is my way of paying tribute to his bitter, ironic, anguished

* Foreword to O.V. Vijayan, *The Tragic Idiom: A Cartoonist Remembers*
(New Delhi: Rupa, 2002).

sensitivity to the nature of the human predicament in this part of the world. Above all, I want to celebrate the blessing of his intellectual and moral presence among us at this moment. That presence has made it more difficult for India's urban middle classes to be self-certain and self-righteous at the same time. They must choose between the two.

Vijayan's self-definition as a cartoonist is clear. He states it in his customary, acid style:

> It is an unutterable sadness which punctuates the reality that I am called upon to portray, and yet the dominant superstition of my profession demands that I raise a laugh. If you are depressed and morbid, I am reminded, there is a custom-made laugh even there, for did not Thurber mourn his epoch with laughter? But I am what Thurber could never understand. I am a Third World cartoonist. In my world there are children who are fed on grass, and whose eyes, as they peer out of an Oxfam ad, are full of an infantile senility that Thurber might never have encountered.
>
> .... I think of this tryst with grass, and when I do that, I want, in one suicidal sweep, to repudiate all those who lied to me about the tryst with destiny. Now how do I make that into a political cartoon?

I do not think Vijayan has told us the full story when speaking of this strange paradox, sired by the clashing demands of a conventional professional identity and inescapable life experiences. He is certainly not a clown forced by circumstances to nurture a tragic vision of life—a Thurber obliged to work from a particularly nasty slum in the hot and dusty tropics—though that is the way he might like to put it. True, after seeing some of his cartoons, smiles quickly turn to grimaces, followed by embarrassed silence. Some are even forced to pretend that they have not noticed the cartoons or found in them anything worth noticing. But that is not because they are driven to silence by imageries of starving children.

Vijayan's forte is not tragedy; it is sarcasm—bitter, venomous sarcasm. His drawings always have sharply defined targets and they are never safely institutional, even when he targets the military–industrial complex, capitalism, Western imperialism, international terrorism, or nearer home, Third-World despotism and controlled, house-broken democracy, or India's enduring public institutions—structured by formalized hypocrisy, hyperbole, and corruption. His villains are usually real-life persons and clearly identifiable. Yet, there is something unidentifiable in them that makes the viewers feel complicit with the villainy. Indeed, many viewers get the uncanny feeling that they are the actual butt of the cartoonist's jibes.

That is why, after seeing his work, his targets are unlikely to flaunt their generosity and democratic temper by congratulating and thanking him, the way Jawaharlal Nehru and some others reportedly did with Vijayan's mentor, the famous cartoonist K. Shankar Pillai, in the 1950s and 1960s. Nor are the targets likely to have the temerity to buy the originals and proudly hang them in their drawing rooms, as Lord Linlithgow did in the case of Shankar and many others do in the case of R.K. Laxman. Vijayan's targets are more likely to slink away from him if they accidentally see him at a public function or avoid eye contact if they have to meet him face-to-face. That is the difference between, say, Vijayan's or Rajendra Puri's cartoons on the Emergency and suspension of civil rights in India during 1975–7 and those of Abu Abraham or R.K. Laxman on the same subject. Prime Minister Indira Gandhi, I am sure, would have tried to maintain civilities if she met Abraham or Laxman, at least publicly. She would have not felt obliged to do so in the case of Vijayan and Puri. In an age that has no place for what Vijayan calls 'the graceful callisthenics of struggle' and the 'twilight glow' of liberal transition, Vijayan certainly leaves no escape route for his targets; they have no option but to confront themselves.

Seeing Vijayan's drawings and laughing—some of them do elicit wry, cramped smiles—is a way of hiding one's embarrassment. It is an attempt to deny that the barb has gone home, that one feels accused of culpability, and angry that someone has seen through one's pretensions and humbug, and has gone to town with them. The laughter, when it comes, does not come naturally and easily; it comes painfully, and the strain shows.

That apology of a laughter comes despite oneself because, after seeing his cartoons for the first few times, almost none expect them to raise a laugh. Not even when Vijayan depicts the laughable. If the viewers belong to India's sophisticated, urban middle class, with its distinct normative biases and ideo-logical crutches, they soon come to suspect that Vijayan's real goal is to make them, his viewers, look dishonest and laughable at the same time.

They, therefore, go to him the way one goes to a psychoanalyst or psychiatrist—or, some might say, a dentist—unwillingly and often only because they find him morbidly fascinating. There is also the lingering hope, lovingly nurtured by the dominant style of cartooning and unwillingly selling the line that a cartoon is a minor morality play—an easy, painless guide to contemporary politics that can cure the ordinary citizens of their nightmares and inner doubts, and allow them to live with their own selves undisturbed by the demands of a brutalized public life. The encounter with Vijayan, they know, would be unpleasant but they hope that he would not make it too starkly self-confronta-tional. There is also perhaps a vague expectation that he, being from their class, would be kind towards their favourite defensive shield, what psychoanalyst Wilhelm Reich used to call, charac-ter armour. They give up soon enough, when they find Vijayan reluctant to play footsy with their secret fears and hopes, and dub him an eccentric nihilist.

I am afraid I cannot recommend *The Tragic Idiom* as an easy anodyne or a cure for insomnia. I suggest that you use it in homeopathic doses, as an occasional mirror for the country and the class to which you belong, particularly when you feel you have had enough of orchestrated nationalism and the media-soaked, over-fed, self-certain politicians vending their hollow visions.

* * *

It is a pity that ill-health has forced Vijayan to lay aside his brush at a time when India's dominant public culture is going through a phase of pathological self-righteousness and seems eager to induct—indeed push—the rest of society into a consensus on the pet aversions and addictions of the country's quickly expanding middle class. I wish Vijayan was working at a furious pace now, to debunk the certitude that has flooded India's public life. And I hope that this collection will partially bridge the gap that has opened in our political culture. It is a powerful and captivating commentary on the past of India's future.

In the end, I must admit that this is one foreword I always wanted to write, ever since Vijayan once made me write a few lines on his cartoons many years ago. I belong to Vijayan's tribe, comprising those who have betrayed their class, and I have watched in rapt admiration the demolition job he has done for our generation. It covers not merely targets that are easy and fashionable to attack, but also ones that are politically incorrect to touch. The latter include the slogans that have helped our class to establish its stranglehold over the culture of Indian politics and the media. These slogans—national security, development, and progress are the foremost among them—also include old favourites like class struggle, revolutionary violence, and the vanguard of the proletariat. Together they serve as the constituents of a new secular religion. In the name of that religion, one can now inflict any amount of suffering on the new untouchables of our times, on those who can cope neither with the market nor with our concepts of progress and nationalism, nor even with the ornate, exclusive vocabulary we have developed in the name of emancipatory ideologies. It is easy to take a position against the usual suspects, more difficult to take a hard look at one's own kind. By embarking on that more difficult task, Vijayan has only reconfirmed his stature as one of the foremost social critics and chroniclers of our times.

BOOK III

THE WORK OF CULTURE

18

The Fear of Plague

*The Inner Demons of a Society**

Plague activates anxieties and imageries like few other diseases do. Tuberculosis invokes images of dissipation and waste, occasionally even intimations of nineteenth-century romanticism and self-destruction. John Keats suffered from tuberculosis; so probably did Saratchandra Chattopadhyay's hero Devdas. Cancer has become associated in recent years with mindless over-consumption and the revenge of nature. It is mainly seen as a disease of the rich and the powerful who, after getting the best of health care, have to find some reason to die after a robust hospital bill. Plague activates more primitive fears, particularly in Europe. There are countries in Europe that have lost more than half their populations to plague in the past. The continent has lost, at some points of time, as many as one-fourth of its inhabitants to different versions of the Black Death. That memory survives.

* An earlier version of this chapter was first published in Vinay Lal and Ashis Nandy (eds), *The Future of Knowledge and Culture: A Dictionary for the 21st Century* (New Delhi: Penguin [now Penguin Random House India], 2005), pp. 222–6.

The primeval European fear of plague has got entwined with the fear of the Third World. There may no longer be a proper second world any more, to guide the poor and the dispossessed towards an expert-driven proletarian utopia, but the Third World survives as a concept for the First World and the modern elites of Asia and Africa. In that meaning, the Third World is the abode of the third rate, where a surplus of obsolete people, living in dirt and penury, provide a fertile breeding ground for pestilences of all kinds. Poverty is a crime and a proof of one's worldly failures and sinful ways. The ungodly are also the god-forsaken, and hence, pestilence-prone. The best one can do is to avoid their contagion.

Albert Camus's novel, *The Plague* (1947), is set in Algeria, and its white doctor–hero, working among Arab victims of plague, symbolizes a person seeking existential meaning in a battle against an epidemic that did not have an established cure when the events in the novel supposedly take place. He acts out the philosophy of life spelt out in the author's *Le Mythe de Sisyphe* (1942). As is well known, Sisyphus was condemned by the gods to roll a stone uphill for eternity. *The Plague* is the story of a modern Sisyphus battling the random suffering of a people and, in the process, giving meaning to an otherwise meaningless life.

The fear and the fantasies associated with plague, particularly in European Christendom, cannot be contained by any discovery of plague vaccines or of antibiotics effective against the disease. Most Europeans are not impressed that the mortality rate for plague has reportedly come down to below 5 per cent the world over, and in well-equipped West European or North American hospitals, that rate cannot but be even lower. We are told that in the United States, every year one or two persons are either infected or die of plague. No one notices that, and the epidemiologists do not seem to be bothered.

However, the older associations of the disease survive. As Ingmar Bergman shows so elegantly in *The Seventh Seal* (1956), plague is located in a melancholic, grey, mental landscape where it cohabits with ideas of sin, moral responsibility, death-defiance, repentance, and expiation. That landscape remains, but has become invisible in recent centuries, thanks to the overdone festive style of modern capitalism. Europe's post-medieval prosperity promises perpetual happiness in a deathless society. Instances of plague, remembered there primarily as a medieval disease, are a reminder that death *does* come, even in a world of plenty, dominated by mega-science and fool-proof rationality, packaged in hyper-consumption.

The fear of plague in Europe, however, is not only the fear of death. It is the fear of death that comes as the Biblical wage of sin. It carries the load of one's own past—when life was nasty, brutish, and short—projected on to the Third World. The Third World is living in abject misery because that is what the heathens deserve in God's scheme of things. The misery is also read as Europe's past that survives and haunts the modern, desacralized Europe and its godless ways. The Third World visits Europe as the plague when European Christendom fails to maintain its purity of body and of mind.

Plague also gives ample scope for heroism. The knight who plays chess with Death in *The Seventh Seal* is not a mere cinematic figure. He lives in the unconscious of all Europeans. He is a crusader who has already risked his life for his faith. His decision to take on Death in plague-ridden Europe cannot but acquire heroic proportions. Likewise, the doctor in *The Plague* battles an epidemic as the ultimate symbol of heroic resistance to the vagaries of fate. As befits an existentialist hero, he creates his morality out of essential meaninglessness.

* * *

The fear of plague in India is of a different kind. Here too, plague connotes moral waywardness and divine retribution, but the disease does not invoke the inner demons that haunt Europe. Small pox and cholera are the prototypical diseases of the tropics; without learning about them no student can graduate from a school of tropical medicine even today. Even tuberculosis has acquired a mythic status over the last 150 years, in at least South Asia. Plague, though it has sometimes been called a great killer or *mahamari*, remains for Indians, rightly or wrongly, an imported epidemic. It seems to thrive in cold weather, not in the torrid summers of India. Nor does it have, like Shitala and Olaichandi or Olaibibi, any goddess or god presiding over it or the fate of its victims, except in Karnataka where a Pilague-amma has a small, modest space in the pantheon. It certainly does not have any distinctive, traditional ritual to go with it in the rest of South Asia.

Hence, in India, it is more difficult to acquire mastery over plague by appeasing or establishing a contractual relationship, through a *manat* or *mannat*, with any particular deity. For the only deity associated with plague in Karnataka survives perhaps because Karnataka along with Kerala has port cities connected with Europe and West Asia. Perhaps, there is no felt need to have that sense of mastery over fate through a steady compact with divinity in the case of plague. Like malaria and unlike small pox and cholera, plague is probably an outsider in South Asia.

This is implicitly admitted by many Indians. Plague has been seen by them mainly as a scourge of urban India, marred by its dirty streets; mixed populations drawn from diverse, often unknown sources; unhealthy lifestyle; and crowded slums. Public hygiene and modern preventive medicine, combined with some degree of caution, are supposed to take care of plague when a specific threat exists. Hence, even at times of great pilgrimages like the Kumbha, efforts to inoculate pilgrims against plague are rare; they are mostly inoculated against small pox, typhoid, and cholera.

Yet plague has been visiting urban India on and off to take its toll. In recent times Surat, and to a small extent metropolitan cities like Bombay and Delhi, have been its main victims. I do not know how the residents of Surat explain the epidemic—as a failure in civic management, government apathy to prior warning by experts, or as the natural fate of a city that had no time to build a civic culture because it had lost its soul to Mammon and chose not to look beyond commerce.

I have a fair guess what the greatest Gujarati of all times might have said on Surat's encounter with plague in 1994, which killed only 52 persons but led one-fourth of Surat's population of nearly 4.5 million to flee from the city. He would have almost certainly invoked his notorious theory of collective *karma*, the one he had coined at the time of the Bihar earthquake in the 1920s. As we know, he blamed the earthquake on the practice of untouchability, to the utter chagrin of rational humanists like Rabindranath Tagore. Perfectly comfortable with the moral universe of pre-modern Europe, Mohandas Karamchand Gandhi would have, I am sure, held the particularly cruel communal riots of Surat in 1992 responsible for the outbreak of plague in the city.

19

Consumerism

Its Hidden Beauties and Politics*

Consumerism is not the first choice of human beings. Nor is it a basic need. There is not an iota of evidence in contemporary psychology, anthropology, or ethology that consumerism is a part of human nature, that we cannot survive without unending consumption. Not even the great champions of the free market have dared to claim that human happiness is inescapably hitched to the kind of consumption that the prosperous are encouraged to practice in the name of development today. Even much of the West, identified the world over with infinite consumption, had no genuine tradition of heavy consumption before the beginning of this century, probably not till the 1940s.

Consumption was discovered as a value and a lifestyle only about five decades ago. Previously, it had been a character trait of profligate rulers and the spoilt children of a few super-rich; now

* First published in Vinay Lal and Ashis Nandy (eds), *The Future of Knowledge and Culture: A Dictionary for the 21st Century* (New Delhi: Penguin [now Penguin Random House India], 2005), pp. 43–7.

it was made a marker of social achievement, and thus, a part of everyday life. People now consumed stories of super-consumption through newspapers, journals, and television—the way they earlier read of, fantasied about, and vicariously entered the harems of Oriental potentates. Earlier, the aristocracy, when it consumed mindlessly, did not dare to advertise the fact, for it was incongruent with class status. Only the newly rich were expected to flaunt their wealth. High consumption now became a marker of social status and success, and a patented remedy for feelings of social inadequacy and personal inferiority.

Perhaps no other country has become so deeply identified with consumption in our times as the United States, though some of the most powerful critiques of consumption, too, have come from that country. Perhaps the reason for both is that in no other country has consumption been so systematically institutionalized as a need in itself. A few city-states like Hong Kong and Singapore, and a few small kingdoms acting as city-states, such as Dubai, have also jumped on the bandwagon of 'consuming societies'. These are societies where not only is consumption an end in itself, but the entire country often looks to a casual observer like a huge supermarket, and the country's political economy, if not life itself, is organized around consumption. However, the global cultural impact of such city-states is not even a fraction of that of the United States.

In the United States, the successful institutionalization of consumption might have come about perhaps because it is mainly a society of immigrants that has tried to build a public culture hitched to the psychological and social needs of the exiled and the decultured. The institutionalization of consumption is an incidental by-product of this larger cultural process going on for the last 200 years. As I have said elsewhere, consumption has anxiety-binding properties, particularly in the lives of the uprooted, the lonely, and the massified.

This culture of exile also provides a clue to the unique status that the United States has begun to enjoy as everyone's second country.

In pre-War Europe, Paris claimed the status, I am told, of being every European's second city. For many subjects of British and French colonies, too, Paris, and to an even greater extent, London, had a similar status. Today, it seems that only the United States can claim that status. The size of the American market (including the market for conformity and deviance, and for new faiths, ideologies, and creeds) has a role to play in this. The United States is the consumer's paradise. Even dissent has a better market there than elsewhere; it is consumed more avidly and widely there than almost anywhere else. Even this critique of consumption can be consumed.

* * *

In the 1940s, Erich Fromm coined the term 'marketing orientation' to describe a personality type that included persons who sold their selves rather than things in the modern marketplace. He did not foresee that one day we shall have another personality type that would consider it 'normal' to consume for the sake of consuming. The consuming orientation is now a hallmark of style and high fashion; there are persons and groups in the world famous only for their flamboyant consumption. These hyper-consumers would have put to shame the greediest rich before World War II.

Usually while justifying consumption, marketeers claim that it will lead to greater consumption of the physical essentials of life by the poor. Alternatively, they extol the technological growth or economic modernization that follows a consumption explosion, allegedly serving as an engine of development. It has, however, already become obvious that the kind of consumption they have in mind—or are comfortable with—has nothing to do with any such grand social vision. For once built, a culture of consumption becomes a self-perpetuating affair. As has been the case with the super-consuming rich, it becomes an end in itself. This is not unknown to development experts; they expect consumption to lead to consumption-oriented development and technology. I am not saying that their economic logic is faulty. I am arguing that their justifications for consumption capture only a small part of the phenomenon and spirit of consumption.

To understand that spirit, one must first face the fact that to make consumption a value, human beings have to be re-engineered. The first step in it is to isolate or uproot a person from his or her community, traditions, and family. In their place, he or she has to be given a large, anonymous quasi-community called the nation; a more manageable set of cultural artefacts called traditions (artefacts that can be consumed in a theatre, gallery, classroom, or a tourist resort); and a nuclearized unit called a family where the elderly and the underaged both become either intrusions or liabilities that have to be sometimes borne but never treated on the same footing as the conjugal pair, bonded together by a commodified concept of sex.

Simultaneously, an ideological basis has to be laid for consumption. The possessive individual who, according to many European scholars, provides the very basis of modern liberal capitalism, has to be redefined as the consuming individual. Simultaneously, the right to property has to be redefined as the right to consumption. And the full sovereignty of this consuming individual has to be declared. So that the apparent sacredness that attaches to the individual in many theories of the state, freedom, and rights begins to attach to the act of and the right to consumption. Some social and political activists claim that standardized production systems are producing standardized consumption patterns, for only such patterns now make economic sense. Many popular ideas of democracy in the global mass culture seem, on closer scrutiny, to be an attempt to protect this pattern and the particular form of individualism that goes with it. As some put it, 'dollarized poverty' is now matched by dollarized wealth and dollarized individuals.

To such an individual—lonely, narcissistic, and decoupled from community ties—consumption becomes the ultimate value, a guarantor of social belongingness and status. He or she compensates for an empty social life by consuming. One is because one consumes.

This lonely individual is the basic constituent of all projects of global marketing. Marketing is all about creating needs. Basic needs do not have to be advertised; people automatically try to meet them and are willing to work or pay for them. Advertisements become necessary to create artificial needs. Marketing is the art and science of creating such needs by linking them to basic human needs. This linkage is often not noticed. Many talk of consumerism as a form of a conspiracy to cheat the ordinary innocent citizen with the help of smart, high-pitched advertisement. The ordinary citizen is not that easily cheated. They are influenced by advertisements but first a void has to be created in their lives, so that the magic of advertisement and its seductiveness can work on them.

The creation of that void is crucial. Only when his or her life is emptied of a deep sense of belongingness to a community, family, or tradition does the atomized individual begin to seek meaning in various pseudo-solidarities, one of the most important of which, today, is the solidarity of consumers. Presidents and prime ministers in the first world are now made or unmade on the basis of the threat they pose to—or the promises they offer of—mega-consumption. Consumption, or the hope of it, now gives meaning to the lives of many, however odd that may sound to a large proportion of the world. This has even produced a new internationalism which, paradoxically, relieves one from any responsibility to learn about other countries or communities. You do not have to, for others also consume, and therefore they are. They also can be known through their consumption patterns.

* * *

Yet, consumerism is not anti-cultural. Being a worldview, it has a place for culture. That place is not for culture as we have known it—vibrant, unmanageable, fuzzy, and often suspicious or subversive of the projects called progress and development—but for a consumable culture. Once such a culture becomes triumphant, many known entities in our world acquire new meanings. For instance, I notice remarkable and rapid changes taking place in ancient civilizations such as China and India. There are already signs that, under a consumerist dispensation, the Indianness of India may become a liability and yet, at the same time, a capital. Much effort, we may presume, will be made in the coming years to encash that Indianness as a form of commodified classicism or ethnic chic, 'viewable' on the weekends and saleable in the tourist market.

Do cultures resist consumerism? I do not really know. But I like to believe that they can hit back when threatened with extinction, whether the threat is real or imaginary. Human biology can be even more aggressively resistant. A large majority of the killers in the first world have to do with over-consumption. Worse is the fate of those ethnic groups in the First World which have not developed any scepticism towards consumption. The incidence of cardiac diseases among expatriate South Asians in some Western societies today is three times that among the native Whites.

20

Coca-Cola*

The first principle of the philosophy of Coca-Cola is that Coca-Cola is substitutable only by another cola. The substitute may be Diet Coke at some point of time (indicating a concern with health) or Pepsi at another (indicating a subtler sensitivity to taste), but it must be a cola. For, once exposed to the world of cola, life in a community cannot be defined any more without some version of a cola. The spectrum of human needs in the community expands permanently and can never again contract to what it was before cola drinks entered it. Everything else about Coca-Cola is negotiable but not the issue of non-substitutability. A cola can never be replaced by tea, coffee, beer, wine, fruit juice, or water. That is why, in the global scene, Coca-Cola's archetypal Other, its chief competitor, is Pepsi.

Many of my cleverer friends—South Asians, Americans, and citizens of other countries—tell me how autonomous they are of what they contemptuously call the Coca-Cola culture. They do not

* An earlier version of this chapter was published in Vinay Lal and Ashis Nandy (eds), *The Future of Knowledge and Culture: A Dictionary for the 21st Century* (New Delhi: Penguin [now Penguin Random House India], 2005), pp. 37–42.

drink Coca-Cola; they do not even like its taste. In some cases, they also force their children to be abstemious. Proud of their dissent from the global mass culture, they flaunt their 'deviance' by talking about Coca-Cola the same way others talk of McDonald's and Woolworths, or red meat, hard liquor, and tobacco. Their attitude to cola is a mix of contempt (towards what they see as an important aspect of low culture) and fear (towards a caffeine-based drink which, according to some experts, is bad for health).

I doubt if such deviance is as deviant as many think. The very fact that one must flaunt such dissent, that the dissent is confined only to cola drinks and does not extend to other items of useless consumption, tells us something. It tells us that Coca-Cola is a worldview, a philosophy of life, within which there is ample scope for variation and even some scope for dissent.

This is what was forgotten during the brief tenure of the Janata Party at the helm of the Indian polity during 1977–9. The then minister of industries, George Fernandes, threw the Coca-Cola Company out of India. Fernandes thought he was being true to both his socialism and Gandhism, apart from contributing handsomely to India's drive for self-reliance. He was operating faithfully within the given framework of the philosophy of Coca-Cola. For Coca-Cola was duly substituted by Campa Cola, the product of an Indian corporation, and by Thums up, produced by another multinational. Now, more than a decade afterwards, to spite the likes of Fernandes, Coca-Cola has re-entered the Indian market triumphantly. It is also triumphantly competing with Pepsi to provide the ultimate prototype of market competition that is supposed to be the salvation of Mother India soon.

The secret of Coca-Cola, closely guarded by the company, and an object of greedy curiosity for every other producer of cola drinks, also constitutes a paradigmatic puzzle for our times. Many other companies the world over have come close to Coca-Cola's unknown formula, to judge by the tastes of their products. Others have often deliberately come close to, but not duplicated, the formula. They have sought to create a distinct or unique place for themselves in the cola market, a place not occupied by Coca-Cola itself. The success of these competitors has occasionally been spectacular. But that does not—in fact, cannot—detract from the mystery of the formula, the code still waiting to be cracked, the standard waiting to be approximated. No argument about local, regional, or national variations in taste can ultimately work in such cases. Any such argument must fail as decisively as the touch of cinnamon and cardamom in some Indian cola drinks has failed to attract Indian customers in the long run. The philosophy of Coca-Cola has no place for—and does not have to bother about—popular cultures of different societies or regions. It bases itself on the global mass culture of consumption, apparently unaffected by local cultures, levels of economic activity, and political preferences. Local cultures may be hostile to the strangeness of Coca-Cola, the economy may not be able to sustain its production or import, and politicians may for symbolic reasons seek to 'clean' a society of its colaphiles. But remove the external compulsions, and the attachment to or love for Coca-Cola comes back in its pristine purity.

Everyone knows this, though only a few acknowledge it. Thus, when India threw out Coca-Cola, Air India, which had to woo Indians in competition with other international airlines, understood the logic of the situation perfectly well. It was neither impressed by slogans of self-reliance and basic needs nor by the industrial policy of the airline's owner, the Government of India. Air India never served its passengers any of the Indian versions of cola.

Coca-Cola touches something deep in human existence. Like many other elements of the presently dominant global mass culture—such as pop music, jeans, and hamburgers—it reminds its consumer of the simple, innocent joys of living, which might have been mostly lost in the modern world but which survive in symbolic form in selected artefacts of modernity. Hence the difficulty of giving up Coca-Cola and the fanaticism of the lapsed colaphiles. Like a heavy smoker who gives up smoking and becomes an anti-smoking activist, those rejecting Coca-Cola on ideological grounds or fulminating against the Coca-Cola culture must fight against a part of their own selves.

Coca-Cola, of course, is the ultimate symbol of the market. You cannot have a cola without a market. You can have orange juice or tea or beer without going to a market. Theoretically, you can grow oranges and squeeze their juice manually at your home. Theoretically, you can grow your own tea and drink it, if you happen to be at the right altitude and in the right kind of territory, or brew your own ale, if you have the patience. None of these are possible in the case of a cola. There is no territory or altitude in the world where you can grow your own cola and consume it. You have to have your cola in some readymade form, you do need a franchise for it, and you have to be part of the global market to have access to the world of Coca-Cola.

* * *

I need hardly add that the philosophy of Coca-Cola is not confined to Coca-Cola alone or to colas in general. It informs many areas of life, and the votaries of the philosophy would like it to ultimately inform all areas of life. They do not have to work hard for that, because the philosophy is blatantly phagocytic; it eats up all other adjacent philosophies, or alternatively, seeks to turn them into ornamental dissenting philosophies within its universe.

A neat example is American politics, and for that matter, much of liberal–democratic politics the world over. The most remarkable aspect of democracies, today, is the way they are abstracting all politics out of elections. Elections are now primarily media ploys and secondarily politics. They are fought the way giant corporations fight media wars—through advertisement spots, with droves of media experts and public relations consultants remote-controlling the battle from the side-lines. The voters are given a choice between images, sold as alternatives to one another, while being only each other's flip side.

The candidates think that the 'political' needs of the electorate can be engineered through experts. The experts think all candidates are edited versions of each other; only their public images differ. For both, the ultimate model of political contests is not the boxer's ring but the advertisement battles between popular brands of consumables, none of which could be called essential except in terms of needs artificially created in the consumer. The strategy is borrowed straight from the titanic battle between Coca-Cola and Pepsi for higher market shares.

The consumers—also called the electorate—are never given a chance to stop and think or confront the possibility that they might be deciding their own fate. The philosophy of Coca-Cola insists you never acknowledge that the game might have ended or changed for you. It insists that you go on playing the game, for worse than losing is to opt out or own that your needs could be or have become so different that the game is not relevant to you.

The philosophy of Coca-Cola is the paradigmatic social philosophy of our time. Those who talk glibly of the Coca-Cola culture subverting other 'superior' cultures know nothing of its appeal. Coca-Cola happily grants such superiority when the market or advertisement policies require it, for its appeal is nothing less than an invitation to worsen it at its own game. Japan, which can be called the Pepsi of the world economy, has shown that Coca-Cola can be 'defeated' if one joins the game sincerely and recognizes that the real battle is on TV, in our drawing rooms and in our hearts. It has also shown—as the five little Far Eastern economic dragons are doing now—that one can win only if one retools oneself to withstand the rigours of fighting Coca-Cola on its own terrain.

Academician Primakov, the Russian social scientist, seemed surprised in the 1980s that, in Düsseldorf, McDonald's employed more people than the steel industry and Coca-Cola paid more tax than Krupps. An old-style Marxist scholar, he failed to appreciate that mass culture was not only sane politics, but also rational economics, that defiance of mass culture was already defiance of sanity and rationality. To have the luxury of that defiance, you must take on not only the world of mega-consumption but also the worlds of normality and rational knowledge.

Many years ago, when as a new scientific and cultural innovation, Coca-Cola began its journey through the corridors of time, it allegedly included cocaine as an ingredient. If true, some may like to read this history as a standard example of corporate greed and immorality, as proof of how little the Coca-Cola Company cared for its consumers. I read it differently—as proof of how little the company itself understood the product it was unleashing on the global culture. The company, following the tenets of nineteenth-century capitalism, was selling something addictive to hold on to its clientele and to make the demand for its product artificially inelastic. It had no idea that it was a pioneer selling a worldview and a lifestyle. It did not know that even without using a physically addictive ingredient, it had produced a culturally addictive brew that could ensure as inelastic a demand as any bootlegger or drug peddler might want.

In the mass culture that has begun to engulf the urban, media-exposed, modernizing South, Coca-Cola is an epistemological, not ontological statement. It is a way of thinking rather than thought; perhaps even a way of dreaming that subverts other kinds of dreams.

21

Sugar

*An Incidental Obituary of the Humble Jaggery**

Some decades ago, Mr Kalpnath Rai, India's food minister, banned
the production of *gur* (molasses, treacle, or jaggery) in India.
All sugarcane would be diverted to the production of sugar, he
declared, to meet the shortage and the rising price of sugar in the
country. Whether temporary or permanent, this edict probably
marked the final decline of a dietary tradition that was at least two
millennia old in India. It is a tradition that is already dead or mori-
bund in most other countries of the world.

The attack on gur is not new, and Mr Rai and the Indian state,
not being particularly imaginative, have only followed conventional
wisdom. Sugar is a cash crop that fetches higher prices, stores better, and is an industrial product. It can also be used for producing
high-priced alcohol, and the global food industry loves to put it in
as many industrial food products as it can think of—from ketchups

* An earlier version of this chapter was published in Vinay Lal and
Ashis Nandy (eds), *The Future of Knowledge and Culture: A Dictionary
for the 21st Century* (New Delhi: Penguin [now Penguin Random House
India], 2005), pp. 317–21.

and potato chips to breads and jams. Naturally, sugar-making is seen as a form of development, and international bodies like the World Bank have always been partial towards it, often investing millions of dollars in the growth of the sugar industry .

The production of gur, on the other hand, is a low-brow, non-polluting cottage industry and family skill. It is seen as a surviving custom that has little to contribute to a country's growth rate. One indicator of this way of thinking is that, for the last so many years, when farmers get loans for producing sugarcane in India, they cannot use their crop to produce gur; they *have* to produce sugar.

White, crystalline, refined sugar is a relatively new entrant on the world scene. The older civilizations did not use it, though some of them almost certainly knew how to make it. It became a part of the West's staple diet only in the seventeenth and eighteenth centuries. Its production got a boost after African slave trade began and brought to the cultivation of sugarcane in the Americas, particularly North America, cheap labour. Even after slavery was abolished in the British colonies in the Americas, in some places in the Caribbean islands, farmers cultivating other crops were often forced at gun point to cultivate sugarcane.

With the expanding production of sugar and dramatic fall in its price, the popularity of sugar in Europe increased, not merely among the elite but also among the hoi polloi. Something that was sweet, pure, and white could not but be good for health, the argument presumably went. By 1815, per capita sugar consumption in Britain, at the time the most industrialized country in the world, had risen to 33 kilograms per year. However, it was still a far cry from the present average of over 55 kilograms per person in highly developed countries.

Sugar consolidated its position as the main sweetener and drove out jaggery from the diets of most Asian and African societies only in this century. In parts of India, jaggery was used in tea till quite recently. Even in the so-called advanced societies of the West, only in this century has the consumption of sugar reached pathological levels. Despite the growing popularity of various sugar substitutes and growing health consciousness, each day, the average American, for instance, still consumes a gargantuan amount of sugar, to equal which he would have had to eat roughly 30 kilograms of beetroots daily before the popularization of refined sugar.

The human body is not built to bear such a massive assault. By all accounts, such rates of consumption lead to a quick 'high' in blood sugar levels, followed by the pancreas trying to feverishly break it down by secreting insulin, thus creating an artificial 'low'. According to Dag Poleszynski, that low blood sugar level produces a 'severe state of stress', giving rise to 'emotional instability in the form of depression, anxiety, irritability', and predictably, a craving for more sugar. He traces the high rates of mental illness and the spread of various forms of drug addiction in the West to the mindless consumption of sugar. Others hold the body's inability to cope with huge fluctuations in blood sugar responsible for fatigue, nervousness, inability to handle alcohol, lack of concentration, and allergies.

In much of West Europe and North America, mortality patterns are now quite similar. About 55 per cent die of cardiovascular diseases, and about 35 per cent of cancer. (The figures should not be very different for South Asia's westernized elite, for available data suggest that the incidence of heart diseases is higher among the Indian immigrants than among the natives in the First World.) Of these, while cardiovascular ailments have been linked directly to over-consumption of sugar, some forms of cancer have been linked to sugar more indirectly, through the changes in dietary habits that have accompanied the popularization of sugar. Apart from the well-known side-effects of sugar like obesity and diabetes, its overuse has also been linked to a variety of social pathologies, including non-specific violence. High intake of sugar is not merely a marker of modernization; it is also, it seems, a pathway to self-destruction.

In the meanwhile, as with other pathologies of modernity, the problems created by sugar have encouraged the corporate world to generate, and then cater to, a new set of needs. Markets are now flooded with all kinds of remedies designed to cope with the ill-effects of sugar. They range from a variety of sugar substitutes to a large number of drugs that are advertised as certain protection against over-indulgence in sugar. For example, the same companies that produce sugar, which damages teeth, often have a stake in companies that produce fluoride toothpastes designed to redress the situation. The medical establishment is also all too willing to discuss the hazards of eating sugar and the problems created by obesity. But nobody, or almost nobody, dares to suggest that the production of sugar need not be encouraged.

The Atlantic slave trade was one of the most tragic and violent chapters in human history; it is a story of unbelievable human cruelty towards fellow humans. By some estimates, about one-third of all captured slaves died in transit during the passage from Africa to the Americas. They died like flies from epidemics and ill-treatment, and no dignity was granted to them even in death. The spread of slavery owed much to the demands of the sugar plantations in the new world.

The cultivation, production, and popularization of sugar—which in turn owed so much to the slave trade—is now repaying that blood debt with interest. My guess is that if one takes into account both direct and indirect victimization, including the abridgement of life and degradation of its quality, the number of people killed by sugar during this century may well turn out to be larger than the number of Africans killed on the way to America's sugar plantations. As James Ridgeway, the author of *It's All for Sale:The Control of Global Resources*, sums up the story, 'No agricultural crop has brought such misery to the world as sugar. Sugar has ruined land from one end of the earth to the other.'

There is more than poetic justice in this. There is in it the lesson that oppression always has, in the long run, proved as disastrous to the oppressors as to the victims. In the short run, however, this may not be much of a consolation to the defeated cultures. All they can do is to marvel at the fact that what the white plantation owners and promoters of sugar did at gun point about two centuries ago, the overweight Mr Kalpnath Rai and the dumb bureaucrats of the food ministry were trying to do by pushing files.

22

Solitude*

Solitude as a moment of inner stillness, touched by a sense of inner composure, has been traditionally a cradle of artistic creativity and great thought. In many cultures, solitude is sought and cultivated by creative artists, thinkers, mystics, and world-renouncers. In some others, solitude is associated not only with gifted artists and artisans but also with shamans and philosophers. But even in such cultures, ordinary mortals can hope to cultivate or snatch moments of inner stillness or serenity by distancing themselves from a dense, crowded, interpersonal world or a raucous public domain. Indeed, this capacity to snatch solitude from unlikely places is said to be in these cultures a vital clue to happiness and a definitive marker of wisdom.

Note that solitude must be 'cultivated' and sought even by those who are usually identified with solitude; it is not a natural

* This note has grown out of preliminary comments made at the seminar on Solitude, organized as part of the Fifth *Cinemaya* Festival of Asian Cinema on 22–3 July 2003 at the India Habitat Centre, New Delhi. It was published subsequently in *Cinemaya*.

attribute of even philosophers, mystics, shamans, or gurus. Only a few of them can be called recluses. Many of them have a rich interpersonal life.

The opposite of solitude, from this point of view, is not multitude, human company, or a crowd. The opposite of solitude is loneliness. Loneliness is never cultivated, though it can sometimes be sought. Loneliness is usually avoided and fought, directly or indirectly, except when it is a component of solitude or is seen as such. Many today do not distinguish between loneliness and solitude. There is also a vague awareness that loneliness today is becoming a major civilizational problem; it is no longer an individual predicament. No one, to my knowledge, has yet claimed solitude to be a social problem.

Nor can being alone by itself be a problem, unless it is seen as a synonym of loneliness. My colleague and friend Rajni Kothari, the eminent political scientist and futurist who lived alone in his last years, once seemed slightly offended when a friend visiting him remarked, 'You must be lonely'. Kothari said, rather firmly, 'I am *not* lonely; I am alone.' Unknowingly, he was making a sharp distinction between being alone and loneliness the way some psychoanalysts have done in the clinical context.[1]

In many traditional societies, the scope for loneliness was limited and usually came from external sources such as bereavement, imprisonment, or exile. The problem most people faced in such societies was perhaps not loneliness but an excess of human company. You lived in a community and a family, and the preponderance of primary over secondary social ties—to use an old-fashioned sociological classification of human relationships—ensured that you could not easily withdraw from the interpersonal world to have some time for yourself and with yourself. Hence,

---

[1] For an overall picture of the psychoanalytic position on the subject, see, for instance, Myer D. Mendelson, 'Reflections on Loneliness', *Contemporary Psychoanalysis*, 1990, 26(2): 330–55.

the high value that attached to solitude and the association that solitude had with major forms of human creativity and intellectual achievements.

That connection and the styles of creativity associated with solitude persist, but their scope and range have diminished drastically. Often, those who use solitude as the base of their creative life seem cut off from mainstream public life and its concerns. There are apparent exceptions, though. The great mystic Jalaluddin Rumi is enjoying a renewed vogue today, and there have always been small bands of admirers of Ralph Waldo Emerson and Henry David Thoreau. Likewise, in cinema, there are a few like Andrei Tarkovsky, and cinema aficionados in India might add, the gifted Malayali director G. Arvindan.

Such people have a very distinct place in our intellectual landscape, but we also know that the more glittering stars in our times have always been those whose creative styles owe something to their titanic struggles with loneliness. Perhaps because, in modern times, most of us are grappling with an inner sense of loneliness even when immersed in a lively interpersonal world, organized thought or artistic self-expression based on a sharp awareness of human loneliness has a natural appeal for many. Fyodor Dostoevsky, Charles Baudelaire, Vincent Van Gogh, and Albert Camus among writers and artists, and Ingmar Bergman, Rainer Fassbinder, Jean-Luc Godard, Guru Dutt, and Ritwik Ghatak among filmmakers, are examples of creative minds that have openly battled loneliness. Of course, there is much diversity among these artists and thinkers. The desolate landscape of Bergman differs from the carnivalesque celebration of life mixed with self-pity in Guru Dutt. But they have all flirted with desperate, depressive isolation, and self-destruction.

In the normal rhythm of unheroic, everyday life, the battle against loneliness takes a different form. Many fight loneliness—and the fear of nothingness that loneliness often triggers—by seeking some degree of love, fame, or adoration. That is their version—Ernest Becker, author of *The Denial of Death* and *Escape from Evil* might say—of death denial.[2] Such defensive manoeuvres do not necessarily cure the inner sense of loneliness, but give one the feeling that one is wanted, and hence, not lonely. Even great revolutionaries and populist heroes are driven by fears of such inner loneliness and abandonment.

Two standard remedies for loneliness in our times are entertainment and consumerism. By former, I mean entertainment that turns the person being entertained into a passive consumer of messages. A novel at least forces readers to imagine the characters and the events in their minds. In television and popular cinema, that option narrows; they are closer to being total media. Virtual reality is exactly what its name suggests. Only a deliberate, personal act of will allows you to escape its seductive charms. Empirical surveys suggest that, for many Indians, television is crypto-human company. In some households, the TV is switched on mechanically during certain hours of the day, not so much for viewing but as an additional social presence. It wards off, if not loneliness, at least fears of loneliness.

The other time-tested and popular means of fighting loneliness in our times is, of course, consumerism. For millions, consumerism has become almost a personal existential statement that serves as an endorsement of individualism. Indeed, consumerism is often read and promoted as the ultimate expression of individualism, even though it can be argued that individuals are driven to consumerism through media management in a way that paradoxically reduces the free play of individualism. Not merely is consent manufactured, conforming to Erich Fromm's formulation ventured in the 1940s, people in a consumer society choose what they are prompted to choose. Fromm's diagnosis finds indirect endorsement from David Riesman, Nathan Glazer, and D. The derivative nature of contemporary individualism—and

[2] Ernest Becker, *The Denial of Death* (New York: Free Press, 1973); *Escape from Evil* (New York: Free Press, 1985).

the element of dependency built into it—are underwritten by an ontological self-affirmation that glibly proclaims 'I consume, therefore, I am.'

Given the scope of loneliness and the sugar-coated pills often vended as sure-shot, magical cures for it, it is not surprising that some of our great cultural heroes are those who have used loneliness as a base for their creativity. Using such a base means being in touch with a central crisis and global concerns in our times; it resonates. Because neither entertainment nor unthinking consumption can truly cope with the inner sense of loneliness; they only provide temporary respite. Even when we entertain ourselves to death or shop till we drop, in one corner of our minds, we are vaguely aware of what is happening to us (as in one of Godard's films where the protagonists commit suicide by eating themselves to death).

Against this backdrop, I dare venture my belief that there is still scope for another kind of creativity that has closer links with solitude. Filmmaker T.V. Chandran, echoing an entire school of thought, has told us that most Indians are poor and cannot afford the luxury of loneliness or solitude. Frankly, I suspect that his movies themselves show that even the poor and the dispossessed, defying their well-wishers and other 'vanguards' of the poor and the exploited waiting in the wings, not only search for but also find moments of inner stillness and composure which have traditionally shaped the nature of human creativity. That is what allows them to retain their humanity and sanity and their 'gift of the fight'.

In this respect their position blends seamlessly with what might have already become the central challenge of our times. The challenge today, Frédérique Apffel-Marglin says on behalf of PRATEC (the Andean Project for Peasant Technologies), a radical activist group in Peru that mainly works on traditional agriculture but also doubles as an intellectual movement, is 'to rediscover the centrality of silence, of contemplation, of reverence, of receptivity; of knowing how to nurture the beings of the world and knowing how to let ourselves be nurtured by them in turn.'[3]

If the search for solitude survives in a culture, perhaps the culture can be said to be vaccinated against any serious epidemic of loneliness.

[3] Frédérique Apffel-Marglin, 'Knowledge Systems', in Vinay Lal and Ashis Nandy (eds), *The Future of Knowledge and Culture: A Dictionary for the 21st Century* (New Delhi: Penguin, 2005).

23

Ethnic Cuisine*

We can take the easy way out and answer Arjun Appadurai's question—why a pan-Indian cuisine did not emerge—by pointing out that even 50 years ago, to a non-urban Indian, no cuisines other than his own region's looked decisively Indian or, if you so prefer, ethnic. Most descriptions of inedible food that I have heard from Indians involve 'strange' Indian cuisines, not foreign ones. But that does not mean that there was no concept of other kinds of food, but to qualify as such they had to be the cuisine of one's significant others.

There *were* ethnic cuisines, but no one called them so. The cuisines of others were always a part of one's life—as markers of cultivation and class; as indicators of social status; or as esoteric rituals, meant for adventurers, travellers, and beginning in the nineteenth century, anthropologists. French cuisine did traditionally perform

* Extracted from the keynote address at a conference on food organized by Rachel Dwyer at the School of Oriental Studies, University of London, 22 November 2002. It was originally published in Vinay Lal and Ashis Nandy (eds), *The Future of Knowledge and Culture: A Dictionary for the 21st Century* (New Delhi: Penguin [now Penguin Random House India], 2005), pp. 90–5.

an important function for the European elite. For a long time, it had a particular cultural role to play, for instance, in English public life, despite widespread stereotypes of English insularity. English cuisine, in turn, had a place in colonized societies like India where, to spite the detractors of English food, many Indians accepted it as a marker of cultivation and others developed its more labour-intensive, spicier, tropical versions.

However, in the civilized world, ethnic styles of cooking were mostly organized within a stable, hierarchical frame. Even in bland Scandinavia and in the gloomy, self-sure ambience of Victorian and Edwardian London, the cognoscenti, the learned and the beautiful people served French food or some domesticated version of it on formal occasions. It is true that some members of the gentry seemed committed to good old healthy English food, but that was often a self-conscious gesture rather than a matter of preference. British Islanders in general, and not merely the English, have, for centuries, lived with feelings of inferiority as far as food and wines are concerned; even their love for their own food is tinged with a certain ambivalence. This is best reflected in Somerset Maugham's well-known saying that one could eat very well in Britain if one decides to have breakfast morning, afternoon, and night.

In the United States too, despite occasional paeans to the beauties of home-grown, wholesome American food, there has been a similar bent towards French and, to a lesser extent, Italian and Viennese cuisines for a long time. On formal occasions, presidents, members of the cabinet, generals, and university professors have tended to serve French food or some fusion of French and domestic fare. Sometimes, as an elegant variation, it has been Italian food. Everyone sings the glories of the American mom and her exploits in the kitchen, but formal, public banquet is another matter. There you stick to cuisines that are recognized as appropriate for such occasions.

Many societies have similar ideas of occasion when it comes to food. In my native Calcutta, Bengalis have always sung the glories of Bengali food, but when it comes to eating outside the home in a restaurant, they tend to choose some version of Mughal, North Indian, or, less frequently, European food (by which they usually mean Indianized British food, given fancy French or Italian names). The famous clubs of Calcutta, true to their colonial heritage, also serve English food that, some might say unfortunately, often tastes like English food. The city's first recognized Bengali restaurant was founded in the 1960s and it was a particularly modest affair, run by a women's cooperative. The city's first up-market Bengali restaurant opened in the 1990s. Kasturi in Dhaka, the capital of Bangladesh, is arguably the best Bengali restaurant in the world. At least one distinguished non-Bengali Indian editor, Dilip Padgaonkar, who is also a gourmet and a food theorist, has said so publicly. But it also is relatively new; my suspicion is that it began to function in the 1980s. There persists the belief that you do not eat Bengali food in a restaurant; you eat it at home or on formal occasions like marriages and anniversaries, as long you do not organize them as events in restaurants. Bengali food is only now becoming restaurant food.

Sometimes, it could be a mix of the occasion and the life cycle of the host. For a long time, Chinese food in the United States was meant for university students with meagre budgets, eating out on the weekends or playing host to their friends and teachers. It was different and it was cheap. For decades, Indian food has played a roughly similar role in London and other large cities in Britain. An entire generation of British women has been brought up, thanks to their boyfriends and classmates, with random but sustained exposure to an amalgam of Mughal and Punjabi curries, cooked mainly by Bengalis. Exactly as an entire generation of older Americans now lives with their memories of Chinese food consumed in their student days in the company of their dates.

Things have been changing gradually but radically during the last three decades or so. Ethnic food is now serious business. It has made deep inroads into the global metropolitan culture. It has become a marker of the width of one's cosmopolitan experience. You can now talk with erudition and sensitivity on ethnic food for hours, and listeners are unlikely to be bored. Ethnic food as a public concern now occupies the same place that health food did three decades ago. The ability to discriminate amongst the different shades of a specific ethnic cuisine and the ability to have an informed chat with waiters before ordering food in a restaurant that serves lesser known fare like Ethiopian, Moroccan, or West Asian food have become signs of learning, elegance, and sophistication. These abilities are now analogous to the older status game that became popular in Edwardian England—the ability to address waiters by name in well-known restaurants.

Exogenous cuisines are now acquiring the status of African safaris, and are becoming the arena of a different kind of power play. No cuisine, however limited or flat, is considered inferior, except probably a few European ones, and certainly they cannot be called so in polite company. Though mainly tourists and the brave at heart are expected to frequent restaurants serving local fare in places like Scandinavia, the Netherlands, or Scotland, if you find Argentinean, Philippine, or sub-Saharan food uninteresting or not distinctive enough, you are supposed to keep your feelings to yourself.

Ethnic food has become the measure of one's tolerance of cultural diversity. Only philistines are supposed to grumble about any ethnic food served to them. You make a social and political statement if you dislike any cuisine, not if you like it.

At the same time, some of the old cast of suspects have acquired new stature and cultural meaning; they are basking in re-invented glory. Eating Chinese food in Chinatown is no longer a lowbrow or downmarket venture, nor is eating Indian curry in an Indian restaurant in a university town like Oxford in the United Kingdom. However, you may convey something about the level of your cultivation and cosmopolitanism if, when your business partner or research collaborator asks what kind of food preferences you have, you blandly proclaim your love for Chinese or Indian food. You are expected to specify what version of Chinese or Indian food you like. Your host will have much more respect for you if you suggest a Hunanese or Szechwanese restaurant or if you specifically demand that he takes you to a Malayali joint for *appam* or even to a Gujarati fast-food stall for *bhelpuri* or *khandvi*. (Indeed, ethnic fast foods are never stigmatized, unless they get associated with multinational chains. They are not even called fast food.)

Because everyone is looking for newer, stranger, and rarer kinds of ethnic eating places, the variety of ethnic cuisines available in the global metropolitan culture has proliferated enormously in the last 20 years. So have the skills demanded from the guests in these restaurants. On the one hand, customers visiting a Sri Lankan or Thai restaurant are expected to order the fierier versions of curries and not their domesticated editions that try to be kinder to one's palate and taste buds by avoiding an 'excess' of chillies. On the other hand, such restaurants have to distinguish or distance themselves from their more familiar neighbouring cuisines so that their customers do not feel cheated. Nepali restaurants in Manhattan naturally try to avoid preparations that are close to or indistinguishable from some forms of Indian food, however central to Nepalese cuisines these preparations might be in real life. In a global metropolis, a Cambodian restaurant just cannot serve the same fare as the Laotian or Vietnamese restaurant next door. At the same time, the former must cleverly include a few familiar things from the neighbouring cuisines to give itself a wider range and a longer menu, perhaps even a touch of familiarity.

There are other subtle shades in the canvas that cannot all be listed here. However, a couple of examples should give the reader a flavour of how, in the global cosmopolis, the expanding tradition of ethnic dining has become an institution and a billion-dollar enterprise. All visitors to ethnic restaurants in North America and Europe must have noticed the growing tendency to serve or demand country-specific beers with ethnic food. In general, you may choose your wines from all over the world, but you are supposed to drink Ethiopian beer with Ethiopian food and Japanese beer with Japanese. The demand is relaxed only in the case of American food; no one insists that one must only have American beer with it, though that also is coming, with more exclusive brands of American beers being identified. There may be some justification for this practice in the case of cuisines that use less spice and depend on flavours that are not overwhelming. But a good case can be made that in the case of cuisines that have 'overwhelming' tastes and flavours, the choice of beers becomes partly notional. Before you dip into a fiery Thai curry, you might legitimately claim to enjoy the subtleties of the Singha beer, which is after all a light ale, as the British call it. But once you start eating, nearly all beers should taste the same. Perhaps a Guinness with its strong taste will survive the onslaught of chillies and spices better. At least, there is some chance that one's palate would be able to savour the stout's personality. But drinking a Guinness with a Tom Yum soup would be considered blasphemous in the present dining culture of global metropolitanism.

Likewise, for years, experts on food and gourmets have advised those eating Indian food to opt for beers, not wines, because the heavy spices used in such food drown the flavour of wines. But that is no longer considered acceptable in the new global food culture. It is an insult to Indian food—and to the Indian civilization—to say that it is not compatible with a sophisticated, expert choice of wines. A plethora of columnists on food and wine have begun to dole out a plethora of advisories on how to choose the 'correct' wines for different kinds of Indian food, to the utter surprise of Indians, accustomed to drinking mainly plain water with their meals and having learnt, during the last 200 years, that gallons of Scotch whisky of dubious quality, and in its absence, arrack—the poor man's tequila—is the ultimate in dining pleasure.

One suspects that the culture of ethnic cuisine and ethnic dining has become more and more sophisticated and complex because it has become a major symbolic substitute for the cultures it is supposed to represent. This culture of food is paradoxically becoming more autonomous of the cultures from which the cuisines come and the civilizations or lifestyles they represent. And that is way things should go, most people seem to believe. Ethnic cuisine is expected to survive the demands of culture, and as the contemporary world pushes more and more cultures into extinction, talking incessantly of multiculturalism and democratic tolerance, ethnic cuisine becomes more and more like a museum or a stage on which a culture writes its name or signs an attendance register for the sake of appeasing our moral conscience and declaring its survival.

The Los Angeles Museum of the Holocaust displays some artefacts of Jewish culture thoughtfully collected by the Nazis for a projected museum on an extinct race after the Final Solution. Those were not the days of ethnic cuisine. Otherwise the Nazis would have surely added a wing to their museum where one could go to a well-appointed restaurant serving traditional Jewish fare from all over Europe.

24

Satyajit Ray's India

*Cinema, Creativity, and Cultural Nationalism**

Even before his death in 1992, Satyajit Ray aroused mixed feelings in a sizeable section of Indian film critics. Few denied his pioneering role in Indian cinema, but towards the end of his life, some serious film critics seemed to be in two minds about his overall vision and long-term influence. At least some of them resented that Ray's India had in effect become international cinema's India. The notorious outburst of film actor Nargis in Indian Parliament, that Ray was exploiting India's poverty in his films for the sake of his foreign audience, was only an obtuse expression of that unhappiness.

* This chapter has grown out of a brief article published as 'How Indian Is Satyajit Ray?', *Cinemaya*, Summer 1993, 20; and *Deep Focus*, 1996, 6. I am grateful to Aruna Vasudev, not only for her comments on an earlier version but for posing the original question to which this chapter is an extended response.

There were many reasons for that ambivalence. Ray was a humanist at a time when the perils of homocentrism were becoming more glaring, a modernist when the crisis of modernity was deepening, and a realist when the certitudes of realism were collapsing. However, the most important reason for the ambivalence always remained doubts about Ray's Indianness. Was Ray truly Indian? Or was he basically a highly Westernized, deracinated cosmopolitan who dealt with Indian themes merely because he happened to live in India? Was he, to use the contemporary buzz-word, a dark-skinned Orientalist? Were his films made mainly for Western film critics and a Western audience?

These questions acquired sharper edges with Ray's growing fame and influence. Cinema everywhere is a bewitching medium, and famous film directors are invariably subject to detailed biographical inquiry and persistent journalistic curiosity. In addition, Ray was a cultural hero, and came from a family of legendary literary figures. As people came to know his personal history and got accustomed to his public presence, they also came to know of his lifelong fascination for Western classical music and literature, his early indifference to Indian music and Bengali literature, his tenure in a fashionable advertising agency, and even his sophisticated English accent and Anglicized manners. (He reportedly ate even the Bengali staple, fish-curry-and-rice, using cutlery.) Ray *did* give the impression to many that India, and even Bengal, were for him an acquired taste.

I am, however, not concerned here with that part of the story. For me, these questions subsume more important concerns. I shall raise a few of them here to clarify the nature of the main question that underpins them, not to answer it, but to problematize the links between the politics of cultural creativity, public ethics, and aesthetic experiences of large segments of living Indians. For, questions about Indianness can be raised not only in the case of Ray, but also in the case of any one who does not self-consciously fit in with that model of creativity which refuses to pay homage to the acceptable cultural format of this generation of

Indian bourgeoisie. This acceptability is built on the increasingly narrow definition of public self the Indian middle class has chosen for itself in recent decades. To this class, some like novelist R.K. Narayan seem too tame and apolitical in their invocation of non-metropolitan India and, thus, arouse one kind of anxiety in the critics about their own critical self. Others like painter Ravi Varma arouse another kind of anxiety in the art historian by being too blatantly a 'mimic' and revealing the foundations of the historian's own aesthetic and political self.

* * *

On one plane, when one questions Ray's Indianness, it boils down to a latent, unsettling question about the nature of creativity in India: Can a highly Westernized, urbane Indian, fully cosmopolitan by global standards, be creative when dealing with something culturally typical and seemingly outside the reach of one who knows little of village India, caste society, or India's stylized modes of artistic self-expression first-hand? And that question, in turn, is part of the disowned, unresolved self-doubts of the Indian middle classes and their own cultural roots.

The same question can be raised in another form. Not in the form cultural anthropologists raise it when talking of categories internal to a culture and categories that are not, about the emic and the etic, but the way Robert Merton once did years ago.[1] Can, for instance, a White American write creatively about the American Blacks, whether using etic or emic categories? Structural–functionalism is terribly unfashionable these days, but one line of argument that Merton recognizes but does not pursue beyond a point seems particularly relevant in societies like India, honeycombed by myriad diversities. Namely, that the idea of the outsider

---

[1] Robert K. Merton, 'Insiders and Outsiders: A Chapter in the Sociology of Knowledge', *American Journal of Sociology*, July 1972, 78(1): 9–47.

and the insider can only end, logically, in a *reductio ad absurdum*. For instance, once you have argued that an American White scholar cannot truly write creatively about the American Blacks, because empathy has limits and cannot substitute for direct participation and experience, historical or contemporary, the same cultural argument can be pushed further. One can then say that the Black man cannot, in turn, write creatively about the experience of the Black woman. And, among Black women, the adult Black woman cannot fathom the anguish of the adolescent Black woman. And so on, till one is left with the proposition that no one can cross cultural boundaries to write about someone else's experience, that we live in a culturally solipsistic world. To adapt Berkeley's much-used aphorism, nobody can feel another person's toothache.

The second way of finding out the depth or reach of Ray's cultural roots is to look at the internal evidence of his films. Here we confront the remarkable fact that Ray's greatest and most creative films are the ones in which he deals with periods, social segments, and problems about which he had the least direct or personal experience. The Apu Trilogy, *Jalsaghar*, *Devi*—they are all far removed from the world in which Ray lived.[2] It is even doubtful if, before he made *Pather Panchali*, Ray had enough first-hand experience of an Indian village to qualify as a social anthropologist from even the most disreputable department of anthropology.[3] This anomaly remains to be explained.

---

[2] Writer Sunil Gangopadhyay says that Ray read for the first time the famous Bengali novel *Pather Panchali*, the basis of his first film, when he was invited by publisher Dilip Gupta of Signet Press, Calcutta, to illustrate the children's version of the novel, *Am Antir Bhepu*. The film version of *Pather Panchali* follows *Am Antir Bhepu* faithfully. Sunil Gangopadhyay, 'Priya Lekhak Satyajit Ray', in Shyamalkanti Das (ed.), *Lekhak Satyajit Ray* (Calcutta: Shivrani, 1986), pp. 17–20.

[3] Satyajit Ray, *Apur Panchali* (Calcutta: Ananda Publishers, 1995), esp. chapter 3. At one place Ray says: 'Till that time I had no direct experience of what one means when using the expression village life... I *had* once written in *Sight and Sound* [a film journal] that I had no explicit idea of

But then, this is an anomaly only to film critics, not to students of creativity. For in this respect Ray is no exception; many writers and artists show the same pattern. Joseph Conrad in *The Heart of Darkness* comes off as a better novelist than when writing novels set in locales better known to him; Pablo Picasso made a more creative use of African tribal arts than many African modern painters themselves have. The logic of fantasy life and self-transcendence is not the same as the logic of everyday life and common sense, Freud or no Freud. The absence of direct experience often allows a freer imaginary, and therefore, deeper access to the shared myths and experience of a culture, transmitted through channels other than what we like to call direct experience or academic training. Through an exercise of creative imagination, an artist is often capable of partially transcending the barriers imposed by the lack of direct experience and empirical knowledge, and even by the social determination of art. In some contexts, liminality can be an asset.[4]

Can the question of cultural authenticity and grounding then be raised in a third way? Can we say that whereas Ray's subject matter and treatment were Indian, his aesthetic, especially cinematic, values were Western? After all, cinema is not only a discovery of the modern West, it has become a paradigmatic mode of self-expression in the twentieth-century West.

---

what constituted the core of the story. Consequently, I had to depend on the descriptions in the original novel. The book, however, was an encyclopaedia of village life. But I also knew that I could not depend only on it. There were many things that I would have to discover myself. In an effort to understand village lifestyle, I found out that in front of my own eyes were opening up the doors of an astonishing world. I am born in a city and have grown up in a city. To me the taste and structure of this [lifestyle] was entirely new; its values were also entirely different.'

[4] See also Ashis Nandy, 'The Imagination of the Village', Lecture at the *Samskritishivira* (workshop on cultural studies) organized by Ninasam, Heggodu, Karnataka, 10–20 October 1994. Published in Vinay Lal (ed.), *Emergences*, 1995–6, (Special Issue Nos 7–8).

This question is important, at least prima facie. One can make, I suspect, a reasonably good case that some of the guiding principles of Ray's aesthetic passions and even some of the core values of his life were drawn from the European Enlightenment. Ray *was* a product of the cultural implosion that took place in Bengal in the nineteenth century, triggered by the British colonial presence, and Renaissance Europe was certainly a massive presence in his consciousness.

Two qualifications, however, should be kept in mind in this connection. First, there *are* many elements in Ray which cannot be explained in terms of Western aesthetics at all. If Indian aesthetic concerns do not explain all of Ray, their Western counterparts, by themselves, explain even less. A film like *Charulata* or *Devi* is certainly not a product of Western aesthetic values alone, though Western social values have a major role to play in each.[5] This is especially true of movies in which he was at his creative best. Elsewhere I have argued that in these movies Ray virtually created a powerful anti-self which defied his entire background, personal philosophy of life, and even his ideas of social and political rationality. As if he set up this anti-self to give fuller expression to his under-socialized imagination and reach down to his latent cultural self. Ray's values, the values that he would have owned up to self-consciously, found much more direct expression in his less serious work—in his children's stories, science fiction, and crime thrillers. It is in them that one finds him giving full play to his modernist self.[6] The

[5] For instance, part of the aesthetic appeal of Ray's *Devi* comes precisely from the director's—and the writer's—total unawareness that the interpersonal dynamics they portray in the story—the dynamics that guides the story to its tragic end—is built around the unacknowledged eroticized relationship of the heroine with her father-in-law.

[6] Ashis Nandy, 'Satyajit Ray's Secret Guide to Exquisite Murders: Creativity, Social Criticism, and the Partitioning of the Self', in *The Savage Freud and Other Essays on Possible and Retrievable Selves* (New Delhi: Oxford University Press, 1995), pp. 237–66.

most one can say is that, like many other creative people, Ray too perhaps lived with a plurality of selves, and a part of him was as deeply Indian as a part of him was Western.

This is not a casual, throw-away comment. If Satyajit Ray could not sustain such plurality within himself, he would have fulfilled the criteria laid down by some of our more noisy and self-righteous film theorists searching for a 'pure' India and Indianness in cinema—the way Rudyard Kipling, repelled by the bicultural babus questioning imperialism, searched all his life for genuine Indians in the form of apolitical, noble savages, the Gungadins—but he would have been untrue to his cultural and urban middle-class heritage. After all, Ray was an authentic Calcuttan babu and could not but be true to his cultural self without being bicultural—and to that extent untrue to traditional India—in his art. Paradoxically, that was his 'vernacular' inheritance.

Seen thus, our reformulated question becomes a pointer to a clash between authenticity and Indianness in a situation where every middle class Indian, to be truly Indian in his or her creative style according to the dictates of the new votaries of ethnic *chic*, must disown the entire experience of being Indian over the last 200 years. It is that 200-year-long experience—including the ambivalent affair with the West—that has ensured that all Indians have within their personality a significant bicultural component. What was once learnt as a technique of survival has now become a character trait, a part of the society's cultural repertoire, and a person's 'character armour'.[7]

---

[7] Recently, Gustavo Esteva and Madhu Suri Prasad have objected to my use of the term bicultural, especially since it seems to imply that one can simultaneously live with the mythological frames of two cultures and creatively use both. See Gustavo Esteva and Madhu Suri Prasad, 'Introduction', in *Bonfire of Creeds: The Essential Ashis Nandy* (New Delhi: Oxford University Press, 2004). For the moment, I shall bypass this issue by only emphasizing the integrative potentialities of a vision that simultaneously 'makes sense' to peoples rooted in different, often incommensurate cultures.

It is my belief that a less defensive use of this bicultural component will continue to be a major source of Indian creativity
even in the foreseeable future. True, this 'biculturality' was once
an imposition. It is also true that it has acquired depth in Indian
culture and consciousness because of the record of colonialism in
this part of the world. But it is pointless to deny that the society's
suffering has opened up the possibility of cultural experiments in
this part of the world that are no longer possible in the culturally hegemonic, increasingly monocultural West. We even hold in
trust parts of the West lost to the West itself. While being aware of
the pathology of cultural mimicry that colonialism endorsed, one
cannot ignore the creative potentialities that have often constituted
the obverse of that mimicry.[8]

Two other less important issues. First, those who criticize Ray
for not being adequately Indian are themselves often a part of the
high-flying world of film criticism, deeply obligated to Western film
writers for both their molar theories of cinema and their micro-
theories of cultural analysis. Even in Ray's life time, as the ethnic
began to become more fashionable in the West, as the Western art-
film establishment began to talk more and more of 'voices from
the Third World', the demand on Ray to turn more Indian grew.
So did the demands on him to be more socially relevant that were
being made since the 1960s, by both Western and Indian radicals.

The impact of these twin demands on Ray's work was not
happy. They occasionally pushed him towards self-conscious, perhaps even slightly cramped social comment. I am not concerned
with that impact here. I am only drawing attention to the fact that
the demand arose as part of the same tradition which the critics
accuse Ray of being a part of.

Second, all said, cinema is a total medium, the technology
of which has grown mainly in the West. However, cinema is
also in many ways an open medium that allows alien forms of

---

[8] This has been discussed in greater detail in Ashis Nandy, *The
Intimate Enemy: Loss and Recovery of Self under Colonialism* (New Delhi:
Oxford University Press, 1983).

consciousness to gatecrash into it under certain conditions. Other cultures *qua* cultures have influenced the medium mainly through its—forgive the inelegant expression—'alliance or convergence of aesthetics'. A film is plural not only through the way the director conducts and integrates diverse aesthetic forms, but also by virtue of the scope it gives to the other participants in the creative process—the music director, the photographer, the performers, the art director, and so on—a certain artistic autonomy (even if, as in the case of Ray, that autonomy was granted as if by default). Cinema may be primarily a director's medium, but the organizing principles the director employs may be culturally defined. (For instance, the roles of the music director and the lyricist in commercial Hindi cinema are entirely different from that in cinema elsewhere, and even from that in an Indian art film.)

In such a context it is always unclear, when one questions a work of Ray using a molar category like Indianness, which constituent medium of cinema one is talking about. Presumably one is not speaking of the cultural sensitivities of writer Rabindranath Tagore's 'Nashtaneer'or the classicism of music director Vilayat Khan's *Jalsaghar*. What weightages must one give to the different components in a total aesthetic statement called cinema? Does culture have a role in determining the weightages, too? If the answer is yes, do we have to seriously take into account Ravi Shankar's musical score when evaluating the cultural status of the Apu Trilogy, and, for that matter, Ray himself? Can the concept of direction itself, particularly the priorities it sets for the different elements in the craft of film-making, come to reflect something of India's cultural style? I leave the answer to be given by those more qualified to give it.

Can our original question be cast in another form? Can it be stretched to cover what a few committed critics have always been tempted to ask: were the myths and archetypes Ray projected into his work any less Indian than, say, those used by that other stalwart of Indian cinema, Ritwik Ghatak? Here we enter even more difficult terrain. The best test of whether a creative work is authentically Indian or not can only be through the nature of the reception the work gets from other Indians. It has little do with textbook definitions of Indianness and film craft. For ultimately the judgment on the subject cannot be only artistic, nor can the judgment be passed by a specialist; it has to be cultural. If Ray made sense to, and if his art resonated with, his fellow Indians, he has answered the question in one way. If he did not make that kind of sense, he has answered the question in another way.

This is not mindless populism. I am not talking of box office success, though Ray had his share of that, too.[9] I am speaking of the acceptance Ray won from a wide range of creative Indians who often had nothing to do with films. I am speaking of the very presence of Ray on the Indian art scene for nearly four decades, a presence that is automatically acknowledged by even those who have to criticize him four decades after his entry into the world of films, decades during which many once-acclaimed directors have gracefully sunk into oblivion. Does that 'unavoidability' of Ray have something to tell us?

This question is important in another way. When one raises the issue of Indianness, one can obviously speak of at least two forms of Indianness—one identified with myths and archetypes, the other with political ideology. Usually Ray is accused of not being sufficiently Indian in the first sense, not the second. On the contrary, he is often accused of being insufficiently ideological, and that judgment is backed by the tenets of Western radicalism. There is a contradiction here and it must be spelt out. The experts who have faulted Ray usually derive their emphases on myths and

[9] Even ignoring the box offices successes of films such as *Charulata* (1964), a film like *Pather Panchali* (1955) may not immediately equal the performance of a blockbuster like Ramesh Sippy's *Sholay* (1975) at the box office, but if one takes into account the slow but steady revenue from the former for nearly 40 years from all over the world, it should certainly match the earnings of most successful films coming out of Bombay's film bazaar. Popularity is not only what a cross-section of people at any one point of time chooses. There is a temporal dimension to it, too.

archetypes from imported film theory, having close links with contemporary Western psychology and anthropology on the one hand, and political ideology on the other. They have condoned, as in the case of Ghatak, the heavy and often clumsy use of Western political ideology, often working at cross-purposes with the core theme and moral thrust of his films. That, however, is not seen as Ghatak's deviation from Indianness, apparently because it allows one to stress the Indianness that is in conformity with the newest concerns of Western film theory. Ray, despite all his Westernness, was a less tamed political creature in this respect. He *had* his political ideology and it *was* Western, but it shaped his cinematic dream work and vision to a lesser extent.[10]

Two final words on the nature of the creative process. The culturally shared myths we are talking about are only partly conscious; they reach down deep into our personality and unconscious. A creative person is one who has some access to that unconscious—Freud sometimes used the term 'archaic traces' in such a context—and can dredge out the relevant fantasies to serve as new, 'sharable' cultural myths. And because this entire process is not usually under one's control, there are limits to which a creative person can be self-conscious about his enterprise. The creative process is always likely to retain some of its ancient mystery. One can be fully transparent only about its final product and arrive at a *post facto* consensus about its quality. This is merely another way of saying that one cannot expect a made-to-order conformity to predefined standards of culture. That which is culturally or socially significant or functional can be artistically shallow.

For example, I am convinced that commercial Hindi and Tamil movies have much more to say to us about Indian society and politics than art films do. Unlike some recent critics, however, I do not believe that this makes commercial films creatively more acceptable than the movies that are more serious artistic ventures. There is a qualitative difference between the likes of Ray and the

---

[10] Nandy, 'Satyajit Ray's Secret Guide to Exquisite Murders'.

likes of the Manmohan Desai and the Ramesh Sippy. That does not, however, mean that Ray had nothing to do with Indian commercial cinema. He hated such cinema, but did not realize that hatred can bind one very deeply to one's target. Ray's cinema, for much of his Indian audience, remains a systematic and spirited negation of virtually every aesthetic value commercial Indian cinema lives by. Recently I heard Charles Long, the distinguished scholar of Afro-American subjectivities and spirituality, comment on Patrick Chamoiseau's celebrated novel, *Texaco*, written in both Creole and French. Long claimed that Chamoiseau could be so daring in the use of language in his novel because, after showing that he could write elegant Parisian French, he could afford not to depend on French and switched to Creole. Roy's response to the same cultural hierarchy is different. He participates in the culture of world cinema by self-consciously using the cinematic language that the other greats of world cinema use. But his language does not become a mimicry because, unknown to him, it is a systematic negation of the Creole that commercial Indian cinema self-confidently uses and celebrates. The ultimate clue to Ray's distinctiveness lies in that culturally specific negation of a vernacular medium that supplies a lowbrow mix of village fare, folk theatre, and carnival.[11]

On one plane, Ray is less informative about contemporary India because he is more a master of his chosen mode of self-expression; and as a master *he* participates in defining the spatial and temporal dimensions of his culture; he stretches the boundaries of his culture to make his understanding of India a lasting part of the culture. The critics of Ray are doubly handicapped; they have to judge him by standards that he himself had altered to suit his creative style. Whether his culture shaped him adequately or not, he shaped his

---

[11] See Ashis Nandy, 'The Popular Hindi Film: Ideology and First Principles', *India International Centre Quarterly*, 1981, 9(1); and Ashis Nandy, 'An Intelligent Critic's Guide to Indian Cinema', in *The Savage Freud and Other Essays in Possible and Retrievable Selves* (New Delhi: Oxford University Press, 1995), pp. 196–236.

culture by altering its contours. That ability to transcend or redefine one's world and the accepted idea of the contemporary—and
even the criteria for judging the contemporary—is nothing to feel
sorry about. It is something to celebrate.

Second, because human creativity is *by definition* a psychosocial
process—that is, if the psychosocial determination of creativity is
not a matter of only individual volition—certain social demands
may be suspended when it comes to artistic efforts. A culture or
a particular culture–personality bonding, or if you so prefer, a
culture–personality system, uses art to experiment with its own
repertoire of psychological skills, awareness, and visions. That is
not all there is to art, but that is an important role of art in any
society. In such a bonding, there can be nothing called socially
irrelevant art, even if the artist himself declares his art to be so
from the rooftop. The presence of a culture in a work of art is
a given, independently of the artist. Self-conscious efforts to be
socially relevant can only end in comic monstrosities like socialist
realism. Satyajit Ray came close proving that in his *Ganashatru*
(1988) which, he was convinced, was one of his socially most relevant films. And which, others are as convinced, was one of his
most 'oversocialized' efforts.

First of all, the original of the story of *Ganashatru*—Henrik
Ibsen's *An Enemy of the People*—just did not have the creative
power which allows some works of art to gain from new interpretations offered from outside the culture of origin (such as
Akiro Kurasawa's interpretations of Shakespeare's *King Lear* and
Macbeth). More important, however, is the fact that, in the context
of Ray's own life and political values, *Ganashatru* can be read as
a story of religious superstition in ordinary people being hood-
winked by a greedy, small-time crook speaking in the name of
religion and the heroic defiance of this dyad by a modern doctor.
Unfortunately, it is set in times when modern medicine itself has
become a trillion-dollar, multinational, corporate enterprise, with
larger sharks playing for larger stakes, protected by the irrational
search for perfect health, medicalized cosmetics, a fully painless

life, and immortality of the consuming classes. It is set in times when it is becoming increasingly difficult to convince the viewers that any village confidence trickster, exploiting the superstition of innocent believers, can ever match the greed of giant, multi-national pharmaceutical companies and suave, highly professional doctors in the business of medicine.

However, more importantly, Ray had enough resilience left in his failing body and mind to retrace his steps, hesitantly in *Shakha Prashakha* and more self-confidently in his last movie, *Agantuk*, which directly defied the politics of *Ganashatru*.[12]

Agantuk, whatever may be its status in world cinema as a creative venture, is a milestone in Ray's journey towards cultural authenticity. It is simultaneously a statement on cultural survival, and a story of his last effort at self-transcendence. The film sets up through its main protagonist—a globe-trotting anthropologist who is no longer taken in by the European Enlightenment's vision of the world—a powerful anti-self of Ray's that negates many of his own core values, so as to be true to his essential but partly disowned creative self. In his great movies, too, Ray defies these values but that defiance is unintended, and one is tempted to add, often against the grain of his self-definition.[13] In *Agantuk*, that defiance no longer remains tacit—one can no longer call it the self-expression of a latent self that Ray would have loved to disown. *Agantuk* may not be great cinema, it may not even be the last word on cultural authenticity, but it is certainly a moving testament and an impressive attempt at self-confrontation.

It was as if Ray, at the end of the road, in the last few years left to him, rebelled against the earlier organization of his personality and his own idea of 'sanity' to reconcile, through a supreme act of creative courage, the division between his cinematic self and his more controlled public self.

---

[12] It is an indicator of the same resilience that Ray's unfinished last film, too, was a clear negation of the ideological thrust of *Ganashatru*.

[13] Nandy, 'Satyajit Ray's Secret Guide to Exquisite Murders'.

25

Hindi Cinema and Its Half-Forgotten Dialects

*Christopher Pinney Interviews Ashis Nandy**

India as a culture area will be nowhere, I think, in the world of knowledge, the sciences and arts, if it does not first defy the European monopoly of the scientific method established in modern times.[1]

These words are by the anthropologist J.P.S. Uberoi, but they can also be used to adumbrate one of the starting points from which the cultural critic and historian Ashis Nandy has set about investigating the 'vestigial dialects' that have remained beneath the

* This interview was originally published in *Visual Anthropology Review*, 1995, 11(2):7–16. My principle gratitude is to Ashis Nandy who saw and commented on this text. I am also indebted to Rachel Dwyer and an anonymous reviewer whose perceptive and challenging comments will perhaps be addressed on another occasion.

[1] J.P.S. Uberoi, *The Other Mind of Europe: Goethe as a Scientist* (New Delhi: Oxford University Press, 1984), p. 9.

mimicry with which India has responded to the West. In certain idioms of popular culture, Nandy has recovered what might—in other contexts—be termed a Ginzburgian subaltern subconscious with which to attack the simplicities of colonialism. He is searching for 'an ethically sensitive and culturally rooted alternative social knowledge' and believes that this is 'already partly available outside the modern social sciences [among] those who have been the "subjects," consumers or experimentees of these sciences'.[2] Nandy—who might be caricatured as a neo-Gandhian[3]—is intent on recovering a third space from which an assault can be made on the West and the West's slavish imitators who have been largely responsible for the current state of the world:

> It has become more and more apparent that genocides, ecodisasters and ethnocides are but the underside of corrupt sciences and psychopathic technologies wedded to new secular hierarchies, which have reduced major civilizations to the status of a set of empty rituals. The ancient forces of human greed and violence... have merely found a new legitimacy in anthropocentric doctrines of secular salvation, in the ideologies of progress, normality, and hyper-masculinity, and in theories of cumulative growth of science and technology.[4]

[2] Ashis Nandy, *The Intimate Enemy: Loss and Recovery of Self under Colonialism* (New Delhi: Oxford University Press, 1983), p. xvii.

[3] Though note that he has declared that he is not a Gandhian (Ashis Nandy, 'Satyajit Ray's Secret Guide to Exquisite Murders: Creativity, Social Criticism, and the Partitioning of the Self', *East-West Film Journal*, 1990, (4)2: 14–37, 16; reprinted in *The Savage Freud and Other Essays on Possible and Retrievable Selves* [New Delhi: Oxford University Press, 1995]). For some sense of his criticisms, and also of Nandy's affinity, see Ashis Nandy 'From Outside the Imperium: Gandhi's Cultural Critique of the West', in *Traditions, Tyranny, and Utopias: Essays in the Politics of Awareness* (New Delhi: Oxford University Press, 1987). The tenacity of the 'neo-Gandhian' label is understandable in the light of many of his public statements and indeed some of the conversation reported here.

[4] Nandy, *The Intimate Enemy*, p. 10.

This quote comes from his significant and best known book, *The Intimate Enemy: Loss and Recovery of Self under Colonialism* (1983), which has established Nandy as a leading theorist of colonialism as it impacted upon both quotidian and remarkable Indians.

A seminal idea proposed in *The Intimate Enemy* which has subsequently come rather to define Nandy's (frequently mis-represented) public political stance concerns the disjunctions imposed by colonialism which have returned to haunt contemporary India. The penetration of the West has created a class of mimic men, 'modernists, whose attempts to identify with the colonial aggressors has produced pathetic copies of...Western man in the subcontinent',[5] and Nandy places his hopes with a different class of Indians who are 'Neither pre-modern, nor anti-modern but only non-modern'.[6] It is here that Nandy's essentialism ceases to look merely 'strategic' as he seeks to ontologize his preferred brand of wisdom ('perfect weakness') in the depths of the Indian tradition. He concludes *The Intimate Enemy* with the observation that in some cultures (that is, India), 'ancient wisdom' is also 'an everyday truism'.

'The nineteenth-century dream of one world has re-emerged', he continues, but 'this time as a nightmare'.[7] Cruder forms of racism on which colonialism was dependent are on the retreat, but for Nandy there is a second, more insidious form of colonization which must now be confronted. This is a techno-rational vision of the world (a 'secular hierarchy') the internalization of which by nationalists was a pre-requisite for liberation,[8] but which is now in permanent conflict with a more enduring order which Nandy is content to call 'tradition'. 'The West is now

[5] Nandy, *The Intimate Enemy*, p. 74.

[6] Nandy, *The Intimate Enemy*, p. 74.

[7] Nandy, *The Intimate Enemy*, p. x.

[8] For a very recent elaboration of this, specifically in relation to Rabindranath Tagore's later work, see Ashis Nandy, *The Illegitimacy of Nationalism* (New Delhi: Oxford University Press, 1994).

everywhere, within the West and outside; in structures and in minds',[9] and Nandy's concern has been to both trace how this came to be and also to discover those areas of daily life in which Indians have sought to resist this ongoing colonization. One of these areas of daily life with which Nandy has recently become increasingly concerned is popular Indian cinema, in some of which, he argues, can be found 'vestigial traces of dialect which everyone had half-forgotten'. This phrase comes from a remarkable Gandhi Memorial Lecture, delivered in 1987, 'The Discreet Charms of Indian Terrorism', in which he traces the events surrounding two hijackings of Indian Airlines jets by Sikh militants in 1984. For Nandy, the interior of a hijacked aircraft is a kind of laboratory in which his suppositions about morality and politics can be tested. What he finds is that in this claustrophobic space, external identities quickly start to break down. There is no Hobbesian jungle: instead a co-operative pattern of behaviour informed by a sense of common humanity starts to emerge.[10] Following the hijacking, events unfolded within 'the limits imposed by another moral order'.[11]

This moral order was quite different from that of the state, and quite different also from that of Nandy's other detestation, the middle class, although he sometimes singles out what he terms the *haute bourgeoisie*. A significant element in the articulation of this new morality was the meeting ground afforded by popular Hindi film music. A young hijacker sang 'melancholy songs of separation and love from Hindi films', and the passengers asked him to sing more.[12] Nandy detects here a sub-strata of popular culture with dialogic possibilities: '...the maudlin and comic aspects

[9] Nandy, *The Intimate Enemy*, p. x.

[10] Ashis Nandy, 'The Discreet Charms of Indian Terrorism', *The Journal of Commonwealth and Comparative Politics*, March 1990, 15: 25–43, 35; reprinted in *The Savage Freud and Other Essays on Possible and Retrievable Selves* (New Delhi: Oxford University Press, 1995).

[11] Nandy, 'The Discreet Charms of Indian Terrorism', p. 37.

[12] Nandy, *Traditions, Tyranny and Utopias*, p. 32.

of the air piracy, the aspects most likely to jar on the sensitivities of the urbane Indian *haute bourgeoisie*, were exactly the ones that helped to establish the links among the three parties involved'.[13]

At this time of crisis, in which everyone was staking their lives, learned techno-rationalist codes were jettisoned, and 'real convictions about the nature of the interpersonal world' and 'deepest private theories' were tested. And, Nandy concludes, they were not found wanting. He finds it enormously significant that at such times of testing truth, it is not the statist bourgeois sentiments of the editorial pages of national dailies to which people appeal, but the sentiments to be found in commercial Hindi movies.[14] This suggests that such movies are something much more complex and relevant than 'half-digested global mass culture', and Nandy proposes that: 'in trying to cater to the lowest common denominator of popular taste, the popular movies in the subcontinent have unwittingly established an intricate relationship with some of the deep but marginalised sources of Indian culture'.[15]

---

[13] Nandy, *Traditions, Tyranny and Utopias*, p. 38. It is interesting to note in this context Nandy's disparagement of Salman Rushdie, whom he concedes has—in his fiction—uniquely captured the elements of the new urban Indian popular culture, but whose social and political writings are 'terribly like what someone like Jawaharlal Nehru would have said about the public realm today if he were recalled in a séance by an enterprising medium'. Nandy, 'Satyajit Ray's Secret Guide to Exquisite Murders', p. 16.

[14] Elsewhere he suggests a broader realm of the 'vulgate' which acts 'as a cultural "underground" rather than as a legitimate form of popular culture'. Ashis Nandy, 'An Intelligent Critic's Guide to Indian Cinema', in K.S. Singh (ed.), *Visual Anthropology and India* (Calcutta: Anthropological Survey of India and Seagull Books, 1992), pp. 43–76, 42; reprinted in *The Savage Freud and Other Essays on Possible and Retrievable Selves* (New Delhi: Oxford University Press, 1995). This would include '*bat-tala* [popular Bengali publishing], calendar art and the bow-tie wearing waiter in the cheap back-street restaurant who has been simultaneously attracting and intimidating the first-generation immigrant to the city since the last century. Nandy, 'An Intelligent Critic's Guide to Indian Cinema', p. 45.

[15] Nandy, 'The Discreet Charms of Indian Terrorism', p. 38.

This is an interpretation which Nandy himself concedes may appear 'romantic or mystifying'.[16] Like much of his work from the *Intimate Enemy* onwards, it can be charged with being essentialist and highly romanticized (and when I interviewed him, he was notably less willing to make such claims for Hindi films), but it is also an argument that I have found enormously seductive, a typically perceptive and intriguing insight from a remarkable mind.

* * *

As we sat in the garden of the Centre for the Study of Developing Societies in Delhi,[17] I asked first about one of Ashis Nandy's current projects, an edited volume of essays on films in India.

AN: Originally, the idea was to interface film theoreticians with political and social analysts but that misfired. The environment [during the preceding conference in Mysore] didn't trigger an interesting enough dialogue, and in retrospect I came to the conclusion that the problem was not so much with political and social analysts, who want to get on with the job, but with film theory which for many has become a more esoteric specialized genre.... I have reconstituted the book primarily as an attempt to look into the politics and sociology of popular films, in some cases through highly personalized narratives.

CP: **How do you see this approach to film fitting in more generally with the theoretical thrust of your work? I see a Ginzburgian attachment to popular culture which you describe somewhere as a 'vestigial dialect' through which local discourses become apparent.**

AN: My primary concern is with the unique situation which prevails in India—the clash between popular and mass culture. In the West, popular culture and mass culture are one. That's the

16 Nandy, 'The Discreet Charms of Indian Terrorism', p. 36.
17 17 November 1993.

way that they have been traditionally viewed during the last several decades. The implicit assumption is that popular culture is mass culture—because these societies are primarily urban and primarily massified. In other kinds of society, popular culture can be seen in terms of three aspects:

First, popular culture—as folk culture—is neither dead nor marginalized. Seventy-five per cent of Indians are still in rural areas where folk culture is popular culture. Grandmothers' remedies might be a marginal or vestigial form in the West, surviving in the interstices of Western life, because modern medicine dominates life. Here, modern medicine does not dominate life, even in urban areas; according to available estimates, 85 per cent also use some form of traditional medicine. So the popular is not dead or marginalized—it is the dominant system.

Second, there is the popular culture of the Indian middle classes, which has grown out of the last 150 years of encounter with the West. This is often very carefully developed by some very gifted individuals looking for new modes of articulating their concerns.[18] For instance, the novel came to India in the middle of the nineteenth century, mainly through the English language; I doubt if many Indians think of it as a foreign medium today—it has been totally integrated. Similarly, other forms of visual arts, the cinema for instance, borrow elements from Indian folk traditions, Indian classicism, Western folk traditions, Western classicism, in order to grapple with certain kinds of popularity—tradition, modernity, and so on.

Because this form of popular culture is an adaptive genre, it also has very distinctive styles of adaptation in different parts of

---

[18] Here Nandy acknowledges the productivity of what he elsewhere calls a 'bicultural...technique of survival that has now become a character trait' (Ashis Nandy, 'How "Indian" Is Satyajit Ray', *Cinemaya* (1983), 20: 40–5, 43), as embodied in figures like Satyajit Ray. At other times (and later in this conversation), such hybridity is castigated for empty mimicry—what he calls 'the pathology of cultural mimicry that colonialism endorsed' (Nandy, 'How "Indian" Is Satyajit Ray').

India—Bengali, Marathi, Hindi, and Tamil films are all identifiably different, though that difference has been diminishing during the last two decades. They are products of distinct regional cultures which have experienced modernity in different ways. The regional films have developed forms which incorporate the new experiences of these cultures in ways folk cannot always do—the folk just doesn't have the resilience to do it, nor the elasticity. This is the domain of popular culture as opposed to the domain of folk culture. This is popular culture proper.

Third, there is popular culture as mass culture in the genuine statistical sense, and like all forms of mass culture, it is exportable and is fully universal. It doesn't matter whether you buy McDonald's hamburgers in Tokyo or in Delhi.

CP: Except here it's made of lamb.

AN: I'm told that they're going to make it from buffalo meat here; McDonald's is coming to India in style. The aim in mass culture is always to reproduce the original standardized product. The lamb or the buffalo-meat hamburgers will also be made to resemble beef hamburgers. Coca-Cola is the same whether you buy it in Rio de Janeiro or Helsinki.

CP: But doesn't everyone drink Coca-Cola in a different way?

AN: They do, but they have to drink Coca-Cola in different ways. It is a tamed plurality, and there are limits to such plurality. India, for a while, tried to produce local variants of Coca-Cola—Campa Cola and other such stuff. One producer tried a touch of almond, then another had success with cardamom. But they did not last. The point I'm trying to make is that mass culture usually doesn't brook many differences; it has its own distinctive style and sticks to it. It can be Catholic, but it always moves toward standardization because it is oriented to atomized individuals, not to communities. When the airline Pan Am experimented with Indian cuisine as its vegetarian option, it did so not only in India but all over the world.

To return to our main concern, I locate Indian commercial films in a matrix defined by the popular, the folk, the classical, and mass culture. It is a third dimensional space between the folk and the classical, and the popular and the mass. And when we say that there is homogenization in these films, it is because the mass element becomes dominant. In this respect, there *is* a difference between the films of the 1980s and the films of the 1950s or 1960s; Raj Kapoor and Guru Dutt are typically 'popular'. Earlier you could easily distinguish between a Bombay style, a Madras style, and a Bengal style. Even that is becoming difficult today, though there is still a North Indian and a South Indian style.

Today, Bombay cinema has become hegemonic. There is no longer a regional cinema left. Hindi cinema has become Indian cinema, and the rest are now its regional variations. Something similar is happening in the Indian political culture. In a democratic order, certain kinds of voice, language, and styles of articulation should have a natural presence, however local. And they *did* have such presence until the late 1960s and early 1970s, but since then they have been constantly losing ground. Indian political culture, too, has increasingly become more open to dominance by smaller segments of society which previously dominated public life only in areas which were marked out as specialist domains.

CP: You recently said that Hindi film 'asks the right questions but arrives at the wrong answers'.

AN: I meant that with every issue these films have handled, implicitly or explicitly, they have consistently touched the heart of social or psychological problems because they have to survive at the box-office. Their treatment of core myths and cultural concerns is conventionalized in ways that are more acceptable to the dominant culture of the state. But they do not shirk the issues South Asians are most concerned with. Take, for instance, a movie like Amitabh Bachchan's *Deewaar*,[19] which can be thought of

---

[19] Directed by Yash Chopra in 1975.

as a remake of *Mother India*.[20] The convention of this genre is that there are two brothers—one an upright police officer, the other a criminal who has entered crime out of frustration with the world and in response to the injustices he or his family has suffered. This is an old story which has been told hundreds of times and usually it's a great success. The movie examines the conflict between the upright brother and the criminal brother as a moral struggle over corruption—one brother seeking revenge and the other seeking to reaffirm social norms. But if we look at the story, it's also obvious that this is a battle over the mother. The moral brother gets the mother; the immoral one does not.

CP: So what is the connection with the dominant culture of the state?

AN: It is turned into an argument between the brothers over public norms, what the police should do, what is their duty as against that of the criminal. They discuss public norms within a framework of whom the mother should endorse. The treatment of the movie is in terms of moral choices between public and private norms, conformity and dissent, and the latent message is that moral choices have to be endorsed by the primordial authority of the mother, not by the impersonal authority of the state and civil society.

CP: *Deewaar* would be an example of the 'lost and found' genre. Why are these so popular in Hindi film?

AN: The brothers are actually the same persona deliberately divided and then put back together again. That's the inner logic of the film. The crucial strategic device is that of doubling. Nowhere else in the world will you find such an enormous fascination with doubling. In India, *The Prisoner of Zenda*, which has two or three versions in English, has not less than 20 direct versions, probably more than 30. And if we take into account other kinds of doubling—two brothers getting separated at birth, by

[20] Directed by Mehboob Khan in 1957.

accident, in a storm, and so on—they are even more numerous. Doubling is a means of handling psychological qualities which one is forced to negotiate and with which one is uncomfortable. You exteriorize the qualities and turn them into sociological factors, so that the qualities which are inside you can be projected outwards as another person with whom you apparently come to terms sociologically, not psychologically.

CP: **Sudhir Kakar would explain that in terms of traditional Indian family values, the split from the mother, and so on. Would you give it a much more historical explanation in terms of colonial mimicry, and so forth?**

AN: Yes and no. There's a contradiction between tradition and modernity so that the modern brother gets a traditional village girl as his lover, and the traditional brother, a farm hand in some obscure village, gets an ultra-modern woman doctor, and these two kinds of liaisons establish a new relationship between the old and the new, tradition and modernity, the East and the West. Later in the film, when the two brothers come to each other's rescue (the traditional brother rescues the modern brother, or vice versa), a new relationship is established between the two sets.

CP: **But it does always seem to be that the traditional overpowers the modern, rather than the other way round.**

AN: Not always. If the parents are objecting to the heroine's marriage on caste grounds, then usually it is shown that the young couple triumph over caste norms. Tradition is given a special place when it seems to stand against the anomie and normlessness of the city-slick, street-smart brother who is also modern. In that case, the traditional brother comes to the rescue to establish a dialogue that lets him have the last word. Traditional virtues triumph. The innocence of the village—the innocence of the child.

[Elsewhere, Nandy writes of the 'ultra-modern, arrogant, super-competent, western-educated professional {who} has to ultimately turn to his twin—a rustic...to defeat the hardhearted smuggler or black-marketeer, who in turn is a negative model of modernity and a negative mix of the east and west'[21]].

CP: You're suggesting that the resolution is not so much a conservative triumphing of traditional order as the triumph of innocence and local discourse.

AN: Yes, of course. It's only recently that people have begun to take some serious interest in these movies. Previously a standard criticism by those who dismissed them was that they were conservative. But they are not conservative. They have, even if by default, their own conception of limits, and the films can be seen as an exploration of these limits—limits of modernity, of tradition, of mothering; limits of evil and tolerance. It was this model which began to dissolve to some extent in the late 1970s with the entry of mass culture—in which the violence is more realistic, more gory.

[This particular notion of 'innocence' is developed in *The Intimate Enemy* where Nandy writes about an 'authentic innocence, which finally defeated colonialism, however much the modern mind might to like to give the credit to world historical forces, internal contradictions of capitalism and to the political horse-sense or "voluntary self-liquidation" of the rulers'.[22]]

CP: Can that local discourse hold up in the face of Zee TV?[23]

AN: It will be placed under greater pressure, but it will come back just as it is coming back in the West. It will take time for people

[21] Nandy, 'An Intelligent Critic's Guide to Indian Cinema', pp. 70–1.

[22] 1991: xii–xiii. For more on Nandy's argument on the contrasting approaches of 'art' and 'commercial' cinema to the victims of Indian modernity, see 'An Intelligent Critic's Guide to Indian Cinema', p. 49, where he argues that 'commercial cinema romanticizes and, given half a chance, vulgarizes the problems of the survival sector but it never rejects as childish or primitive the categories or the world-views of those trying to survive the processes of victimization let loose by...modern institutions.'

[23] A Hindi satellite channel.

to develop the kind of scepticism which people in the West have already developed towards television. Doordarshan makes people sceptical because they have made a mess of their ham-handed propaganda, but in India, there's no scepticism of the media as such. For instance, the BBC is trusted much more in India than it is in England. On the whole, there is no genuine scepticism of the media. This will take more time. People must sense the threat that the local and the vernacular face from a universalized total medium for there to be a space for both.

CP: **What would your response be to a future historian of film who, 10 years hence, argues that two singularly important factors explain what has happened in Hindi film of the 1990s: First, that the audience has changed, and that increasingly films have been directed at the urban single male migrant in search of sex, violence, and the remembrance of his absent family; second, the rise of Hindutva, which has created a complicity between popular Hindi film and contemporary popular chauvinist politics? Would this convince you?**

AN: I would be convinced on both points. If by *Hindutva* you mean the ideology of the state which goes with *Hindutva*, frankly it's no different from the ideology of the state which has come to dominate Indian conservative, liberal, and Leftist thought—a standardized theory of the state which was very popular in India until the late 1980s. The *Hindutva* view is totally 'statist'—totally convinced that a homogenous national culture is necessary to ensure that the state does not collapse, totally convinced that the culture has to be hard-boiled, hard-eyed, realpolitik-based, and fully secular. It is in this sense that the ideology of *Hindutva* is paralleled by the ideology of the state which the Hindi film has propagated over the last 40–50 years, or maybe even longer, from the 1930s onwards. But then, this has been the dominant message in Indian public life for a long time, that we have everything in our civilization but a proper state. The state is essentialized and it is assumed that the more centralized the state, the better because you cannot trust the local *satraps* and notables who are more exploitative and bloodthirsty than the centralized leadership can ever be, and that all concepts of village republics and local democracy are Gandhian hogwash, mystification propagated by parts of the freedom movement, the time of which is past. This theme has been part of the folk-wisdom of modern Indian politics in general. From the politics of the extreme Left to those of the extreme Right, there has been almost no dissent on this score. The *Hindutva* movement is a by-product of this dominant ideology.

But Indian cinema is one of the few places where there is natural tolerance of diversity, particularly religious diversity. Partly because the film world does not bother who is a Muslim, who is a Hindu. *Mother India* is a very Hindu film only if we forget that it was a Muslim who made it and that a Muslim immortalized its central character. To deny this authorship is to deny that the communal confrontation we are seeing is partly a by-product of secular politics.

[Just recently, Nandy has further stressed *Hindutva's* distance from popular religious culture: '*Hindutva* which comically mimics 19th century European nationalism, also carries in its veins a deep hostility towards everyday Hinduism and ordinary Hindus, inherited from its unofficial European parentage'.[24]]

CP: This suggests quite a profound contradiction: you are saying that on the one hand, the Hindi film is a vehicle for vestigial discourse—local voices—but that it's also a vehicle for pro-state statements. I'm thinking in particular of your 'The Discreet Charms of Indian Terrorism' lecture in which you argue that through film songs people found a medium for non-modern communality.

AN: Well, yes, there is a latent message. Even the violence is stylized—in one film, *Don*,[25] when Amitabh Bachchan fights a

---

[24] Nandy, 'The Fear of Gandhi: Nathuram Godse and His Succesors', *The Times of India*, 27 April, 1994.

[25] Directed by Chandra Barot, 1978.

climactic fight with the villain—a life and death battle—he stops and says—'hold on, let me chew *paan*'—and then resumes fighting. Even within contemporary realistic violence there is something playful about it, clues are continually given to the audience that the violence is not serious. *Naseeb*[26] would be a very good example of this.

Let me make an autobiographical statement. I came to these films because of my interest in middle-class culture and politics. I see a lot of the problems in Indian politics arising from middle-class attempts to prevent the hoi polloi from getting their due under democratic politics. Demographically and electorally, the middle class is a small minority in India— for that matter in the whole of South Asia—and it can only legitimize its disproportionate power through ideology, an ideology that allows the middle class to believe that it stands between the barbarians outside the city walls and the citizenry inside. The ideology functions in another way. It allows you to take out of politics, sector after sector, and hand them over to experts—from development and planning to diplomacy—on the grounds that the ordinary politics demanded by ordinary people cannot work and the sector must be handed over to professionals, all naturally drawn from the middle class. There is a widespread belief in the Indian bourgeoisie that ordinary Indians are not fit to be full citizens of a modern nation-state because they don't understand what modernity is, and the middle class must become the new vanguard for the masses. The state has been beautifully retooled for this particular purpose; it keeps in check the full political conse- quences of the democratic process.

A critique of nationalism is, therefore, also a critique of the Indian middle class which has lost its confidence and is feel- ing marginalized. They find any critique deeply disturbing. For instance, that article you mention, 'The Discreet Charms of

[26] Directed by Manmohan Desai, 1981.

Indian Terrorism', the kind of attacks I faced over that—I was accused of 'romanticizing' terrorism; some asked me, 'what about the human rights of the passengers'; others said, 'you are supporting separatism'.

CP: The argument about specialism suggests a paradox in your own engagement with the Hindi film. There's always a danger that you are going to turn this popular myth into a domain of experts.

AN: Yes, that's right, and I am afraid of it—actually my questions to the Hindi film are simply political ones.

[Subsequently, I was struck by an interesting contradiction in Nandy's own methodology which, through its conscious myth-making, attempts to remove him from one forum of cultural criticism (conventional academic debate) and establishes him as a different kind of inviolable expert (a shaman). In *The Intimate Enemy*, he writes that a 'purely professional critique' (by social scientists) will not do; rather it will have to be fought 'the way one fights myths: by building or resurrecting more convincing myths'.[27] Parallel to this, Nandy states in a collection of essays: 'I shall not grudge it if some enterprising reviewer finds unconvincing history in the following pages, as long as he finds in them convincing myths.'[28]]

CP: How should people be approaching film? I was struck when recently reading Dissanayake and Sahai's *Sholay*—which is methodologically excellent—how difficult it is to produce really exciting analysis through audience response. Do you think in the future you may do an ethnography of film-viewing? I've been struck by the fact that often you've alluded to your viewing of these films on video rather than in the cinema—your experience of film is in this privatized context?

---

[27] Nandy, *The Intimate Enemy*, p. xviii.

[28] Ashis Nandy, *At the Edge of Psychology: Essays in Politics and Culture* (New Delhi: Oxford University Press, 1980), p. vii.

AN: Yes, it is. But a few of my students have taken an interest in this. And if I had thought of it earlier, I would have encouraged a study of audience responses to *Khalnayak*.

Films, however, are not only for viewing; the film industry, what the stars do in public, film music—they all have a cultural presence. For instance, I've also taken an interest in the uses of astrology in the film industry. Astrology is used mechanically in traditional India—for a daughter's marriage, choosing the right moment for a *puja*, the time of a journey, but elsewhere in the modern sector its presence is enormous, especially in the stock market and among politicians, sports stars, and film stars.

CP: **But beyond the timing of the *muhurat*,[29] how does it affect the timing of anything? Everyone is juggling his/her dates on an entirely pragmatic basis.**

AN: The astrologer may say that the title of a film must have 14 or 11 letters, because it is a lucky number, or that the name must start with a 'K' because an earlier film starting with a 'K' was greatly successful. Then there are the heroes and the heroines, the lucky ones and the unlucky ones. The producers take their astrological charts and consult the astrologers about that too. But despite this, I do not see any great contradiction between pragmatics and astrology. Film-making in India is a terribly uncertain profession, like politics. Even the most rational choice cannot guarantee you success. So you need to justify your rational choices. Mrs Gandhi was a hard-boiled, highly calculative politician, but she also visited the necessary temples to ensure success.

CP: **Do you see this as a defiance, a positive strategy, a vestigial trace?**

AN: I see it as a strategy for survival. And as a rational adaption to one's environment.

---

[29] An auspicious period during which important and uncertain work can be inaugurated.

CP: Throughout your work there is a parallelism between the 'non-modern' and the 'postmodern'.[30] This reminds me of Arjun Appadurai's recent comments on the parallels between non-modern magical realisms and postmodern varieties ['the forms of "magical realism" are many...the traditions in which they have been produced and enjoyed are multiple...it is not just a modern privilege to have blurred the line between fantasy, history and satire'[31]].

AN: Yes, I think that this is a search for—an attempt to rediscover—alternatives, which in the West have been pushed to the margins and are almost non-existent, and have to be recovered or recreated through novels or through postmodernist theory or some other attempt to transcend contemporary times. Whereas here [in South Asia] these options are present, right at the centre, often among a majority; they are not marginalized. The range of choices is wider. This is a complex and diverse civilization— and this owes much to traditional texts and forms of awareness and even forms of self-mocking wit. There is a beautiful example Ananthamurthy [the Kannada novelist] gave me once. In the Kannada Ramayana, as in other Ramayanas, there is a dialogue between Sita and Rama. Rama doesn't want to take Sita with him to the forest when he goes into exile because she would face discomfort and hardship. In every Ramayana there is this argument, but its contents vary. In the Kannada Ramayana also, Sita says to Rama that it's her duty to be with him, and that she won't enjoy the comforts of the palace without him, so it doesn't make any difference if she's in the forest with him, but at the

---

[30] See Bhabha's (Homi Bhabha, 'Conclusion', in *In the Location of Culture* [London: Routledge, 1994], p. 251 ff) use of this to understand more fluid, hybrid contexts than Nandy has in mind.

[31] Arjun Appadurai, 'Afterword', in A. Appadurai, F.J. Korom, and M.A. Mills (eds), *Gender, Genre, and Power in South Asian Expressive Traditions* (Philadelphia: University of Pennsylvania Press, 1991), pp. 467–76, p. 474.

end she adds, 'Besides all this, in every other Ramayana, Sita goes to the forest with her husband, so how can you stop me from going.' It's an elegantly self-reflexive Brechtian comment and Indian diversity includes that, too. This diversity and local critical traditions are not dead. Many people have argued that irony is the central theme of Hindi movies—for instance *Hero Hiralal*[32]—is basically just a take on Hindi movies.

CP: There is lots of exciting work coming out of Public Culture, but it seems to be privileging the urban and the global as against the local.[33] That becomes problematic in India because then everyone just does studies of cinema hoardings and no one wants to look at different kinds of *matkas* (earthenware pots) in obscure villages.

AN: Yes, an ethnography of film viewing could transcend some of these problems so that one could see what a film means at different levels. I would be most sympathetic to that sort of effort.

CP: You once wrote that you are more interested in having a dialogue with the person in the street rather than with other academics.

AN: Well, I'm not making a populist argument. I'm making an argument of a different kind, and perhaps I should spell it out. I think that in every society, the overlap between the intellectual and the academic is never complete. But in some societies at certain points of time, the overlap can be very little or it can be immense. The United States and France, at the moment, are in a phase where the overlap is almost total. If you thought very hard you might get three or four intellectuals who are not academics. But there the list would more or less end. In these countries, there are not many influential intellectuals who are not academics. But things were very different a couple of

---

[32] Directed by Ketan Mehta, 1988.

[33] A reflection, I believe, of the contributors, rather than the editors (Carol Breckenridge and Arjun Appadurai).

decades ago. America had the likes of Lewis Mumford, and the French intellectual scene was dominated by Sartre. But in India, at this point of time, for some reason, the overlap has diminished, instead of increasing. There are many human rights activists, social activists, and political activists who are doing fantastic work at the ground level, and with whom I have been involved on and off, and from whom I have learned more than from academics who approach their problems as if it was a matter of cognitive puzzle-solving. It was to that difference that I was alluding. Even those who call themselves academics in India should know which way their intellectual survival lies.

Maybe in the future the Indian academe will incorporate more intellectuals. Meanwhile, it seems to me that many scholars don't have enough imagination and sense of survival. After all, the academic game can be played by Indian scholars in American universities much better than by established scholars in India because of easy access to other facilities. Yet Indian scholars pathetically try to replicate what is done in universities in the United States. They are in no position to compete in, say, a conventional study of the hermeneutics of *Naseeb* with the right kind of referencing to Jameson or Hall, or Derrida or Lacan.

CP: So what should they be doing?

AN: I'm not saying that they should ditch the Western academe entirely, but they would be much better off trying to enrich their work by looking around them and listening to the intellectual debates going on in their own society and other Southern societies. For instance, they might do an ethnography of say, *Naseeb*, or a particular genre of films in comparison with the currently popular Pakistani television series. They will probably learn more and be able to say more. But because of their infatuation with Western scholarship, they have nothing to share with the Pakistanis next door or with the Bangladeshis. There are fantastic comparisons to be made with cinema in Egypt,

Algeria, Hong Kong, and so on. There is no attempt to explore experiences. Most academics like to make books out of books, not even books out of books and life. I would very modestly plead that there is a place for both in Indian intellectual life. But, I mostly see only a pathetic attempt to mimic. In reaction, there is in my works probably an overdone or studied underestimation of Western academic works.

CP: You don't then see it as strategic mimicry to survive in an international academic market? In _The Intimate Enemy_[34] you referred to Illich's account of how Aztec priests were thrown to the dogs because they had said that if what the Spanish priests said about their gods being dead were true, they too would rather be dead. You hypothesized that a group of Brahman priests in the same circumstances would have embraced Christianity, written elegant praises to their rulers and their gods, while all the while their Hindu beliefs remained unshaken. Isn't this part of that process?

AN: No, I'm afraid it's not that.

* * *

Nandy dedicated a recent volume (1987)[35] to 'those who dare to defy the given models of defiance', and as I left this garden in Delhi, I was struck by the power of his own noble brand of essentialism. Subsequently, in the _Times of India_,[36] Nandy wrote the following commentary on Mahatma Gandhi that was pregnant with parallels to his own work, and gave me a sense of the 'everydayness' within which Nandy himself has chosen to operate:

> He stands for the unheroic [and] represented the ordinary, 'superstitious', sceptical, tradition-bound, wily Indian.... Whatever touch

---

[34] Nandy, _The Intimate Enemy_, pp. 107–8.
[35] Nandy, _Traditions, Tyranny and Utopias_.
[36] Ashis Nandy, 'The Fear of Gandhi: Nathuram Godse and His Successors', _The Times of India_, 27 April 1994.

of heroism we see in the Gandhian political style is built paradoxically on the assumption of that unheroic everydayness.... Anti-Gandhism springs from the awareness that while we can elect our leaders every five years, we cannot elect our people....

Nandy concludes that 'We are stuck with the Indians as they are. And most westernized and semi-westernized Indians, including the votaries of *Hindutva*, resent that.' Many readers may have reservations about this putative perpetuity, but they may also come to value the wisdom of those vestigial dialects that lie at the heart of some peoples' everyday heroism.

BOOK IV

THE CLINICAL GAZE

26

Infantilization

The Nineteenth-Century Ghosts Haunting
Twenty-First Century Democracies*

Infantilization, a time-worn technology of self, acquired a different kind of salience in the cultures of governance and social knowledge systems of Europe and North America in the mid-nineteenth century. This was in response to two developments: the consolidation of the Atlantic slave trade and modern colonialism. Both were primarily European and North American enterprises, and infantilization legitimized, ethically and scientifically, the two new institutions and created space for them in European thought and political culture. Later, the technology was to acquire global currency through the spread of modern knowledge and the idea of

* This is an expanded version of a presentation made at a conference on Politics and Paranoia held in New York, and later published in the *New Internationalist*. I am grateful to Alan Roland and the editor of the *New Internationalist* for their direct and indirect help in making this chapter come to life. Reprinted by kind permission of *New Internationalist*: www.newint.org.

scientific rationality, both heavily tinged with various versions of social Darwinism.

Incidentally, both slavery and modern colonialism were also, arguably, the first serious attempts to globalize. If a cross-continental trade, that too in live human beings, and a new political economy fathered by colonial empires, touching six continents—on one of which the sun reportedly never set—are not global, what is? Fittingly, it required a global war to bring about the end of colonialism and remove blatant institutionalized racism that was the bequest of slavery in North America.

Lest we forget, slavery and colonialism became global systems after Enlightenment values had made deep inroads into European society and after republicanism and ideas of scientific rationality and progress had become part of the everyday language of politics in the West. Indeed, it was the Enlightenment connection that distinguished modern colonialism from its older cousins specializing in open exploitation and pillage, and seeking legitimacy in religion. The new colonialism talked of a civilizing mission and the White man's burden, offered new options of secular salvation, and saw itself as an agent of progress, historical laws, and scientific rationality.

In a secularizing world, infantilization quickly became a moral posture and a theological necessity. It allowed the main actors in slavery and colonialism to make peace with their conscience, and the intelligentsia and the Church to produce a powerful mix of secular and sacred justifications for the new world order. It allowed one to talk glibly of the historical necessity to take care of the backward-looking, irrational, ignorant savages, and about the Christian responsibility to guide them towards a better future.

* * *

However, the middle-range legitimacy for these brand-new institutional initiatives came from a new, scientized language of the body and a new politics of life cycle, riding piggyback on it. In this language, the metaphor of gender was supplemented by a bifocal metaphor of human life cycle.

First, childhood lost part of its shine as an intrinsically valuable stage in the human life cycle. It was redefined as a stage of incomplete, imperfect adulthood. In that imperfect stage, child-likeness continued to be valued as a symbol of Biblical innocence, purity, and authenticity, but childishness emerged as a marker of the child that needed strict discipline and ruthless, authoritarian control. Once the metaphors became common currency, the likes of Cecil Rhodes could speak of the African as 'half-savage, half-child' who needed close supervision and re-socialization, so that one day in the distant future they, the Africans, would grow up to bear responsibility for their own lives. That process of growth was to be later given many attractive names—modernization, development, and progress being the best known among them.

Second, older societies like China and India, brought under the dominance of the emerging global order, were reclassified as ancient civilizations that had seen better days but were now decrepit, decadent, and disposable, and had to be, naturally, run by youthful nation-states that had become the carriers of the ideology of productive, masculine adulthood. Their obsolete, yet occasionally lovable cultures were to be now museumized, to be viewed and marvelled at on weekends.

The dominance that the masculinity principle established in the public sphere in the nineteenth century is well known. Less known are the authoritarian upbringing, exploitation, and sheer cruelty towards children in the Victorian age. Phillip Aries and Lloyd deMause have told the story in lurid detail.

* * *

No one emerges from large-scale violence and oppression unscathed, certainly not the perpetrators. Victimhood is indivisible. Once you turn institutionalized violence into a system and run it, your self-definition and subjectivities begin to adjust to the system you have set up. Predictably, the hierarchies based on gender and life cycle not merely became metaphors of inescapable stages of history and a new language of triumphalism for the European civilization, but also shrank the roles of women, children, and the elderly in Europe and the Americas. Some in the backwaters of the Southern world were ungracious enough to suspect the various theories of stages of history to be actually mouse-traps of history, but that was to be expected and no one paid any heed to them.

The seductive charms of infantilization today, tacitly shaping the idea of modern citizenship, are a direct product of this psychological and cultural journey. So is the contemporary idea of democracy, championed by societies that have a long, not-very-enviable record in the matter of democratic rights in the Southern world. The violent, oppressive past survives in both the rulers and the ruled. For the rulers, it survives as academic history, manicured and washed clean of all emotions. As if that past was a record of when someone did something fishy to someone else. For the ruled in the ahistorical, darker continents, it survives as timeless, shared memory that underwrites cynicism and frequent attempts to turn against one's own self, and also as part of an epic consciousness that is yet to find full expression in music, art, and literature.

Four clear traces are already visible in the dominant strain of democracy. First, after their momentous triumph at the end of the 1980s, the victors in the Cold War are now more confident that it is the end of history for the world. Hence, they are less sceptical about the production process that ensures a steady supply of 'normal' citizens as part of normal democratic governance. They have even less reason to feel diffident about deploying the same vague social evolutionary principles that first legitimized their global dominance. Indeed, there has grown a deeper suspicion of their own 'immature' ordinary citizens and a fear that, left to them, they will not exercise their political choices wisely.

Second, during the long Cold War, some democracies came to feel that they were handicapped in the battle against the communist regimes by the freedoms and rights their citizens enjoyed in open systems. They tried to build closed systems within an open, democratic order. Years ago Robert Jungk argued that all societies, democratic or totalitarian, had the same authoritarian culture of secrecy, surveillance, and censorship built around their nuclear establishments. Such closed systems within open societies have now become standard in domains such as national security, foreign affairs, technological choices, and even development, increasingly outside political debates and legislative control. These domains are now presided over by experts who are supposedly above politics and beyond criticism. What the authoritarian regimes failed to do through the coercive machinery of the state, the victors in the Cold War have done without much effort, with the consent of a passive, carefully depoliticized citizenry. The moral of the story probably is: countries can be careless while choosing friends; they cannot be too careful about choosing their enemies.

Third, the explosive growth of the media and the idea of perpetual entertainment—if not in real life, at least in the virtual world—have brought governance within the ambit of what can be called the happiness industry. This has helped politics to become a 'manageable spectacle', and to enter the living rooms of citizens to turn them into receivers of one-way messages and willing captives to a virtual world of politics that promises to exile all death and suffering from politics. Simultaneously, politics has become more open to those from the entertainment industry than to those coming through the representational process, for the former are seen as more adept in the technologies of psephocratic systems.

In large parts of the world, citizens are now primarily spectators of politics, with only the right to vote once every four or five years. The rest of the time they see politics as spectator sports on television, enjoying vicariously a feeling of active participation in public life. Even the electoral process is becoming more media-sensitive and turning into brand wars over market shares. The de-politicization of politics is no longer a catchphrase in the 'advanced' democracies. It is reflected in the increasingly poor voter turnout in some of the most powerful democracies in the world. In the United States, voter turnout is usually half of what it is in India, and increasingly, some of the central political problems of our time—such as mass poverty, loss of security at the bottom of society, threats to life-support systems and the environment, and loss of vocations—are routinely pushed out of political debates in many democracies. The sense of sheer impotency and irrelevance forces many to opt for ideologies that seek to restore agency to the individual, if not as a responsible, self-conscious citizen making personal choices, at least as an agent of a trans-human, cosmic power presiding over a moral universe.

Four, the definition of a happy citizen itself is changing in modern democracies. Citizens are the ones who are free to vote, consume, travel, and entertain themselves to death. These activities mark one out as an active, responsible, happy citizen and keep him or her occupied. Those unhappy despite these freedoms are seen as maladaptive discontents, forever looking for reasons to be disgruntled. The Soviet Union used to get them certified by psychiatrists and put them in asylums. They were unhappy in a utopia and that was culpable. In open societies, they are advised to go to psychotherapists or are prescribed anti-depressants.

Even democratic initiatives in matters of democratic rights and disaster management in distant parts of the world have been fitted within this model, and have led to the infantilization of entire populations. Whether it is food shortage in sub-Saharan Africa or tsunami victims in South and Southeast Asia, it is the same story. Even survivors of genocide are quickly classified as traumatized and incapable of taking care of themselves. Post-traumatic stress disorder (PSTD) has become a handy diagnostic category that deprives traumatized communities of all agency, which is then transferred to experts belonging to international bodies.

* * *

If infantilization has been so central to violence and oppression in our times, should not there be a history of infantilization? Of course, there can be. That is what we are moving towards now. True to the Enlightenment heritage, that history will dutifully exile all human subjectivities as so much of flotsam of our times, and confine itself to the archives so adored by historians. To spite them, in the post-War era, some psychoanalysts *did* try to sneak into history to de-sanitize it, but their efforts have widened psychoanalysis more than they have broadened academic history. Once a 'proper' history of infantilization takes shape, once the history of the new post-Enlightenment forms of violence is written up, without any reference to the inner world of the victims and the categories they use, the experience of suffering of millions will have to survive at the margins of human awareness the way it usually does—as fading memories handed down from generation to generation and as fragments of an unwritten epic that cast their shadows on some vernacular modes of political and cultural self-expression.

27

Ajita Chakraborty

*The Psychiatrist as a Social Critic**

In tune with my guru...R.D. Laing, I would say it is only the psychiatrist who retains the possibility of transcendence.

—Ajita Chakraborty

No account of a society is complete without a profile of its subjectivities. This is particularly true of India, which has, for centuries, lived with diverse, highly developed theories of mind and techniques of intervention in human consciousness. Sadly, the very existence of these theories and technologies has also posed a problem for the country's modern literati during the last 150 years. Modernity entered India riding piggy-back on utilitarianism, British empiricism, and Baconian science. All three traditions of knowledge had a clear touch of suspicion, if not fear, of the subjective. Much later, when Leninism became a major presence

* Reproduced from 'Psychiatrist as Social Critic', Foreword to Ajita Chakraborty, *My Life as a Psychiatrist: Memoirs and Essays*. © 2010 Ajita Chakraborty's literary heirs. By courtesy.

in Indian theories of progress and a bastion of dissent for a while, this fear of the subjective became, under the reign of a positivist strand of Marxism, a phobic reaction to the inner life of citizens. This unleashed two tendencies among Westernized Indians, especially among those looking for new baselines of social criticism, and seeking legitimacy for the various modern reform movements launched in India. First, there emerged the tendency to believe that Indian thought had traditionally overemphasized the subjective and was, by nineteenth-century European standards, idealist. As a corrective, some like Debiprasad Chattopadhyaya were to later construct, based on the works of relatively minor, ancient Indian philosophers—works mostly available second-hand—an alternative, materialist school of Indian thought. They saw the theories and technologies that constituted India's psychological traditions as contaminated by the mainstream culture of Indian philosophy, and hence, hopelessly regressive—anti-science and anti-empirical, designed to legitimize the existing social order, particularly its unequal, oppressive elements. Chattopadhyaya himself, a Freudian who psychoanalyzed Ajita Chakraborty, disowned Freud, embraced Leninism, and began to look at all psychological life as an epiphenomenon. Others of his persuasion, even more aggressively positivist, goaded succeeding generations of Indians to conceptualize society the way architect and town planner Le Corbusier later advised us to conceptualize a house—as a man-made machine in which to live, work, and die.

Second, political and social realities began to be discussed within the expanding modern sector of India not only in mechano-morphic, scientized terms but also in a language that reflected the increasingly popular ideas of development and progress. The new passion to historicize everything under the sun also contributed to these changes. All past was now seen as leading up to the urban-industrial society and the actualization of Enlightenment values. As in the case of science, history, too, was expected to demystify most things Indian, and to encourage the emerging urban, modernizing middle class to look at all local knowledge as contaminated by the legendary and the mythic, serving as repositories of the superstitious and the magical. In reaction, many who disagreed with such simple-minded constructions of Indian thought went to the other extreme. They either proudly embraced the new stereotype of Indian thought as a marker of India's spiritual and moral superiority or made comical efforts to read into Indian epics recent discoveries of science and technology.

Despite a few valiant efforts to strike a dissenting note, these two tendencies made it almost impossible to seriously study India's psychological traditions since the first department of psychology was founded at the University of Calcutta in the early years of the twentieth century. In such a culture of knowledge, the psychological disciplines were bound to have a paucity of clinical and archival materials on those who built these disciplines. They were seen as professionals producing disposable clinical case reports, meant at best for other practising Indian psychiatrists. Psychological theory had to come from the West, and Indians were expected to supply empirical footnotes based on Indian data and contribute some comparative nuances to existing Western theories.

As a result, we are today left with a very thin database on the pioneers who struggled to reconcile the new sciences with our multicultural, multilingual, non-modern society and tried to make sense of their vocation in its new social milieu. Only scattered, half-hearted efforts have been made to access the experiences of psychologists, psychiatrists, and psychiatric social workers or study the debates within these disciplines on crucial social and cultural issues. Given that the traditional healers and their methods have also mostly escaped the attention of social scientists, we were left with predominantly de-cultured, asocial, overly medicalized psychological disciplines studying human subjectivities in this part of the world.

It is not, however, easy to exile the inner life of a people. No amount of ideological fervour can turn human beings into predictable robots, nor is it possible to understand the inner life of a society in technocratic terms. The everyday life of ordinary citizens quickly learns to bypass such stylized interpretations of society, and sometimes, even while paying lip service to fashionable ideologies, maintains its own secret ledger that survives as an underground, contraband social and psychological awareness.

* * *

Against this background must one read this fascinating collection of Ajita Chakraborty's psychiatric reflections on some of the critical social and intellectual issues of our time, prefaced by a long autobiographical essay—one of the very few available to us from a century of modern psychiatry in India. The author's life has spanned many of the tumultuous moments in the life of contemporary India and many of the traumatic events that have shaped the self-awareness of—or its absence in—both the patients and the practitioners of the psychological disciplines: enormous inequities and obscene instances of destitution; famines, including the man-made Bengal famine that killed 3 million; a series of politically inspired riots, beginning with the frenzied, anarchic violence that accompanied the partitioning of British India and took a toll of at least a million lives; and massive uprooting caused by urbanization and development.

Indeed, these events have critically influenced intellectual life, moral concerns, and social knowledge in this part of the world. They have all left behind their psychological footprints, and the inner lives of millions have been indelibly branded by either direct memories of such events, or fictional or mythic accounts handed down by families, communities, writers, artists, balladeers, and film-makers. This book gives the reader a chance to glimpse the same process through the life of a psychiatrist.

Chakraborty tells her life story directly and simply, one suspects, by underplaying the professional and the strictly psychiatric. Though she says in her preface that she has written this book as a social being and a psychiatrist, most of the time the psychiatrist wears the garb of a spirited, independent-minded citizen. This only strengthens the power of her narrative, because the psychologically inclined reader can in any case read between the lines and decipher her professional judgment in most cases—ranging from the author's closest friend in college who had a clear streak of narcissism to some of her well-known professional colleagues, highly manipulative, overly competitive, and almost proudly authoritarian. In her telling, cross-national psychiatric movements such as cultural and transcultural psychiatry do not fare any better. They often look overdetermined culturally, almost ethnocentric.

Even when she talks of disciplinary matters, Chakraborty's story is built around persons and their often strange, anomalous actions, and she is unable to hide her psychiatric diagnoses, even while trying to avoid being judgmental about the characters in her story. It was as if she was deliberately writing a straight narrative, strewing clues all along her way and challenging the reader to imagine what her final diagnoses of persons, events, and movements might be.

The author's struggle with ideologies is another running theme in the book. Her former psychoanalyst, Debiprasad Chattopadhyaya, the one who had jilted Freud as insufficiently radical to become a hard-boiled, positivist Marxist and a docile fan of Stalin, had a role to play in this. Chattopadhyaya had a cynical, authoritarian streak. His 'patronizing', sometimes 'sneering' style, not to mention his private admission later in life that he had to denounce Freud under pressure from the communist party, probably triggered Chakraborty's disenchantment with ideologies. Quite early in her life, she says, she turned both anti-Freud and anti-communist. She was stubbornly seeking intellectual and interpersonal autonomy, and her experience with her psychoanalyst underwrote her stubbornness.

Later, the budding psychiatrist's adolescent nationalism and heroic concept of politics, centring on Subhas Chandra Bose and the Indian National Army, also waned. The case of feminism was no different. From the descriptions of her family life and college days, it is obvious that gender justice was an integral part of her personality long before the birth of feminism as an ideology and a trendy buzzword. But while she has fought for causes dear to feminists, these causes failed to abridge her self-definition. She seems to have even evaded the expectation of her feminist publishers to bow down to fashion, and turn this book into a conventional, 'strongly feminist' tract. 'I suddenly could not turn a feminist', she says in the preface.

This ability to treat ideologies as so many items of disposable baggage, without losing sight of the social problems they address, is remarkable. For Ajita Chakraborty's working life spanned the high noon of the age of ideologies in India, when not having an ideology or having a wrong one was seen as a heinous crime or as crypto-psychopathic. Many destroyed themselves as creative thinkers and proudly wore ideological shackles to be politically correct. Perhaps those living in proximity to applied psychological sciences cannot afford to be so intensely ideological. Particularly the clinical vision, in continuous conversation with live human beings, tends to be, at its best, anti-ideological. Unlike in history, where the subjects are mostly dead, and literary theory, where one writes mostly about texts, in disciplines dealing with mental health, the subjects of your enquiry constantly rebel against your certitudes. Some patients improve when you least expect them to; others betray your optimism as if to spite you. They are concerned with living their lives, not proving your theories. It is for outsiders to discover, according to their needs, the ideological connections of a healing tradition.

This does not mean that Chakraborty does not have an overarching, personal, political–ethical vision. Her presidential address to the Indian Psychiatric Association, 1976, reproduced in *My Life as a Psychiatrist*, proclaims her interest in existentialism and admiration for Hannah Arendt. Elsewhere in the book she expresses her admiration for R.D. Laing, the existential psychiatrist. Strangely, there is no mention of Otto Binswanger and Victor Frankl, the two best known existential psychiatrists, who often grappled with issues of direct interest to her. Perhaps, here too it is primarily non-ideological, philosophical existentialism that interests her, not existential psychoanalysis or existential psychiatry.

As a practising psychiatrist, Chakraborty probably believes that healing is a different kind of enterprise; at best, it can have a worldview behind it, not an ideology. It is the gaze of an empathetic, concerned healer in the guise of an ordinary citizen looking behind the masks of persons and groups as a necessary part of the art of healthy living. The only exception is when she tries to look within; there is often a mix of self-deprecating humour and ruthlessness in the way she identifies her own personality traits and records her own reactions to events and social relations.

The essays in the second half of Chakraborty's book were written on different occasions and at different times. Apparently, they have little to do with the long autobiographical section that constitutes the first half of the book. Nonetheless, I cannot but read them as appendices to the first section. They do throw into relief elements of the autobiography without the author being fully aware of it. I have already given the example of the author's fear of ideologies. But even when she talks of rituals as a manifestation of neurotic disorder, there is the tell-tale evidence in the paper of her belief that ultimately the borderline between neurosis and normality is blurred, that you can read a ritual both ways, as an institutionalized neurotic syndrome that has become a part of normality or as a part of normal life that, when properly understood, alerts us to a false concept of normality. Unlike Thomas Szasz and Ronald Laing in some of their incarnations, she does not try to dissolve the borderlines between normality and abnormality; she retains the difference as a therapeutic reality and a tool of social criticism.

* * *

Is Ajita Chakraborty a maverick psychiatrist, the only one of her kind? It will be a mistake to think so. She represents the chaos, the uncertainty, and the inner conflicts over theoretical compromises and therapeutic experiments that cannot but be the lot of a practitioner of a new discipline in an old society, more so when that society has its own ideas and traditions of mental health and ill-health. Some might build, in such a situation, defensive shields of sterile professionalism or cultivated certitudes. Others grapple with their bitterness and frustrations through free-floating anger or by immersing themselves in the petty politics of the profession. In this book itself there are many instances of this. Ajita is different in that she owns up to these inner contradictions and conflicts in her practice and in her eclectic theoretical stance. She may have her angularities, but she also has the self-confidence and the robust empirical feel to be herself whether she is building an ambitious psychiatric profile of the city of Calcutta or talking of the prospects and limits of cultural and transcultural psychiatry.

28

The Psychiatrist as a Political Critic*

Ever since I read Daya Somasundaram's first book in the late 1990s, I have always looked at his writings with a mix of great anticipation and visceral discomfort. He has a clinical style that, when dealing with gory violence, brings to his intellectual concerns not the calming touch of a family physician but the sharp, this-worldly tone of an engaged epidemiologist. Somasundaram works on the long- and short-term effects of mass violence on communities and persons, and his gaze remains steadfastly clinical, but that clinical gaze has a sharp, clear political and social awareness. And the prognosis—perhaps defying Somasundaram himself—looks pessimistic to most readers.

This pessimism has something to do with the perspective that the psychological disciplines bring to conflict situations in South Asia, a region to which both Somasundaram and I happen to belong.

Though there is a rich tradition of exploring the psychological in South Asia, the public cultures of the region have come to disdain it as soft, impractical, and a hindrance to tough-minded statecraft and political realism. Few in the more articulate and audible sections in our societies and none of the parties involved in a conflict are willing to even listen to the kinds of analysis Somasundaram has ventured in his work. South Asians are becoming, unapologetic, hard-eyed, masculinized devotees of realpolitik, and have begun to look at anything dealing with human subjectivities with suspicion. In the process, we are cut off from serious, in-depth studies of mass violence done during the last four decades.

As a clinical discipline, modern psychiatry has consistently emphasized the suffering of the individual patient. This is as it should be. Most traditions of healing observe this rule, even when they underline the roles of society and culture in shaping the context and the source of a patient's suffering. In the southern hemisphere, such contexts and sources can be formulated more directly and even brashly. One could say, for instance, that cholera in the tropics is caused first by poverty, and only then by cholera bacteria. You and I and our kind do not die of cholera, even if we are careless. Our environment and our class status sanitize and protect us, sometimes even when we are casual or careless about our personal hygiene. People living in slums must take care of their personal and family hygiene, food preferences, and lifestyle more self-consciously.

We also know by now, thanks to Ivan Illich, the author of *Medical Nemesis*, that no epidemic except small pox has been eradicated by drugs and vaccination. Public health and hygiene and improved quality of life have played a larger role in each case. And Illich, in this instance, is unduly modest in his claim. For, even in the case of small pox, subsequent research by the likes of cultural anthropologists Frederique Appfel-Marglin has shown that traditional methods of variolation had kept in check epidemics of small pox in countries like India and China.

However, if you are a physician facing a case of cholera, your first job is not to enlighten the patient on the subtleties of social epidemiology or social history of a disease, but to take care of the patient. Somasundaram's work has always been a testimony to this double-edged responsibility of psychiatry, which cannot be shelved by giving a few ritual lectures on social psychiatry to students of medicine the way business schools teach business ethics and the social responsibility of business—as trendy subjects with which future corporate bigwigs are expected to be familiar, so that they can navigate the upper echelons of society politics with confidence.

Those who have read Somasundaram's first foray in the area in 1998, *Scarred Minds: The Psychological Impact of War on Sri Lankan Tamils*, have come to expect from him a heightened sensitivity to the larger responsibilities that disciplines like psychiatry bear in conflict zones. The author wrote that book with what many would consider admirable scholarly detachment, but it was nonetheless a powerful testimony to his awareness of the changing nature of mass violence in our times, particularly the predicament in which non-combatants, trying to live their normal life and protect their familiar moral universe, get caught. The other name for this predicament is collateral damage, and it interests neither the combatants nor the political class and the media. *Scarred Communities* can be read as a companion volume to *Scarred Minds*.

The psychiatrist's job, in recent times, has not been a pleasant one, more so when it comes to the mental health problems that modern warfare triggers. On the one hand, the percentage of non-combatants who die in wars and other forms of armed conflict has begun to rise dramatically all over the world. Some estimates yield figures as high as 85 per cent. In addition, Somasundaram himself has shown elsewhere how civilian populations might be caught in the crossfire between competing forms of ethno-nationalist ruthlessness, paranoia, and systematic onslaughts on a community's way of life. A community can be made to go through multiple experiences of uprooting, when entire villages are resettled and made to walk through corridors of terror, torture, censorship, and surveillance, and forced to see the militarization and brutalization of their children through systematic propaganda, hate speeches, and politically slanted history.

On the other hand, the diagnosis of post-traumatic stress disorder (PTSD), has become not only more frequent but also a double-edged instrument. Post-traumatic stress disorder is no longer only a 'disease' or a handy clinical diagnosis that names the psychological devastation caused by war, both among the victims and the perpetrators; it can also be a means of declaring an afflicted community socially and psychologically challenged and unable to take care of itself. Psychiatrists rarely recognize what is obvious to political analysts and journalists—calling a community traumatized is nowadays also a way of handing over agency to international bodies and outside experts who can then look after the community's welfare as professional social workers and political negotiators. As if war-induced trauma was not enough, the diagnosis of PTSD introduces into the theatre of war a new means of infantilization.

After World War II, civil wars have become a rather distinctive species of armed conflict. Even some of the major wars identified with countries such as Korea, Vietnam, Iraq, and Iran have a large component of civil war built into them. Over the years, in places like China, India, Cambodia, West and East Africa, and in the Balkans, civil strife has taken a huge toll on human life, engulfing entire communities and cultures. One of the main features of such wars is that the high casualties are not only seen as collateral damage, but are quickly written off as 'normal' sacrifices at the altar of state-formation and nation-building. Somasundaram himself has described how, during the Sri Lankan civil war, civilians were caught between the conflicting demands and competing atrocities of the two sides, and were expendable cannon-fodder for both sides. They are still waiting for justice and rehabilitation.

Under these conditions, where does the psychiatrist's professional duty end and his responsibility as a citizen begin? Can resistance to war itself be part of a psychiatrist's intellectual self-definition? Or should he or she consider that to be an avoidable digression that takes a psychiatrist outside the ken of his discipline and the familiar landscape within which professional ethics and the Hippocratic Oath work? Does the psychiatrist's responsibility end at the perimeter of the clinic or does it extend to the epidemiology and the political sociology of the patient's suffering? Can psychiatry claim to be a 'total' discipline, for which there is no alien territory, because human subjectivities, the psychiatrist's preoccupation, recognize no temporal and spatial borders?

These are questions to which there are no simple answers. The disciplines concerned with mental health have seen an enormous expansion in the range of psycho-pharmaceutical drugs. Long-term psychotherapeutic interventions seem to be going out of fashion. The boundaries of the mental health worker's awareness too have widened to include a larger range of social and cultural variables. No psychiatrist can avoid looking at the changing nature of human violence, believing it to be primarily the concern of political scientists and sociologists. Yet, one has the nagging feeling that these expansions are accompanied by an abridgement of the intellectual and philosophical self of the psychiatrist, and in this abridgement a crucial role has been played by a narrow definition of professionalism.

Daya Somasundaram, in this respect, represents neither the conventional boundaries of clinical psychiatry nor the limits of the narrower professional conventions imposed on the discipline. He represents, I like to believe, the future of the discipline in our part of the world, at a time when violence is becoming endemic, predictable, and thoroughly institutionalized as a part of the process of modernization. At this moment of brutalization of our societies, the psychological sciences in South Asia are richer, better equipped, and potentially more self-reflexive due to the presence of this intrepid researcher from Sri Lanka. He has shown that there may still be some life in psychiatry as a critical social discipline in South Asia. *Scarred Communities* should be read not only as a scientific monograph on mass violence in some distant land but also as a disciplinary testimony on what we ourselves have done to our part of the world.

29

The Empire Thinks Back*

In 2006, while attending a literary conference at Hyderabad, I first heard of Durgabati Ghose's travelogue on Europe, *Paschimjatriki*. I had strayed into a panel discussion where Somdatta Mandal, who now teaches at the Department of English in Visva-Bharati, was speaking on travel literature produced in India during colonial times. Her fascinating paper included a section on the writings of Bengali women on Europe. One of these women was Durgabati Ghose nee Bose. Some years earlier, I had worked on Girindrasekhar Bose, the first non-Western psychoanalyst, and Durgabati was his daughter. Like many influenced by psychoanalysis, I felt I had a special relationship with her father. I never met him but encountered him in my teachers and in the works of many first-generation Indian psychoanalysts. Since my teens, I had also been a fan of Girindrasekhar's brother Rajshekhar, better known as Parashuram—famous writer, translator, lexicographer, and social critic—and had often wondered about the intriguing

* This essay was written as a Foreword to Durgabati Ghose, *The Westward Traveller*, trans. Somdatta Mandal (New Delhi: Orient BlackSwan, 2010).

complementarities between the two siblings. I had reasons to be curious about Durgabati and her book. Later, psychiatrist Amit Ranjan Basu, himself a scholar who had worked on Girindrasekhar Bose with distinction, gifted me a copy of *Paschimjatriki*, and I remember the enthusiasm with which I read it.

Somdatta may not agree with this, but it was pretty obvious to me that Durgabati's reaction to Europe was in many ways typical of an urban, middle-class, educated Bengali woman, who was willing to abide by the conventions of such travel writings. She was waiting to be pleasantly surprised by her encounter with Europe, for the Europe she chose to encounter was the Europe her class and her community had already chosen, internalized, and felt they knew. Even the elements of delectable shock and surprise of discovery were built into the design. You were expected to surprise and shock your compatriots, perhaps also yourself, in unsurprising ways.

This is because, as Somdatta's 2006 paper itself indirectly admitted, there was already a tacit comparative frame within which Europe was fitted. Europe made sense to many as India's other, and to a sizeable section of urban, educated, middle-class Indians, India too had begun to make sense as the other of Europe. After all, had not the new breed of theories of progress claimed that India lived out Europe's past, while Europe lived out India's future? Had not all nineteenth-century theories of progress insisted that every society had to graduate through the same historical stages to qualify as properly modern, mature, and 'adult'?

Flouting geography, at the centre of the imagined Europe of that generation was England, surrounded by France, Germany, Italy, and perhaps Greece, as the original source of European modernity. The rest were the other Europe, complete with touches of the fearsome and the exotic, acquired from Edwardian popular literature circulating in colonial India—from Bram Stoker to Arthur Conan Doyle—and from tourist guides and popular travelogues. On one side were Transylvania, Moravia, and Bohemia, on the other Venice, Rome, and Athens. The

Europe I am talking about was mostly a mix of the experiences and dreams of generations of eager Indian students going to Britain for higher studies and sometimes wandering off to the Continent out of curiosity or a sense of adventure. Occasionally the mix was spiced by a touch of the romantic and the heroic, by dreamy revolutionaries secretly training or conspiring to topple the British Empire with the connivance of European powers. Everyone in India's modernizing middle class 'knew' Europe, even the ones who had never been to Europe or read about it much.

Durgabati's Europe, too, tends to be a backdrop for her conversations with her Bengali readers. The romance and awe of Europe she carried within her—which communicates to her Bengali readers in a slightly out-of-breath style—is partly a discourse on India and partly a form of participation in the altercation with the Europe within the reader's own self. If she seeks to infect her reader with a sense of adventure, it is an adventure that comes with controlled risk. It is a bit like the staple suspense of a regular crime thriller in which, despite all the secret conspiracies and hidden evil, all the darkness and the shadows, the reader usually knows how the story will end.

Ultimately, the way Durgabati recounts her adventures in Europe make them variations on familiar Bengali domesticity, interpersonal patterns, and femininity, played out outside their natural locale. This gives the travelogue not merely an odd stamp of predictability or familiarity but also a touch of robust, irreverent charm and self-confidence. What captured my imagination at Hyderabad was Somdatta's brief description of Durgabati's encounter with Sigmund Freud, her father's hero, training analyst, and friend.

Durgabati had dutifully carried with her a letter of introduction Girindrasekhar Bose had written to Freud. She had also read about Freud in newspapers and journals, and had heard about him from her father and his friends. As it happened, she had to make some effort to find the great man, despite his iconic status.

But when she first located him and went to meet him, she felt let down. She had expected him to be 'very impressive', perhaps because she had imagined him as someone who would be a variant of the Englishmen she had met or seen at Calcutta. Instead, he turned out to be a 'simple, ordinary looking, old man who held a burning cigar in his hand and whose teeth were all framed with gold.' (I wonder if Durgabati had ever seen the imaginary portrait of Sigmund Freud that her father and the Indian Psychoanalytic Society had commissioned and gifted Freud. The well-known artist Jatin De, remembered for his drawings done for Rajshekhar Bose's celebrated short stories was the artist. Freud, on seeing the portrait, had exclaimed that it made him look very English, a comment perhaps lost on the first generation of Indian psychoanalysts.)

Freud, however, was very happy to meet his friend's daughter, and after 'exchanging pleasantries', they went out into the garden. Durgabati says,

> After that we came back and sat in the room. Two huge furry dogs ran in. One jumped into his lap and the other put up his two feet on my lap and tried to climb up. I was stiff with fear. I did not have the habit of living with dogs but kept quiet due to courtesy. Picking up an ivory statue of Lord Vishnu from his table, he said, 'Your father had once sent this to me.'
>
> Suddenly the dog gave a loud bark and jumped upon my lap. Forgetting everything and pushing him out of my lap, I stood up from the chair. Dogs in these countries were used to getting hugs from visitors, so why would he listen to me? Considering me a spoilsport, he started barking louder. The professor understood my situation and he quickly locked the two dogs in one room. They kept on barking loudly and banging the door.
>
> 'Are you afraid of dogs?' he asked me.
> 'Yes, I don't have dogs. I am very scared of them.'
> 'Why are you afraid?' he asked further. 'I myself feed the dogs by making them sit on my lap. Your father treats other people's mental diseases, does he know about your fear of dogs?'

'Yes, of course he knows', I added. 'He himself does not have any dog.'

The professor was really surprised to hear this.

* * *

That was the moment Durgabati entered history. For Durgabati concludes the story remembering that she kept thinking in her mind that if she could speak English well, she 'would have asked Professor Freud what his own love of dogs signified. As a famous psychologist, what did he have to say about that?'

The revolutionary healer and thinker, equipped with a concept of dissent in which an enlightened vanguard courageously fights not merely for a new concept of human nature and a new mode of demystification but also for the emancipatory possibilities of self confrontation, missed the chance of listening to his critic from Calcutta. For Durgabati never spoke out. The first psychoanalyst was left with only his fleeting impression of a friend's daughter whose father had avoided his analytic responsibility of interpreting her fear of dogs to her. She must have remained for Freud a transient presence—a complex-ridden daughter of an esteemed colleague, representing uncritical everydayness and domesticity. Durgabati's inarticulate defiance, combined with her ordinariness and diffidence, had doomed her dissent.

Somdatta in her paper emphasizes the diversity of travel literature in colonial times, and gingerly touches upon some of the running themes in them. For instance, she defines the diversity mainly in terms of the empirical details in them, the unifying theme being the assumption that a travelogue must convey information. But what she does not say in her lively analysis of Durgabati's reaction to the Europe of middle-class, educated women in modernizing Bengal is beautifully summarized in an apparently diffident, self-depreciating, mute comment that comes off as an ironic, pithy, sharp counter-discourse and also as an interpretation of interpretation. The Empire may or may not have talked or written back through Durgabati's writing, but at least Durgabati as an analysand certainly thought back and wanted to analyse back.

Durgabati says that she was held back by her inadequate English. Does that also hide a story? She after all was reasonably well-educated and stayed in the capital of British India. Was she trying to say, without knowing that she was doing so, that the metropolis has a language and that language refuses to be your own in crucial moments? Are such inarticulate forms of defiance lost forever? Or do they survive, as in this instance in the interstices of a vernacular text, as the dim memory of a lost folklore?

Somdatta Mandal brings Durgabati's entire travelogue to the English-speaking world. Perhaps in the hope that, eight decades after the event, a new generation of readers may be more adventurous and grant Durgabati's story more dignity, and look behind her silences to explore the extra-ordinariness that underlay her ordinariness. If they decide to do so, they will also have to be beholden to Somdatta for rediscovering Durgabati Ghose as a person in her own right, having her own mind and in full control of her critical faculties.

30

Psychoanalytic Sociology and Postcolonial Predicament

An Interview by Livio Boni*

Gandhism and Freudism

Livio Boni: Ashis Nandy, you define yourself as a post-Gandhian scholar and thinker. Not in the sense that you claim to be an ideological or militant follower of Gandhi, but in the sense that you consider that Gandhism has been a kind of anthropological event, a kind of historical invention which has yet to be thought out. And you consider that, from this standpoint,[1] there is an actuality of Gandhism for the postcolonial understanding.

* Originally published in 'Geographies of Psychoanalysis', International Psychoanalytical Association (IPA): https://www.ipa.world/ IPA/en/en/Psychoanalysis/Geographies_of_Psychoanalysis_folder/ Landing_Page.aspx. The interviewer wishes to thank Nisha Kirpalani for her revision of the original version (in English) of this interview.

[1] For example, Ashis Nandy, 'Gandhi after Gandhi: The Fate of Dissent in Our Times', *The Little Magazine* (May 2000): 38–41.

Could you take us through your singular intellectual approach of Gandhism?

Ashis Nandy: Gandhi was scared of fathering something like Gandhism, and Freud tried to locate his work within the domain of science and would have been heartbroken if his 'science' was pushed any closer to an ideology.

As for Gandhi, he was neither an ideologue nor an Eastern guru dispensing instant wisdom. He was direct in these matters. Any Western admirer who sought his guidance in the matter of non-violence received more or less the same advice. 'Go to your own religious texts and search out appropriate sections.' He was an active politician who, as a politician, saw the horrendous forms violence—hitched to the ideas of conquest, statecraft, and social engineering, and backed by modern science and technology—was taking. He had the foresight and the ethical passion to pursue the logic of this insight throughout his life. There lay his uniqueness. In a century that saw the ravages of ideology, he alone stood bereft of an ideology to allow his listeners full and equal hermeneutic freedom.

LB: In one of your most famous books, *The Intimate Enemy*[2] (until now the only one translated into French and Italian), you consider that the two crucial transformations introduced by Gandhi in relation to colonial ideology have been, on one hand, the revaluation of childhood, and on the other, a refutation of History conceived as an intrinsic rationality. These two points are, of course, a kind of catachresis of the colonial discourse, insofar as they displace the topic of the colonized as a child who needs the assistance of the Master, and the idea of a lack of History in the non-European civilizations. But, by stressing this Gandhian revaluation of childhood

[2] Ashis Nandy, *The Intimate Enemy: Loss and Recovery of Self under Colonialism* (New Delhi: Oxford University Press, 1983).

versus adulthood, as well as its revaluation of 'past' *versus* 'history', you also quite explicitly suggest some affinity between Gandhi and Freud. Does it mean that you read Gandhism from a Freudian point of view? Or Freud from a Gandhian point of view? Or can we imagine some kind of real intellectual encounter between Gandhism and Freudism?

AN: It is probably my attempt to reintroduce Gandhi and Freud to each other, outside the liberal frame of Erik Erikson, Wolfenstein, and Susanne and Lloyd Rudolph. It also is a more self-conscious, South Asian attempt to update Freud for contemporary times by re-equipping him with cultural–psychological sensitivities alien to his European intellectual world but perhaps not to his West Asian ancestors. Psychoanalysis as a critical tool for the new movements of our times then becomes the obverse of the phallocentric Statism that is becoming the preferred consumable in countries such as China and India.

The language of the body that so deeply tinted the colonial ideology had another element, masculinization. Gandhi celebrated the androgynous and had a distinctive gender definition that came only partly from the classical traditions of India. It borrowed more heavily from the vernacular ecumenism of Medieval India, in which spirituality and ethics cut across the borders of caste, religion, and sects, and laid the basis for another cosmopolitanism—more open to radical diversities, greater tolerance of ambiguities, and a robust suspicion of linear theories of progress and the centrality of the state in public life.

Freud becomes relevant to the first part of the story: Gandhi's determined use of a tacit theory of what Western knowledge systems would call reaffirmation of femininity in the public sphere. From his point of view, though, it was also a reaffirmation of a different concept of masculinity that did not negate femininity but had to accommodate aspects of femininity within masculinity to be completely masculine. Such masculinity had its counterpart in an idea of femininity that, to qualify as complete, had to include crucial aspects of masculinity. In addition, Gandhi's femininity, too, had a special meaning, for he often seemed to stress maternity at the expense of conjugality. Gandhi's androgyny was coloured primarily by motherliness. This androgyny was a subversive project. In the colonial discourse, the language of the body became a way of explaining the inferiority of the subjected races and giving content to the ideas of the 'civilizing mission' and the 'White man's burden'. The colonized subject was an incomplete man and an incomplete or lapsed adult. In the Gandhian vision, that became a strength.

Freud approached the problem differently but in a way that was consistent with Gandhi's faith. He too did not see gender differences as sharp disjunctions but as necessary and unavoidable continuities. Gandhi may not have been a vendor of Eastern wisdom, but he did respond to a major civilizational gap in the *modern* West. (The West also had its androgynous Christ and powerful maternal deities in the form of White and Black Madonnas, but they had become recessive in recent centuries.) The appeal of Gandhi's vision to the ordinary Indian was that it looked grounded simultaneously in India's high culture and in its vernacular traditions. Freud was a rebellious son of the Enlightenment, but he was its son nonetheless. Gandhi was an outsider to that worldview. He was a constant reminder of (1) how the Enlightenment vision had been used to justify virtually all the major forms of Satanism of our times—from the four-continent slave-trade to the creation of three new White continents through conquests and genocide; and (2) how all major forms of organized dissent in the West have justified their violence by turning to social evolutionism and sundry theories of progress which remain racist, ethnocidal, and provincial at their core.

The Reinvention of the Feminine

LB: Another crucial point in your interpretation of Gandhism lies in its reinvention of the Feminine. In most of your works,[3] you insist on a transversal trend, during the period of decolonization, based on a kind of revaluation of the Feminine as an alternative to the fantasy of a revirilization, typical of the nationalist discourse. Should we read this revaluation of the Feminine as a cultural element linked to the particular place that maternal deities and symbols occupy in many dimensions of Hinduism, or should we understand this as an original, conjunctural, and event-specific invention linked for instance to the names of Rabindranath Tagore, Girindrasekhar Bose, and Gandhi?

To put it in other words, it seems clear to me that you are not suggesting a kind of eternal and almost Jungian archetype of the Feminine, but that you are trying to explore something like a strategic use and a dynamic re-appropriation of this feminine trope in India's recent political subjectivities. Could you elaborate upon this very fundamental point of your research?

AN: I have already given an indirect response to a part of this question in response to your earlier question. Let me supplement that answer.

You are right, I am not talking of a Jungian archetype, though something like that does shape the underside of the Indian pantheon, presided over by powerful mother deities, in a dynamic relationship with the dominance exercised in crucial sectors of life by feared maternal deities of the left-handed sects. This is not something uncommon in agricultural societies, where human productivity and re-productivity—the fertility of land and the

---

[3] Cf. For example, Ashis Nandy, 'Woman versus Womanliness in India', in *At the Edge of Psychology: Essays in Politics and Culture* (New Delhi: Oxford University Press, 1980), pp. 32–46; and Ashis Nandy, 'The Illegitimacy of Nationalism: Rabindranath Tagore and the Politics of Self', in *At the Edge of Psychology: Essays in Politics and Culture* (New Delhi: Oxford University Press, 1980), pp. 153–233.

fertility of women—are often coterminous. Its underside is the ability to heal and protect, an ability that can sometimes be withdrawn. And such withdrawal can sometimes be seen to converge with the refusal to hold in leash the war horses of epidemics or natural calamities. Power, activity, and play remain symbolically the domain of woman. The warrior communities in Hinduism and the Sikhs, like the Japanese, usually worship warrior goddesses as supreme goddesses. What you might call the fantasy of re-masculinization paradoxically makes way for the fantasy of access to primal power and to one's own creative and destructive selves.

Psychoanalysis in India

LB: In the very interesting and insufficiently known history of psychoanalysis in India between the 1920s and the 1940s, one can find two main trends concerning the relationship with the colonial setting. The first one is embodied by Owen Berkeley-Hill (1897–1944), a British medical officer and psychoanalyst, close to Ernest Jones, who was the head of one of the first psychiatric hospitals in India (in Ranchi, actually in Jharkhand), and who gave a sort of positivist Freudian justification to colonialism.[4] The second trend is associated with Girindrasekhar Bose—'the savage Freud', as you call him in your brilliant essay on Bose[5]—the founder of the Indian Psychoanalytical Society in Calcutta (1922), an original and hybrid intellectual and therapeutic figure, who wrote in English and in Bengali, corresponded with Freud, and built

[4] See his perhaps most famous paper on 'The Anal–Erotic Factor in the Religion, Philosophy and Character of the Hindus', *International Journal of Psychoanalysis* (1921), 2(3–4): 306–38.

[5] Ashis Nandy, 'The Savage Freud: The First Non-Western Psychoanalyst and the Politics of Secret Selves in Colonial India', in *The Savage Freud and Other Essays in Possible and Retrievable Selves* (New Delhi: Oxford University Press, 1995).

his own theoretical perspective on psychoanalysis through a theory of 'opposite wish'.

What do you think of this dual path that psychoanalysis took in India during the colonial era? Could we speak of two different epistemic models, one based on the idea of a simple expansion (a fantasy of *conquistador* that one can easily find in Freud himself), and the other based on the idea of a translation, or even, in reference to Derrida's concept, on a 'graft', a *'greffe'*? More generally speaking, what can we learn from the epistemological case of the double-edged reception of psychoanalysis in colonial India?

AN: Like many other knowledge systems that came through the colonial connection, psychoanalysis in practice promised a theory of liberation as well as a social evolutionary model of liberation that presupposed deculturation and ethnocide on a massive scale for that liberation to be available to the dark-skinned Africans and Asians. But many Indians too found these theories excellent tools of social and political criticism. They did know that these new theories were being picked up by dissenters in the colonizing societies, and perhaps many Indians felt that they too could make creative use of them. They might have been wrong in their judgment, but it was not always the fault of individual thinkers or writers. It was the fault of the intellectual culture European colonialism had assiduously promoted over a period of 150 years. Those who escaped its influence were either fortunate or exceptionally gifted and sensitive.

For instance, Indian psychoanalysts, psychiatrists, and psychologists never warmed up to Carl Jung as much as they did to Freud. Yet, Jung visited India twice, played a role in establishing two new departments of psychology in two major universities, and was better acquainted with Indian thought than Freud was. But at that point of time, Indians were not looking for testimonials on their cultural ancestry but for new frameworks or baselines that would help them to confront contemporary evil. They found Freud more rebellious and more radical.

Girindrasekhar Bose went further. He believed that not only did psychoanalysis have something to contribute to the Indian civilization; the 5000-year-old civilization too might have something to contribute to psychoanalysis. I suspect that this awareness is gaining ground in the Southern world.

LB: Do you see, as Sudhir Kakar does, any actuality of Girindrasekhar Bose's clinical and anthropological views? According to Kakar, in this actuality lie the 'ubiquity and multiformity of the "primitive idea of being a woman" and the embeddedness of this fantasy in the maternal configurations of the family and culture in India'.[6] Do you share this point of view? And what about other possible marks of Bose's influence on contemporary Indian psychoanalytical culture?

AN: I do not see any serious influence of Bose's work on contemporary Indian psychology. I could see such influence in earlier generations of Indian psychoanalysts. There were fleeting glimpses of such influence in some of the works of Tarun Sinha, Phillip Spratt, Haripada Maity, D.B. Desai, and Shib Kumar Mitra. But I am not sure if I would have deciphered such influences before embarking on my study of Girindrasekhar's life and work. Probably I saw them because I was looking for them.

I am inclined to agree with Sudhir's formulation. But it is filtered through Sudhir's own creativity and psychoanalytic sensitivity. I also suspect that some vague awareness of the dynamics you have in mind pervades most psychoanalytic works on India—from Morris Carstairs to Jeffrey Kripal.

Psychoanalysis and Criticism of the Postcolonial State

LB: A point which clearly differentiates your own approach to Freud's work from Sudhir Kakar's is your use of psychoanalysis for a metapolitical analysis of the postcolonial state. In one of

---

[6] Cf. Sudhir Kakar, *Culture and Psyche: Selected Essays* (New Delhi: Oxford University Press, 2008), p. 74.

my favourite books that you wrote, *The Romance of the State and the Fate of Dissent in the Tropics*[7] you suggest a pastiche, readable even in the title of the book, between two Freudian concepts: 'the family romance' and the 'Drives Fate'. This mix of Freudian syntagms indicates your idea of a deep connection between the Oedipus complex of the colonized subject, which implies an idealization of the Master, and the fate of the legitimization of mass violence by the postcolonial state.

Violence in its religious and communitarian forms becomes a tool for the postcolonial state to raise itself to the level of the colonial Master's *imago*, and to repress every heterogeneous and feminine component within itself. In a more recent work, *Regimes of Narcissism, Regimes of Despair*, you consider Indian nationalism as a 'compensatory mechanism' destined to build—if I read you correctly—a kind of 'secondary narcissism' following the narcissistic wound inherited from colonialism.

So, my question will be twofold: Do you think, beyond metaphors, that psychoanalysis can provide a theory of the state *per se*? And, if so, can this theory go beyond the classical psychoanalytical critiques of the fascist state already suggested by Freud and Reich with regard to European fascism? In other words: what does Indian nationalism teach us about the relationship between the state and mass psychology that we did not already know through fascist European experiences and criticisms?

AN: This question is not easy to answer within the format of an interview. So I shall have to give a brief, suggestive answer. The European fascist state was not as disjunctive with the Westphalian nation-state as many European intellectuals like to believe. The psychological bonds between Europe's earlier record of violence and European fascism were deep, though the Fascist political culture did not turn out to be that enduring. In some ways, Fascism took to a logical conclusion some strands

---

[7] Cfr. Ashis Nandy, *The Romance of the State and the Fate of Dissent in the Tropics* (New Delhi: Oxford University Press, 2003).

of consciousness that were already salient under the shadow of the Enlightenment in Europe, that is, *after* the values of the Enlightenment had begun to seep into the culture of everyday life of sizeable sections of Europeans. For these Europeans, the older war cries like 'Christianize the world' or the once-important debate on whether the American Indians and Africans had souls or not did not seem an adequate explanation of 200 years of slow genocide in the Americas that some claim took a toll of some 120 million, arguably the world's most successful genocide ever. Not to speak of the four-continent African slave trade that might have taken a toll on another 12 million (as some African scholars claim), arguably the world's first attempt at globalization through free trade.

The new slogans were 'knowledge is power' (Francis Bacon) and the social–evolutionist ones, 'struggle for survival' and 'stages of history' (Charles Darwin). The modern colonialism of England and France, which could be called the second attempt at globalization—the sun did not set on the British Empire, we were taught in our childhood—had a civilizing mission and carried the onerous burden of not only educating the world but also cleansing the world of inferior races fit only to serve the superior ones. The German state had already been involved in the genocide of two communities in Africa; the British had already discovered the concentration camp and were to discover area bombing as opposed to strategic bombing; and colonial administrations everywhere used racial categories, ethnicity, and skin colour in official classificatory systems. Nazism only built upon this scientization of dominance; its self-justification came not from hatred, but as recent works show, from nineteenth-century biology, eugenics, and twentieth-century public hygiene (see for instance, Robert Lifton, Zygmunt Bauman, Stanley Milgram, for instance). Kant, Hegel, Hume, Jefferson, Marx, and Engels are obvious examples of the new racism that came from the brutalization of both the public sphere and the knowledge systems that dealt with the public sphere in Europe and the brutalization of its colonial subjects. The two World Wars, with a toll of about 100 million human lives, only completed this process of brutalization.

I trace most of the world's present ills to the 250 years of Satanism that has infected many of the global institutes we presently work with. The job of psychoanalytic sociology is to work out the inner dynamics of these connections, and supply a new baseline for social criticism and epistemic ethics.

LB: Let me try a more subjective and lateral question; reading your analysis on fantasies linked to the state in the postcolonial context, I often have the feeling that you try to imagine an alternative to the Oedipian state under the form of something like a good-enough maternal state. Even if you never quote Winnicott, you seem to me quite close to the idea of a maternal mode of the state, not, of course, under the form of the fantasy of a phallic and omnipotent Mother, but under the form of an entity which guarantees to the subject an 'anaclisis' without pretending to embed him. In other words, a Winnicottian mother-like state that could partially disappoint the unconscious demands of the subject, without necessarily turning into a bad state. Does such a question make sense to you? Can we really imagine a maternal style of the state? And, if so, which political shape could it take?

AN: A modern state has individual subjects and wants to have only individual subjects. But whether it wants it or not, a state often has, in the Southern world, thriving communities as its subjects. True, the modern state is synonymous with what is called a nation-state; but there is no guarantee that it will have within its boundaries only one community. Your question presumes some degree of homogenization and shared fantasy life in a state. How does one answer the question in a country with more than 1200 languages, nearly 30 of which are recognized as national languages, and two as official languages? In addition, there are thousands of sects, 330 million gods and goddesses, and an estimated 70,000 castes, which no anthropologist has till now managed to enumerate. There are thousands of varieties of Brahmins and none who knows the names of a sizeable proportion of them. Yet, there are strains of awareness that cut across these divisions. There can be a psychoanalytic sociology of such diversity and what it does to those living in such societies. Maybe some young sociologist will take it up as his or her life's work.

As for the fantasy or vision of a state in India, I suspect that the ideal state is perhaps not modelled on maternity but on a fortunately distant, frequently absent father who does not want to live through his children but finds them amusing and fascinating in themselves and leaves them alone to work out their own destinies. This is because South Asians do distinguish between the Indian state and India, the motherland. The dichotomy between the state and the nation is not that relevant here, for it is not sharply etched out. As Tagore recognized long ago, the Indian nation exists and also does not exist. The motherland is the mother, not the state. But motherland can also mean small territorial units, even one's birthplace or village.

One throw-away comment at the end on the Indian attitude to the modern state. Every ruler of India must be careful when handling the population they rule, for the subjects they rule remain fundamentally ambivalent towards the state. Not only did Gandhi have a clear anarchic streak in him, there is an anarchic streak in most Indians. In no other area of life do they lose patience so easily and quickly as they do with their political rulers. Some rulers have tried to reform the state to counter that ambivalence; others have sought to bypass the state. Still others have experimented with a stricter, more centralized state. Nothing has worked in the long run. The state systems that have lasted long in India have worked with this awareness, knowingly or unknowingly. Perhaps you are not wrong after all. Perhaps this ambivalence towards the state reproduces the ambivalence towards the mother. Perhaps the fear of and hostility towards the state is the underside of the love for Mother India.

Some Contemporary Issues

LB: You are one of the rare postcolonial thinkers who does not come from Marxism or post-Marxism. And you are even, most of the time, very critical towards Indian Marxism. Nevertheless many of your reflections concern, in different ways, the question of what Gramscian Marxism calls 'hegemony'. The relationship between political hegemony and cultural hegemony, the role of 'common sense' and of 'civil society', the refusal to disqualify religion, the presence of the 'Southern question' within the history of Capitalism, and the revaluation of the geographical factors within historical materialism: all these themes, typical of Gramscian Marxism, have had a strong influence on Indian Subaltern Studies, and more widely, on contemporary Indian critical thought. Do you have any interest in Gramsci or Gramsci's contemporary readings?

AN: Yes, I have the curiosity, more so because many of the subaltern scholars are my friends and I consider their work very valuable. Till now we have mostly led parallel lives. I shall like to correct that but that will not be easy.

LB: To move closer towards a conclusion, I would appreciate it if you could say a few words on another important side of your Freudian sociology of contemporary Indian society: the urban question. In many of your writings[8] you analyse some crucial anthropological reversals: for example, how the Indian village—idealized by Gandhi—became a dystopia for a part of

[8] See, for example, Ashis Nandy, *An Ambiguous Journey: The Village and Other Odd Ruins of the Self in Indian Imagination* (New Delhi: Oxford University Press, 2001).

the Indian imagination after Partition (indeed, many slaughters took place in villages); or how the slums of the Indian megalopolis and the Indian diaspora can actually have in common a feeling of uprooting that they try to repress by a demand for identity and homogeneity, thereby creating a new 'social bloc' for the BJP [Bharatiya Janata Party].

AN: India has an ancient urban tradition. The oldest ruins of the Indic civilization are all cities (Mohenjodaro and Harappa, for instance). Cities are also important in Indian epics. They were the centres of politics, trade and commerce, and pilgrimages. And these cities and villages were always in touch. The relationship between the cities and villages represented two distinct but parallel lifestyles that constantly criticized and mocked each other. (See, for instance, translations of Shudraka's ancient Sanskrit play *Mricchakatika*.)

That mutuality and equality began to weaken with the birth of colonial cities like Bombay and Calcutta. These colonial cities, which were sometimes called presidency towns, brought a different imagination of the city into play in urban India. This imagination had two coordinates. First, the cities were seen as a negation of villages, now re-imagined as bastions of Indian tradition, and thus, depositories of superstitions, paganism of all kinds, and the pathologies of a decrepit, decadent Indic civilization. Second, a new evolutionary perspective was introduced which came to see the colonial cities—and the urbanization and modernization that went with them—as the final fate or foreseeable future of all villages. The older mutuality between the village and the city was, as a result, disrupted, and the idea of the disowned village was to re-enter the urban consciousness (through a whole series of freedom fighters, creative thinkers, and social reformers) as a new, decolonized, pastoral utopia. That is the village of Gandhi, Tagore, and filmmaker Satyajit Ray.

However, in a majority of the expanding middle class of India, the colonial imagination of the city has persisted, and to them, the village remains a symbol of backwardness and underdevelopment, and all attempts to re-imagine the village as a living critique of the city appear to be forms of romantic nostalgia and attempts to return to a mythic past. This is a clue to many of the ongoing controversies over development and social change in India.

LB: Finally, I'd like to take the risk of skipping to current events for a moment. The recent cases of violence against women, following the gang rape and murder of a young woman on a bus in Delhi at the end of 2012, have been widely relayed by the European press as well. In an interview given two weeks after the incident,[9] you pointed out the inadequacy of the category of sexual violence to analyse this kind of crime. You put forward the idea of an excess of violence, overtaking the 'traditional' function of rape as a means of asserting social status, and you insisted on the idea of generalized anomic violence which worries the social body because, from then on, everybody can become a victim of it. Could you expand on this idea? How to understand the overexposure of women to anomic violence in contemporary India?

AN: For the moment I shall only say this: Not only did women have power in traditional India, which was a phenomenon natural to all agricultural societies, this power came from the religious and 'magical' equation or continuity made in such societies between women's re-productivity and the fertility of land. In Europe, modern political economy and modern knowledge systems curtailed these powers of women by masculinizing the Christian pantheon and making Protestant Christianity the predominant paradigm of faith (partly because Weber's thesis on Protestant ethics and the spirit of capitalism in particular, and modernity in general, had probably become a tacit part of common sense even

---

[9] Cf. http://www.governancenow.com/views/interview/anomic-anarchic-free-floating-violence-looking-targets.

before Weber articulated it so clearly). But the traditional fear of a woman and her access to the primal magical powers of women remained just below the surface. The growing presence, self-assertion, and self-confidence of women in the modern sector re-activates these fears, and there is a desperate attempt to put the genie back in the bottle. The violence comes from that fear. It is a bit like the European witch-hunt towards the end of the medieval period. As modernity spread, witch-hunting, instead of decreasing, increased between the thirteenth and fifteenth centuries (see for instance, the works of A.J.P. Taylor and Norman Cohn).

BOOK V

SHREDS OF HOPE

31

Beyond Brutalization*

Organized violence and cruelties might have been there since ancient times, but they acquired a new cultural salience after the printing press, especially newspapers, entered the global public sphere. The genocide of native Americans had to some extent escaped harsh scrutiny; it happened somewhere far away and the victims had been demonized rather successfully through a series of intellectual manoeuvres such as the debates on whether they had something akin to souls that could be saved or on where they had to be placed amongst the flora and fauna of the New World. But

* This is a radically revised and expanded version of a paper presented in the inaugural plenary of the Rhodes Forum at Rhodes, Greece, during 8–12 October 2015. Some sections of it borrow from a paper titled '200 Years of Silence on How Theories of Progress Affect Cultural Survival', written for the Conference on the the Notion of Progress in the Diversity of World Cultures, convened by Constantin von Loewen on behalf of the Alliance of Civilizations (UN), New York University, and the Frederich-Ebert Foundation at the United Nations Headquarters, New York (31 May–4 June 2015). Also published in Fred Dallmayr and Edward Demenchonok (eds.), *A World Beyond Global Disorder: The Courage to Hope*, 2017, Cambridge Scholars Publishing, pp. 67–74.

the same strategies did not work that well with the four-continent slave trade and modern colonialism after Enlightenment values had made deeper inroads into Europe's public sphere.

To cope with this 'anomaly', there emerged in the nineteenth century new social theories that supplied three new frames of certitudes. I have always believed that human beings, given long enough time, opportunities, and patronage, can convert any theory of liberation into a new justification for dominance, greed, exploitation, and gratuitous violence. This time it was the turn of modern science, rationality, and secular humanism—three of the core values of the Enlightenment—to be so deployed.

The first frame mobilized the idea of scientific objectivity to establish a continuity between objectivity and objectification. All living beings, including Homo sapiens, were seen as subject to inescapable historical laws and stages of sociocultural and political–economic evolution. At the same time, the frame borrowed from the new sciences of public hygiene and eugenics to produce new stratarchies of peoples who could be contaminated and peoples who could contaminate. Unlike the traditional systems of purity and impurity, touchability and untouchability, this frame supplied clear-cut projects of extermination, and in its more benign form, ethnic cleansing.

The second frame justified a new form of dispassionate, scientized, assembly-line violence that could meet the demands of the scientized laws of biology and history. Later on, during the colonial age, new technologies of violence, from the discovery of area bombing (as opposed to strategic bombing) to nuclear weapons to long-distance assassination through drones gave this form of violence enormous reach, and more recently, a clear touch of cleanliness.

The third frame has built upon the expanding sphere of secularism and the de-sanctification of human life, nature, childhood, and femininity to create new concepts of disposable humans, infra-humans, de-masculinized peoples, and child races. Nothing remained sacred any more in the public sphere, certainly not in international relations. Losses and gains in public life began to be calculated now the way a chartered accountant sums up the gains and losses of a client.

These frames of certitudes are now weakening, if not crumbling. Dominance may not have ended but the politics of knowledge has taken a new turn. Breakdowns could well be, as the old cliché goes, breakthroughs. This chapter is based on that hope, and is a preliminary attempt to briefly spell out one particular part of this story.

I

The world is in disarray in many ways—in the form of roughly 60 wars fought since the end of World War II; emergence of terrorist movements, terrorist states, even lone-wolf terrorists; mishandled environmental crises that have created vast tracts of uninhabitability and massive displacements; a growing proportion of people who live with the feeling of being permanently in exile and are permanently searching for, what Hannah Arendt called, pseudo-communties; consolidation of new forms of hegemony more dependent on 'universal' categories of knowledge and expert-driven technological choices that are seen as outside politics and outside social audit; and persistence of a large number of states where secrecy, surveillance, and censorship continue to be parts of everyday life. The list is long.

Behind these obvious disorders, there are also the more dangerous disorders within, which facilitate the transmission of anxieties, fears, and the experiences of traumata from one generation to another. These are accompanied by the persistence of the easy, escapist solutions of the earlier generations—such as drug-dependent escapism, media- or virtual-reality-driven consumerism, and the manic violence that has begun to come packaged with many of the totalitarian political and religious ideologies of our times. Despite the optimism our political leaders project in public, we are buffeted by incapacitating outer and inner storms, the origins of which remain a mystery to us: the feeling of being an exile, even in one's own country; the loss of old certitudes that is accompanied not by robust scepticism but by a desperate search for new certitudes; the steep growth in the incidence of substance abuse, schizophrenia, depression, and suicide; and above all, the spread of the kind of anomic violence that was unknown 50 years earlier in many countries. This list is also long, and I shall have to spare you the details here.

Here I concentrate on only one small part of the story—on the growing brutalization that is taking place all over the world. By that I do not mean simply wars, genocide, and terrorism, but situations (1) where surplus cruelty and surplus violence do not merely happen but are built into the plans and strategic moves of a state, movement, or army, and (2) where the spectacular expression of anger, hatred, and cruelty itself becomes a part of one's individual or collective self-affirmation, and finding targets of and justification for violence becomes secondary and often a matter of random choice. The discovery by Winston Churchill and Arthur Harris of the psychological pleasures of area bombing, in place of old-fashioned strategic bombing, during World War II, is a good example of the full-blown version of this pathology. The shift was designed to terrorize the citizens of an enemy country.

This change was accompanied by a late entrant into the game of terror, one that George Orwell diagnosed in 1946.[1] He called it Americanized murder, a form of Hollywood-inspired, meaningless, random violence without any genuine depth of feeling backing it. Orwell saw it as an individual act, and implied that such violence was sired by anonymity, identity diffusion, and the casual shallowness of relationships in a mass culture brutalized by World War II. Orwell's essay ends with the case of a young American man, a fake army officer, and his eighteen-year-old English girlfriend who wanted to be a gun-moll, committing three casual, pointless murders, which I am tempted to call a weird, psychopathic style of self-affirmation

[1] George Orwell, 'Decline of the English Murder', in Sonia Orwell and Ian Angus (eds), *The Collected Essays, Journalism and Letters of George Orwell*, Vol. 4 (London: Secker and Warburg, 1968), pp. 98–101.

with perhaps a touch of desperation. America still probably remains the citadel of such murders but others are catching up. In India such murders are no longer serious news. China joined the party in style when, about five years ago, a number of attacks on school children were mounted, most of them random and unprovoked.[2]

If the industrialized, dispassionate, routinized, banal violence that Hannah Arendt brought to our notice—and which later influenced the works of Theodor Adorno and his associates, Stanley Milgram, Robert Lifton, and Zygmunt Bauman—constitutes one axis of the new violence that the twentieth century brought centre-stage, the other axis, we may now have to admit, is the anomic, pointless, surplus violence Orwell talks about. Perhaps many suicide bombers, particularly those coming from the immigrant families in the First World with shallow knowledge of their own faiths but carrying bitter memories of their families and communities. Robert Pepe may be right about the rationality that drives the suicide bombers to self-destruction, but in many of them, there also is a tacit attempt to defy the 'soul-less', modern mass society to self-affirm as a member of a newfound community that legitimizes and—to borrow from S. Balagangadhara,—transubstantiates, the theory and practice of violence-for-the-sake-of-violence.[3] We have been living in denial of both these changes for

[2] Apparently, a majority of these attacks could satisfy the criteria set up by Orwell, but given the scrappy data and the quick death penalties awarded to the killers, we cannot be sure. What we can be sure of was the obvious shock and consternation of many ordinary Chinese citizens who had seen wars, revolution, famines, and genocide. This was one form of violence they were not prepared for. For a brief preliminary survey, see 'School Attacks in China (2010–2012)', *Wikipedia*, https://en.wikipedia.org/wiki/School_attacks_in_China_ (2010%E2%80 %9312) (accessed 25 April 2016).

[3] S.N. Balagangadhara, 'What do Indians Need, A History or the Past? A Challenge or Two to Indian Historians', Seventh Maulana Abul Kalam Azad Lecture, delivered at the India International Centre on 14 November

a long time. As a result, many parts of the world now face a serious problem of de-civilization.

* * *

After the discovery of the Americas, which took a huge toll on indigenous American Indian lives over a period of 150 years—in what at least some scholars have called the world's biggest and most successful genocide that might have killed more than 100 million—and the grisly four-continent Atlantic slave trade, modern colonialism took an even more determined, though perhaps still unselfconscious, step towards a more globalized world. The 6 million lives, which the slave trade is supposed to have taken, grossly underestimates the collateral damage inflicted on African society and culture, not to speak of the families, communities, and villages from which prospective slaves were abducted. No wonder many scholars estimate the toll of modern slavery to be at least double the earlier estimates.

It is doubtful whether we still know the full scope of the damage colonialism did. But we do know that the genocide of some communities left hardly any witnesses to testify to posterity. The Hereros and Namas of West Africa are examples.[4] Nonetheless,

---

2014, under the auspices of the Indian Council for Cultural Relations, unpublished ms.

[4] The rhetoric of social evolution and Malthusian demography reached its zenith in the seemingly less marauding and bloodthirsty colonialism of the British, French, and the Dutch. But the long-term results were the same. See, for instance, two recent books, published half a century after the official demise of colonialism, which bring to the English speaking world for the first time the barbaric side of colonialism: Caroline Elkins, *Imperial Reckoning: The Untold Story of Britain's Gulag in Kenya* (New York: Henry Holt, 2005); Madhusree Mukerjee, *Churchill's Secret War: The British Empire and the Ravaging of India During World War II* (Bombay: Tranquebar, 2010). See also Mike Davis, *Late Victorian Holocausts: El Nino Famines and the Making of the Third World* (London: Verso, 2000).

colonialism could boast of at least two wonderful discoveries that were to prove useful not only to the colonial rulers but also to some of their successor regimes: man-made famines, first deployed in Ireland, and concentration camps, discovered during the Boer war. Finally, the two World Wars that marked the end of modern colonialism themselves took a toll of around 100 million lives; they were, as their very names suggest, the last scenes in that spectacular enterprise 'on which the sun never set'.

Two caveats at this stage. First, this is not an effort to set up an intellectual kangaroo court for a summary trial of the European civilization and its North American variant. We all know that mass violence and wars were not unknown to other civilizations and cultures. Each civilization and each culture has its dark side. I am trying to draw attention to the way the growth of print media and the emergence of a global public and a global idea of cosmopolitanism gave the genocides and ethnic cleansing in which the European civilization participated a new cultural status. These were legitimized as 'natural' collateral damages that took place during the spread of Western civilization in the age of colonialism and the creation of three brand-new White continents. They were seen as part of the attempts to modernize the world and popularize the Enlightenment-driven idea of cosmopolitanism, with the normal share of distortions that any agenda of progress is likely to have.

Second, my focus in this chapter is not on the magnitude of violence but on unnecessary or surplus violence, whether justified theologically or with reference to secular, scientific–rational values, the kinds of spectacular violence that brutalizes its spectators as much as its victims, and thus, has long-term brutalizing affect on societies, and 'normalizes' cruelty not only in particular societies but often globally through mass media, literature, cinema, and children's literature and toys.[5] In other words, I am not discussing

---

[5] If I may take a momentary detour into my childhood memories, even in distant Calcutta, we read tales of adventure written in Bengali by Bengali authors for Bengali children, in which the villains were Pigmies with poison-tipped arrows, fierce Aztec priests looking for new sacrificial

here structural and other such forms of less visible, institutionalized violence, however important or massive they might be and however culpable a political system or political economy might be. For, they involve another kind of 'numbing' or desensitization.

To return to my main argument, the large-scale butchery that went with these geopolitical changes of course brutalized the victims, and many tears have been shed for them. A few like Mahmood Mamdani have even acknowledged and studied the way that the victims of such savagery can turn efficient, dedicated killers themselves.[6] Psychoanalysis has something to say about such identification with aggressors, too. But what about the perpetrators? Were they also not brutalized by what they had done? If they were, did they know it and how did they cope with that knowledge? Is the social knowledge Europe has produced contaminated by this record of three centuries of violence? Are the random racist remarks and formulations ornamenting the works of great European thinkers such as Immanuel Kant, Georg Hegel, David Hume, Thomas Jefferson, Karl Marx, and Friedrich Engels stray comments or parts of a distinct psychopathology of everyday knowledge waiting for a more serious interpretation? Was it the same psychopathology that pushed Heinrich Himmler to speak openly of how the Europeans had to harden their hearts to do their duty to their civilization? (For those concerned with dialogues of civilizations, Himmler moved about with a German translation of the Gita. Obviously he was not impressed with M.K.

---

victims, and opium-smoking Chinese pirates trying to abduct innocent Bengalis for ransom. We did not then know that none of the writers had gone anywhere near Africa, South America, or China. They were presumably happily accessing stereotypes and prejudices floating around them.

6 Mahmood Mamdani, *When Victims Become Killers: Colonialism, Nativism, and the Genocide in Rwanda* (Princeton, NJ: Princeton University Press, 2002). There is been also the remarkable and courageous intervention datelined 12 September 2001 by Richard Falk, 'The Wickedness and Awesome Cruelty of a Crushed and Humiliated People', *Commentary: International Movement for a Just World*, 1(9): 5.

Gandhi's interpretation of the Gita as an allegorical justification for non-violence. Himmler had read the Gita—as many urban, middle-class, well-educated Indians now do—as a sanction for dispassionate, nihilistic, mega-violence for a cause they hold just.) Did the violence and the cruelty exported to distant corners of the world, over generations, alter the algorithm of Europe's own cultural and social life? Apart from a few stray clues, we know very little about that part of the story. For, no serious work has been done on the subject.[7]

This silence, I guess, has something to do with one other contribution that nineteenth-century Europe made to the rest of the world—a two-pronged style of demystification that still dominates the world of social knowledge. First, impressed by the success of modern science in secularizing the world, a series of social thinkers popularized a form of demystification in which manifest social realities had to be unmasked to reveal a deeper 'reality' acceptable to Baconian science and its 'definitive' version of rationality. In quick succession followed a series of thinkers who ventured 'global' theories with presumably perfect knowledge of the globe acquired through their colonial or crypto-colonial connections. Underneath the manifest reality some of them found power relations (Nietzsche), others production relations (Marx), and still others psychosexuality (Freud). Each produced its own partisans who claimed that they had found the master key to human history and/ or human nature and one did not have to further demystify the underlying reality they thought moved the world. Alas, the master key remained mostly in the hands of those who were reared in the culture of the perpetrators.

Second, under the influence of social Darwinism, social knowledge vendors began to talk of societies and cultures in terms of diachronic, evolutionary stages. Some talked of inescapable historical stages of societies, economies, and cultures; others tried

---

[7] For a preliminary attempt, see Ashis Nandy, *The Intimate Enemy: The Loss and Recovery of Self under Colonialism* (New Delhi: Oxford University Press, 1983).

to convert all synchronic experiences into diachronic ones. Their contributions ensured that to Europe, strange countries no longer remained strange, mysterious, and a challenge to the known world of knowledge; they all became parts of Europe's past. And of course, as I have already said, Europe's present was going to be their future. The past and the present of those who did not jump on the bandwagon of progress were to be museumized and turned into 'researchables'.

Please note that each of the searing, traumatizing, world-changing experiences—the American genocide, the slave trade, modern colonialism, and the two world wars—took place *after* Enlightenment values had begun to seep into European middle-class consciousness and European public life had begun to resonate to these values. The changing global sensitivities ensured that the earlier theological justifications for the conquest of America, the Atlantic slave trade, and European colonialism were now an embarrassment. The metaphor of Christianization could no longer satisfy many believing Christians facing the charms of colonialism first-hand in the colonies. This did not lead to any deep self-exploration in intellectual circles. The justifications for colonialism began to get secularized, and modern science and scientized social studies became the main source of legitimacy for the four traumata through which the world had passed. The Third Reich, which knew a thing or two about violence, also knew how to use nineteenth-century biology, Darwinian evolutionism, and twentieth-century public hygiene in matters of ethnic cleansing and genocide.

This secularization and the birth of secular theories of salvation threw up a new set of theories of progress to re-order the world according to a man-made design. In that design, the Christian God, despite protestations to the contrary, had only a subsidiary role. Secular gods like Galileo, Descartes, and Francis Bacon were the ones who shaped the vision of a future that was mostly an ex nihilo product of human creativity. It was a self-confident and self-righteous design, mostly untouched by self-doubts.

In that secular vision, there must have been something especially seductive. For, virtually all subsequent efforts to theorize changes in human affairs, European or non-European, have drawn upon it. Perhaps the continuity had something to do with colonialism. Though the imperial project melted after World War II, it was never fully dismantled. Imperialism did not suffer any decisive, global defeat. The imperial powers emerged weakened but victorious from World War II. The way they loosened their grip on the former colonies also gave the impression that it was a triumph of conscience over self-interest, not of self-interest over the romance of imperial glory. Also, thanks to the authoritarian regimes they fought in the war, the colonial powers looked like champions of democracy and humane governance.

As a result, the culture of imperialism did not face any direct challenge, and did not have to jettison some of the core tenets of its worldview. Indeed, these tenets became an inseparable part of the post-war culture of global politics and the network of international institutions set up after the war. Our ideas of human rights, equality, justice, democracy, and progress, and even our dominant ideas of fighting imperialism are all tinged by the core categories popularized by imperialism. So are our concepts of statecraft, governance, and diplomacy.

Thus, the developing countries are now seen through the prism of two discordant metaphors. They continue to be imagined as dumb, apprentice nation-states, some of them making laboured attempts to enter the big league of nation-states, armed with nothing more than a blood-curdling version of nationalism or religious passion and expensive military toys bought at the expense of their citizens. As for the rest, their current status as modernizing societies have made them look, as a development economist once said, like expectant, destitute mothers delivering their babies on a busy street corner. No vestige of dignity or privacy is left for them. Everybody crowds around them to witness the great event, and give them sage advice, expert consultancy, and development aid.

* * *

Yet, everything is not lost and we are not probably fighting a losing battle. It is true that, mimicking Oscar Wilde, we too can claim that the well-educated, virtuous Indians and Chinese, two billion of them, nowadays have started going to New York when they die. But it is also true that many cultures and communities have maintained double ledgers, one public and one private, often one textual and the other mnemonic. Many cultures are not dead; they have gone underground.

It is certainly not an accident that the new global heroes who have entered the world stage during the last four decades are virtually all votaries of non-violence, and have shown a sharp sensitivity to the growing brutalization around them: Martin Luther King, Nelson Mandela, the Dalai Lama, and perhaps even Aung Sang Su Kyi being the best known among them. On all of them falls the shadow of M.K. Gandhi, disowned by the ruling circles in his own country.

Nor is it surprising that at long last in voluntary movements and in non-party politics, there is emerging a powerful critique of modern science and its culture. A majority of scientists may still be willing to play footsy with their political masters and corporate bosses in the name of the value-neutrality of science, but others are demanding ethical responsibility. Here too, the non-party political movements have taken the lead. Indeed, the role that trade unions and dissenting scholars played in the twentieth century is being in many places taken over by mushrooming non-party formations. As activist–scholar Fred Y.L. Chiu is fond of saying, wherever colonialism went in earlier centuries, syphilis went with it; now wherever globalized capitalism goes, non-party political activism goes with it. For, there is a growing, if tacit, awareness in many that the old means of resistance to uncritical urban–industrialism and corporatized life are not working anymore.

Finally, there is the consolation that intense, clenched-teeth, psychopathic killers and the political regimes they set up, head, or serve do not last very long. There is built-in self-destructiveness in most of them. Space does not allow me to elaborate on this but please allow me to tell a brief story that may or may not be apocryphal.[8]

It seems that Sir Francis Bacon, the father of modern science and the one who believed that knowledge was power, once wanted to find out what would happen if one force-fed a chicken with snow. I believe I could have predicted for him the fate of chicken. But Sir Francis did not believe in speculation; he was an empiricist who trusted only experimental results. So one wintry day at London, when it was snowing, he took a live chicken to his courtyard and began force-feeding it with snow. The chicken of course died but Sir Francis also caught pneumonia and died a few days later.

[8] For a more detailed analysis of the colourful life of Sir Francis, see Jatinder S. Bajaj, 'Francis Bacon: The First Philosopher of Modern Science: A Non-Western View', in Ashis Nandy (ed.), Science, Hegemony and Violence: A Requiem for Modernity (New Delhi: Oxford University Press, 1988), Chapter 1, pp. 24–67.

32

Gandhi after Gandhi

The Fate of Dissent in Our Times*

There are four Gandhis who have survived Mohandas Karamchand
Gandhi's (1861–1948) death. Fifty years after his assassination, it
may be useful to establish their identities, as the British police
might have done in the high noon of colonialism. All four are
troublesome, but they trouble different people for different reasons and in different ways. They are also useable in contemporary
public life in four distinct ways. I say this not in sorrow but in
admiration. For the ability to disturb people—or, for that matter,
be useable—130 years after one's birth and 50 years after one's
death is no mean achievement. Frankly, I do not care who the real
Gandhi was or is. Let academics debate that momentous issue.
Contemporary politics is not about 'truths' of history; it is about
remembered pasts and problems of fashioning a future based on

* This chapter has grown out of a brief note published in *The Times of
India*, 30 January 1996, and was published in its present form in *The Little
Magazine* (May 2000): 38–41. A briefer version was also published in the
New Internationalist (September 2001), 338.

collective memories. For better or for worse, Gandhi seems to have entered that memory.

Two qualifications at the beginning. First, I am no Gandhian. My opinion should not count, but Gandhism, as I understand it, is greater than Gandhi was. Gandhi himself more or less admitted so, when he gave the entire credit for his ideas to ancient wisdom, and he is certainly not diminished by that admission. Actually, he comes off as more human, and for that matter, more self-reflexive. Gandhi could not live up to his principles partly because he was a practical politician, and the job of politics is to dilute ideological and moral purism. To use my favourite commendation, borrowed from the obituary written on him by Arnold Toynbee, Gandhi was one prophet who was willing to live in the 'slum of politics'. He could not afford to be a perfect Gandhian. It is a tribute to his memory when one calls him an imperfect Gandhian.

Second, I should clarify for the sake of the incurably scholarly that the Gandhis I discuss are all Weberian ideal types, that is, they are tools of analysis, and—this Max Weber did not bargain for—caricatures. That means they are unreal but not untrue. In this respect, I have been influenced by literary theorist D.R. Nagaraj who loved to claim, following William Blake, that stylized exaggeration could be a pathway to wisdom.

* * *

Now for the surviving Gandhis. All of them are well known. I am merely bringing to awareness tacit knowledge. However, it is my responsibility as a psychologist to register the warning that the knowledge that exists and is tacit is often the most disturbing and the most painful to own up.

The first Gandhi is the Gandhi of the Indian state and Indian nationalism. I find this Gandhi difficult to gulp and so would have, I believe, Gandhi himself. But many people find only this Gandhi tolerable and live happily with him.

The biography and political career of this official Gandhi began early. After independence, the political presence of the Father of the Nation, his memory, and his writings were proving very problematic to the functionaries of the young Indian state, and to intellectuals who had already begun to specialize in hovering, like so many flies, over the state's patronage structure. Not merely the strong anarchist streak in his ideology, but even his peculiar denial of clear-cut divisions between the private and the public, the religious and the secular, and the past and the present, were proving a real headache. These intellectuals were as disturbed by him as his assassin was. Nathuram Godse, a self-avowed rationalist and modernist, in his last statement in the court that sentenced him to death, claimed he had committed a patricide to save the nascent Indian state from an anti-modern, political neophyte and a lunatic. After independence, Gandhi's own associates would have liked to bury Gandhi six feet under the ground, while keeping his image intact as an icon of the Indian nation-state. Not because they disliked Gandhi, but because he looked such an anachronism in the post-World War II atmosphere of centralized states, social engineering, and 'realist' international politics.

Since then, Indian statists of both the Right and the Left have never acknowledged their enormous debt to Mr Godse for imposing on the Father of the Nation a premature martyrdom that straightaway gave Gandhi a saintly status and effectively finished him off as a live political presence. Their brainchildren still hold it against Gandhi that he has occasionally refused to oblige them and has defied the saintliness imposed on him, presumably as a strategic means of neutralizing him. He would have certainly differed fundamentally from his gifted grandson, philosopher Ramchandra Gandhi, on this issue.

This is the Gandhi, we the residents of the imperial city of Delhi are once in a while told, who is about to be ensconced on the pedestal vacated by King George V at India Gate. It will probably be his final coronation as the patron saint of India's creaky First Republic. It will also be the most comic use of Gandhi since that middle-class, tragic, romantic hero, Subhas Chandra Bose, named one of the brigades of the Indian National Army after Gandhi during the final days of World War II. With the declining status of the Indian state, and with various Westernized versions of Indian nationalism sprouting like so many mushrooms around us under the guise of cultural self-affirmation, this Gandhi is presently not in the best of health. What the late Mr Godse could not do to him, the Hindutva brigade and the two Bombay film buffs turned potency-driven flag-bearers of Hindu nationalism, Bal Thackeray and Lal Krishna Advani, between them have already managed to do through the Babri mosque episode.

* * *

The second Gandhi is the Gandhi of the Gandhians. He is at the moment suffering from an acute case of anaemia. The Gandhians' Gandhi is occasionally quite loveable and has a grandfatherly, benign presence in Indian public lore. But he is often a crushing bore, apart from being a Victorian puritan mistakenly born in India. He drinks *nimbupani*—unlike the Gandhi of the Indian state and nationalism who drinks Campa Cola, technically made by an Indian company, but not Coca-Cola, made by a multinational corporation—and wears home-made Khadi. There is one thing the second Gandhi does not do. He does not touch politics. In fact, he cannot touch politics, lest the subsidies and grants from the Government of India to the various ashrams named after him, to hand-spun Khadi, and to the ritual seminars on Gandhism dry up.

This Gandhi does, occasionally, in this incarnation, convene meetings to condemn the growing criminalization of politics, uneven development, or corruption in the country. In these seminars, everybody sheds bountiful tears about the state of affairs in India without naming any names and without mentioning any party. Everyone is happy after the event; even the corrupt politicians who have criminal connections lustily join in the applause.

The Gandhi of the Gandhians travels all over the world to preach Gandhism or lecture on Gandhian thought. He speaks through the Gandhians to the public in India much less frequently. Rightly so because in India, his audience is usually pathetically small. And even that small audience frequently looks sleepy, inattentive, and tired at the beginning of the sermons. They come because they expect to be seen and because it would not look good if they are absent. The average age of such Gandhians is at the moment about to touch 100, and the average age of the listeners is not much behind. The Gandhians feel that this is because the Indian people have failed Gandhi. Others less respectful towards such Gandhians feel that the Gandhians have actually failed both the Indian people and Gandhi. They point out that those who swear by Gandhi day and night could have walked another kind of road, as the likes of Jayaprakash Narayan, Baba Amte, and Sunderlal Bahuguna had done.

✳ ✳ ✳

The third Gandhi is the Gandhi of the ragamuffins, eccentrics, and the unpredictable. This Gandhi is more hostile to Coca-Cola than to Scotch whisky, and considers the local versions of Coca-Cola more dangerous than imported ones. This is because his objection to automated, over-processed, fast foods is structural, and therefore, he considers it more dangerous if, on nationalist grounds, long-lasting, deep-rooted Indian structures are created to produce superfluous items of mass consumption within the Indian economy. And he says so in so many words. Not given to bogus nationalism, he would rather import Coca-Cola and Pepsi, for those Indians who cannot live without them, than underwrite Campa Cola.

This Gandhi—vintage *Hind Swaraj*—is also bit of a nag and a spoilsport. He loves to be a maverick and an oddity in our public life. It is this Gandhi Vandana Shiva had in mind, whether she knew it or not, when she filed a suit in an American court against the patenting of some derivatives of *neem* alias margosa. It is this Gandhi who has guided the notorious agitation of Medha Patkar against the Narmada dam, Claude Alvares against Operation Flood, and Vandana Shiva against the Green Revolution. And it is this Gandhi who lived in the writer–dancer–thinker Shivaram Karanth, who, in his late eighties, took on the deceit, stupidity, and necrophilia of India's nuclear establishment.

This Gandhi has other subversive affiliations, too. He prefers the company of known critics of his worldview like V.M. Tarkunde and even Pakistanis like Akhtar Hamid Khan and Asma Jehangir to the company of those who claim to bear his name and have had the run of Indian politics for more than five decades. The average age of those who keep the company of this Gandhi is low, and it would have been lower, but for some young-at-heart like Tarkunde and Kuldip Nayar who push it up thoughtlessly. And both this and his young friends are a real nuisance to the Indian state, to the country's officially defined security interests, and scientific establishment. They are a menace to the common sense that passes as sanity but can be actually called, adapting an expression used by my erstwhile guru, Sigmund Freud, the psychopathology of everyday public life.

I have a personal stake in this Gandhi and his terribly irresponsible young friends. Many of the things I have done in my life these youngsters are now doing better. The party of ragamuffins is growing in strength. To spite my numerous enemies, I can say that, even after my death, what I am saying and doing will be said and done more aggressively, confidently, elegantly, and with greater political finesse by them. This thrills me, for even after my death, I should be able to haunt my enemies who survive me.

Incidentally, this Gandhi does not have to wear khadi or abjure alcohol. His usual dress is blue jeans and a Khadi *kurta*, and, to please journalist Raminder Singh, who wrote about it with great relish in *India Today*, he also carries a khadi bag or *jhola*. Many suspect that this Gandhi has now very tenuous links with his birthplace, Gujarat, and that he may disown the state as one that has disowned him.

I am afraid this Gandhi and the evil company he keeps are going to be a real pain in the neck for sane, rational, well-educated Indians in the coming decades. Anthropologist and political activist Fred Y.L. Chiu of Taiwan, frequently reminds me of the old saying that wherever modern civilization goes, it takes with it syphilis. He claims that nowadays wherever global capitalism goes, it takes with it political activism, non-governmental organizations (NGOs), and presumably, those contemptuously called the *jholawalas*, who at the first opportunity begin to harass heroic corporate investors and captains of industry. This, the votaries of global capitalism and business tycoons are tearfully coming to realize, is an unmentionable hidden cost of capitalism. Frankly, I have a secret admiration for the gumption of those who extract this cost.

* * *

The fourth Gandhi is usually not read. He is only heard, often second- or third-hand. While a few like Martin Luther King carefully and critically assess and use his work, the rest do not even know what he wrote. Nor do they care to. Their attitude to Gandhi is similar to that of the late A.K. Gopalan to Karl Marx. Gopalan reportedly once said that he had not read any Marx because he would not have understood him, but he remained a Marxist nonetheless.

This Gandhi is primarily a mythic Gandhi. Unlike in real life, he conforms fully to his own tenets—at least according to his admirers in the environmental, anti-nuclear, and feminist movements. For, the 'realities' of his life are derived from the principles of Gandhism as they have spread throughout the world as a new legend or epic.

Some years ago, an American columnist, Richard Grenier, taken aback by the immense popularity of Richard Attenborough's *Gandhi*, tried to debunk Gandhi by pointing out major discrepancies between Gandhi's life and philosophy. (Grenier of course did not have anything to say about whether he rejected Milton and Beethoven because they had a record of child abuse or Plato because he justified it in the context of homosexuality.) But such attempts at demystification do not work because the Greniers of the world confront the need to believe in human potentialities and a curious compulsion to intercede in situations of man-made suffering that often seems basic to human nature.

When the Polish workers rose against their authoritarian regime in the late 1980s, they talked of Lech Wałęsa as their Gandhi, a description the Vodka-guzzling, tough speaking, moustachioed trade union leader must have found difficult to swallow. But the Polish labourers were not interested in the historical, verifiable similarities or dissimilarities between the two; they were making a different statement. They were saying something about what they themselves wanted, and about how Gandhi with his weapon of militant non-violence had become in our time a symbol of defiance of hollow tyrants and bureaucratic authoritarianism backed by the power of the state and modern technology. For above all, this Gandhi is a symbol of those struggling against injustice, while trying to retain their humanity even when faced with unqualified inhumanity. That is why when Benito Aquino of the Philippines was assassinated, the demonstrators on the streets of Manila did exactly what the Polish labourers at Gdansk did. They shouted 'Benito, our Gandhi', and if this seems only a coincidence, the Burmese students who rose against their military regime some years ago also invoked Gandhi in the same way. Only their leader this time was Aung San Suu Kyi, who had not read Gandhi when she began to be thoughtlessly accused of being an uncompromising Gandhian. At different times, this epithet has fitted different people—from Khan Abdul Gaffar Khan to Nelson Mandela.

The fourth Gandhi walks the mean streets of the world threatening status quo and pompous, glib bullies everywhere and in every area of life. The tyrants undervalue him because he has no arms to back him up, and the professional revolutionaries make fun of him because he talks of non-violence. Both usually pay heavily for this under-estimation. In the long term, the former can only take solace from the fact that sometimes the intended revolution against them fails, paradoxically after succeeding spectacularly. Revolutions, whoever does not know, eat up their children, both physically and morally. The revolutionaries—nowadays usually a motley crowd of middle-aged, arm-chaired, cynical academics, past their prime and enjoying sinecures in universities—can take solace from the fact that they can hold ponderous seminars on the 'historical' limits of Gandhism that should have ensured its death decades ago. But, by the time the seminar ends as a resounding academic success, this mythic Gandhi has moved on to other slums of the world to lead new formations against his erstwhile proteges.

* * *

I have given you four Gandhis and indicated my preferences, so that you can make your choice. But then, you do not have to choose any of the four. Perhaps that will be the wisest course. For Gandhi *can* be dangerous. It is much better for you to hang his portrait in your office or home, like many others do, to show your respect to this new addition to the Indian pantheon, and then take your children to a picnic on the public holiday that his birthday has become.

33

Liberation of Those Who Do Not Speak the Language of Liberation*

Fyodor Dostoevsky has somewhere claimed, social theorist A.K. Saran tells us, that there are only two kinds of people in the world: anthropologists and the subjects of anthropological enquiry. Over the last 150 years, one subset in the anthropologists' world has learnt to speak the language of liberation—a secularized version of the language of liberation once well known in Christendom as part of the theory of salvation. Today, the power of the language has become so enormous that nearly all dissent within the modern world and the modernizing third world has to be cast in that language to be heard or taken seriously.

* This is a revised version of an essay published earlier in The Lelio Basso International Foundation for the Rights and Liberation of Peoples (ed.), *Theory and Practice of Liberation at the End of the XXth Century* (Brussels: Bruylant, 1988), pp. 165–73. Every effort has been made to trace the copyrightholders of the essay. The publisher would be pleased to hear from the copyright owner so that proper acknowledgement can be made in future editions.

In the world of the subjects of anthropology, the rhetoric of liberation is a new import. It is not usually taken seriously and is often seen as esoteric radical chic. There are concepts akin to liberation in some of the major civilizations of the world—the Sanskritic, Jaina, and Buddhist concepts of *moksha* and *mukti* are obvious examples—but they neither enjoy the same political clout nor the intellectual stature to move social and political activists. In fact, many indigenous concepts akin to liberation often carry strong connotations of a theory of transcendence and/or other-worldliness.

Predictably, a plethora of social activists since the last century have been trying to teach the subjects of anthropological enquiry, scattered all over the world—though concentrated in the global South—the beauties of liberation. From St. Marx in the last century to comrade Mao Zedong in this one, from Christian missionaries in the savage world to Reverend Paulo Freire among the volatile, noisy, Latin Americans, none has let go an opportunity to teach the language of liberation to those who do not speak it.

This language of liberation, as it has grown over the last century, is inextricably linked to the idea of revolution. Revolution is what brings about fundamental or radical changes in a society and, thus, the liberation of oppressed peoples. Revolution, therefore, is seen by its votaries as opposed to both status quo and reform. However, revolutionaries are usually harshest not on those who defend status quo but on those who defend democratic reform as a mode of social transformation. To the partisans of revolution, reform is a false mode of transformative politics, dangerous because it can become an easy substitute for revolution in those who suffer from various forms of false consciousness. The best that the idea of reform does, this line of argument goes, is to provide a safe internal critique of a faulty or oppressive system and, thus, strengthen the system.

To those who do not use the language of liberation and/or revolution, these debates read like fruitless hair-splitting. For neither do these outsiders view change as intrinsically valuable, nor do they see any sustainable philosophical ground to presume a one-to-one relationship between change and the language of change.

I

The modern world, including the modern sections of the Second and Third Worlds, is built on the suffering and brutalization of millions. These victims, rebellious only when the stakes and the risks are optimally balanced in their reckoning, seek mainly the right to survive and perhaps some modicum of justice and empowerment. If the moderns want to call this search a search for liberation, it is their look-out, and their tryst with their morality. To the lesser mortals, being constantly targeted for liberation by a minority deeply embedded in the modern world, resistance to the categories imposed by the dominant culture of global politics, including resistance to the categories that come from the mainstream language of dissent, are both parts of the struggle for survival.

This resistance takes many shapes in the savage world. It may take the form of a full-blooded negation of the modern world's deepest faith, scientific rationality. It may take the form of a subtle subversion of the modern world's fondest—I almost wrote cleverest—charity, development. One can never be sure, and the strength of the resistance lies in the fact that one can never be sure.

Note that I am not concerned here with the viability or otherwise of either science or development, nor with the justification for these rejections. I may have something to say about that, but this is not the place. I am concerned here with the politics of these rejections, the way both the acceptance and the rejection of these cognitive and programmatic ventures tell one something about the power relations of knowledge and the politics of knowledge-based social transformation in our times. I am proposing here that, for a large part of the world, the negation of certain universals of knowledge is a natural political corollary of the nature of dominance exercised. For domination today is rarely justified through oracles, ritual superiority, or birth rights. Domination is now mostly justified in terms of better acquaintance with the popular categories of universal knowledge and better access to universal modes of acquiring knowledge. In the world in which we live, without leaning on the rhetoric of scientific rationality and analytic reasoning; without acquiring a progressivist, social-evolutionary idiom; and without a manageable historical consciousness, no human being is truly a citizen, perhaps not even fully human. All oppressed, to acquire the right to our attention and sympathy, have to first show that they are the worthy, deserving oppressed and not a part of the flora and fauna of the Southern world—timeless, unindividuated masses, living in a mythopoetic world.

The popular response in the mainstream global culture to the 'mindless' resistance of the 'infantile', 'atavistic' sector of humanity—when it is not wholly dismissive—is to split the ideas being challenged or resisted. Thus, there is now a modern science dominated by the establishment and a modern science that is reportedly emancipatory. The former constitutes the mainstream; it is wedded to militarism, capitalism, and gigantism. The latter is a form of dissent; it is unconventional, people-oriented, and egalitarian. Development, too, has been split into two: conventional development and unconventional development. The latter has many aliases; it often called rural development, decentralized or community development, eco-development, ethno-development, or alternative development. The current buzzword is sustainable development.

I empathize with many of these efforts to generate alternatives. I have personal links with a number of them. But I cannot for that reason deny that most of these initiatives are also products of the same worldview which has produced the mainstream concepts of knowledge, liberation, and development. Nor can I deny that the political logic of the battle of minds demands that the victims of the powerful, oppressive systems in our times first attack the domination of the ideas of modern scientific rationality, history, and progress as the major, legitimizing principles of all social intervention, and then, only then, seriously consider if some elements from these principles can be safely accommodated in a post-modern science or in a post-development world.

This does not mean that internal criticisms have no value at all. This means that internal criticisms are internal criticisms. They do not exhaust all criticisms. They certainly do not exhaust the criticisms of human violence and oppression which are implicit in the ways of life, myths, legends, and above all, in the spontaneous defiance and rebellions of the oppressed. Most of these self-expressions are not cast in the language of liberation; even less frequently can they be accommodated in a 'proper' theory of liberation. We, standing outside as spectators, can only try to translate these self-expressions into our language and construct for ourselves a tentative theory of liberation out of the 'crude', 'vulgar' theories of oppression that may come to underpin their 'primitive', spontaneous acts of rebellion and subversion. But these are our needs, not theirs.

It is with that awareness that we may have to try to give voice or, still better, to create the space for those who will give voice, to the victims of human suffering in the coming decades. The awareness does not deny that such suffering is a joint product of lifestyles, systems of knowledge, and theories of liberation populating the modern world. It only insists that those trying to give voice to the voiceless must recognize that, after nearly four centuries of presence on the world stage and after about two centuries of hegemony, the culture of modern Europe and North America no longer arouses the enthusiasm which, as a critique of traditions, it once aroused in the third world.

The first generation of social reformers in most colonized societies hoped to use modernity as a vector within Asian and African traditions, something that would, by supplying an outsider's critique, help these societies recover some of the recessive strands of their traditions, and strengthen and revitalize their societies. It is now fairly obvious that such controlled use of modernity has not been possible in much of the savage world. Modernity is not only triumphant in the Southern hemisphere; it has taken over as an Imperial principle in human consciousness in society after society. What was dissent has now become the mainstream.

As in-house criticisms of that mainstream, the theories of liberation may have to learn a lot. Being part of the ruling worldview,
these theories have the idea of historical inevitability to back them
and they have also learnt to ride piggyback on the urban–industrial
vision and the dominant strain of mass culture. Now, they will
have to cultivate some degree of modesty and will have to learn
that all theories of liberation must recognize the existence of dissent that is not only 'insane' and 'infantile' but also flouts the first
canon of all Enlightenment theories of knowledge, namely, that a
dissent to qualify as dissent must be translatable into the language
of modernity.

I doubt if the rebellious spirit of humanity can be ever fully
captured in what is essentially one civilization's concept of rebellion at one point of time. What is dissent if it has no place for the
unknown, the childlike, and the seemingly non-rational? And what
is the intellectual's job-definition if it does not include the ability
to be in a minority and work at the borderlines of the knowable?

II

Everyone in the civilized world is for the liberation of some group
or other. The idea of liberation now cuts across most modern ideologies, and has become common currency over a large cultural
terrain. But the enthusiasm for liberating others has only infre-
quently been accompanied by any respect for the categories, particularly the native 'half-baked' theories of oppression, used by the
others. For, to accept such home-brewed theories is to in effect cut
out the role of the experts in revolution, and de-expertize dissent.
That is why there is such limited acceptance, among the theorists
of liberation, of the categories of those who supposedly are waiting
to be led to their liberation by some specialist ideologue or other.

On second thought, this is not surprising. Ideologues are
always ambivalent towards those whose cause they take up.
Ideologues are embarrassed by the targeted beneficiaries of their
ideologies. The latter too, reportedly stuck in an earlier stage of
history, reciprocate these sentiments; the future beneficiaries of

theorists of liberation rarely show much interest in the good turn going to be done to them by the ideologues. Horror of horrors, the beneficiaries conceptualize the benevolence in their own way. Their gratefulness to their liberators, too, is often shockingly close to zero. Understandably so. Human nature being what it is, while everyone likes to be a social engineer, few relish the prospect of being the objects of social engineering.

Such cynicism of the savage world towards our favourite rhetoric of dissent may not be such a great loss. For all that we know, it may even widen our choices and keep the options for future generations more open. In matters of human futures, there probably can be no final word. And while the quest for freedom is perennial, the present language of liberation may not be the best pathway to it. In fact, as the temporal and spatial limitations of the language become obvious, that which looks like a hopeless case of dyslexia may turn out to be a natural cognitive advantage. In the sense that those who are thoroughly socialized in the presently dominant language of global communications may find it harder to re-educate themselves than those who start from scratch. In the meanwhile, it is possible to venture the proposal that to survive beyond the lifespan of the presently dominant knowledge systems, the language of liberation will have to take into account, seriously, the quests for freedom articulated in other languages and in other forms, sometimes even through the language of silence.

Not recognizing this is not merely a form of the politics of knowledge designed to marginalize large parts of the cultures of the oppressed the world over; it is a form of the politics of knowledge which seeks to abridge the concept of human freedom itself.

Select Bibliography

Bodley, John H. 1975. *Victims of Progress*. Menlo Park, California: Cummings Publishing.

Cesaire, Aime (trans. Joan Pinkham). 1972. *Discourse on Colonialism*. New York: Monthly Review Press.

Churchill, Ward. ed. 1983. *Marxism and Native Americans*. Boston: South End Press.

Coomaraswamy, Ananda K. (ed. Roger Lipsey). 1977. *Coomaraswamy*, vol. 2: *Selected Papers: Metaphysics*. Princeton, New Jersey: Princeton University Press.

deMause, Lloyd. ed. 1974. *The History of Childhood*. New York: The Psycho-history Press.

Dharampal. 1971. *Civil Disobedience and Indian Tradition*. Varanasi: Sarva Seva Sangh Prakashan.

Foucault, Michel. 1973. *Madness and Civilization: A History of Insanity in the Age of Reason*. New York: Random House.

Gandhi. M.K. 1963. 'Hind Swaraj', in *Collected Works of Mahatma Gandhi*. New Delhi: Government of India.

Illich, Ivan. 1970. *Deschooling Society*. New York: Harper.

Nandy, Ashis. 1987. *Traditions, Tyranny and Utopias: Essays in the Politics of Awareness*. New Delhi: Oxford University Press.

Reynolds, Henry. 1982. *The Other Side of the Frontier: Aboriginal Resistance to the European Invasion of Australia*. Harmondsworth: Penguin.

Said, Edward. 1982. *Orientalism*. New York: Pantheon Press.

Shariati, Ali (trans. R. Campbell). 1980. *Marxism and Other Western Fallacies: An Islamic Critique*. Berkeley, California: Mizan Press.

34

Freud, Modernity, and Violence

*Analytic Attitude, Dissent, and the Boundaries of Self in Our Times**

This is my second visit to Jerusalem, and it is with some trepidation that I deal with a subject that may have a distinct resonance in this ancient city of spiritual and moral grace on the one hand, and unthinkable violence, exodus, and divided selves on the other. Simone Weil and Martin Buber, I suspect, lived with the first Jerusalem, the modern Israelis with the second. For the former, Jerusalem not only had secular and sacred geographies but also moral and psychological ones. The latter seem to oscillate between a passion for an Israeli nation-state delicately perched on the desperate denial of a West Asian identity and a fierce commitment to a secular, modern European identity, precariously balanced on

* This is a revised version of the Plenary address at the Fourteenth International Congress of the International Association of Group Psychotherapy, Jerusalem, 20–25 August, 2000. A shorter version of the address was published in *The Little Magazine* (2003), 4(5–6): 8–18.

memories of massive suffering and exterminatory projects, once so lovingly designed by Europe for its Jewish population. The denial goes with a refusal to acknowledge that the Arabs and the Jews are often not divided by distance but by proximity.

The commitment to a European identity goes with the search for a magical remedy for remembered discrimination and genocide in the values of the European Enlightenment, presumably in the belief that a European disease requires European therapy. The search reaffirms an identity that many can neither disown nor fully own up to.

I could have used at this point the relatively better record of the Arabs in the matter of anti-Semitism. (Moorish Spain, arguably, was the one European country that came close to being a multi-ethnic polity. The Ottoman Empire can be accused of many excesses, but anti-Semitism, to the best of my knowledge, was not one of them.) But I shall bypass such historical details for the moment. Instead, I shall use as my baseline what one of the greatest products of Jewish tradition of all times, one who lived much of his life with an ambivalent awareness of his cultural–religious status, might have said about the bitterness that has come to surround Jerusalem. Namely, that the narcissism of small differences and familiarity are often better predictors of ethnic discontents and violence in our age than distance and ignorance. I am told that in the late-nineteenth century a Belgian anthropologist, finding it difficult to distinguish between the Hutus and the Tutsis ethnographically, ultimately decided to distinguish the two tribes based on the number of heads of cattle they owned. When the Rwandan genocide took place, that story became one of the ways of acknowledging what many anthropologists always knew, that the Hutus and the Tutsis were two tribes that, apart from being neighbours, were closest to each other ethnographically. This parallels the Bosnian case, where about 30 per cent of the Bosnian Muslims claim to be related to the Serbs through marriage.

It is in this context that I want to use as my baseline some of the popular forms that the Enlightenment values have taken in the

global middle-class culture to serve as the heart of a global structure of common sense. This is important because these values
now shape our concepts of the normal, the rational, and the sane,
both within and outside the clinic. I shall here lay my cards on the
table and confess that I am suspicious of the claim that Europe in
the seventeenth century discovered all the correct answers to the
basic questions of humankind once and for all, leaving the other
civilizations now to only write occasional blogs, polite letters to the
editor, or useful appendices to these answers.

I

We all live in an intellectual edifice primarily built by the European
Enlightenment. It is not very old, having been given its final shape
less than 300 years ago. I need hardly tell an audience such as
this that our concepts of an ideal society and meaningful social
criticism are coloured by this heritage. However, once we have
said this, we have to confront the painful reality that these concepts of a desirable society and desirable forms of social criticism
invoke altogether different associations in other parts of the world,
including the part where I live and work. These other associations
have acquired new play in recent years because the Enlightenment
vision itself has, finally, come under scrutiny in North America
and West Europe. Indeed, the rumours about its complicity with
the violence of our times have been given a certain edge by a whole
range of work. This body of work, when not directly dependent on
psychoanalytic insights, has borrowed heavily from clinical work
and therapeutic visions. Why?

One reason could be that the first psychoanalyst was a rebellious
child of the Enlightenment. He did not reject the Enlightenment
vision, but the social critique he offered was not from the vantage
ground of the Enlightenment's standard ideas of a desirable society and knowledge. He tried to supply a critique of Enlightenment
reason from within its perimeters but while doing so, often accidentally strayed into strange territories. Indeed, his crypto-Platonic

worldview was more open-ended than it at one time seemed. Scholars have located in Freud's work a whole range of new elements—from German romanticism and *naturphilosophie*, and the more open-ended concept of science associated with that tradition, to the East European, Hassidic–Jewish culture and mystical tradition that occasionally broke through his public self and overdone conformity to the model of the positive sciences.[1] As he gained in confidence in his middle years, he returned to some of the philosophical and civilizational questions that had always haunted him. Books like *Civilization and Its Discontents, The Future of an Illusion, Group Psychology and the Analysis of the Ego, Moses and Monotheism*, and *Thoughts for the Times on War and Death* could be read as 'regressions' to a more defiant and daring mode of psychological theorization. These works are more Dostoyevskyan and more informed with his tragic vision of life. They show that Freud was no intellectual kin of Francis Bacon, though sometimes, in his cultural and intellectual insecurity, he thought or pretended to be so. At least one commentator has felt compelled to say that Freud's tragic vision implied a rejection of 'the simplest Anglo-American belief in the virtues of progress'.[2]

Unfortunately, despite the rediscovery of psychoanalysis by literary theory and cultural studies in recent decades, this other Freud, product of multiple cultural traditions and trying to negotiate cultural borders, remains a stranger to many. The limited cultural sensitivities of some of the mainstream schools of psychotherapy and of psychoanalysis partly derive from this. These schools seem unaware that even modernity is no longer what it

[1] See a more detailed discussion of this in Ashis Nandy, 'The Savage Freud: The First Non-Western Psychoanalyst and the Politics of Secret Selves in Colonial India', in *The Savage Freud and Other Essays in Possible and Retrievable Selves* (New Delhi: Oxford University Press, 1995), pp. 81–144.

[2] Friedrich Heer, 'Freud, the Viennese Jew', trans. W.A. Littlewood, in Jonathan Miller (ed.), *Freud: The Man, His World, His Influence* (London: Weidenfeld and Nicholson, 1972), pp. 22–39; see p. 24.

was, that 400 years is a long time in human history, even the dark ages in medieval Europe did not last that long. Today modernity, to qualify as such, requires an element of self-criticism or at least a sense of loss. The problem is compounded by the various schools of post-Freudian psychology, which are mostly progenies of the theoretical frames that crystallized out as forms of dissent *within* the Enlightenment. Even when they defy the modern, the defiance is primarily addressed to and remains confined within the citadels of modernity. The ones that try to break out of the grid often turn out to be transient fashions with brief shelf lives. A culture not only produces its own ideas of conformity but also its distinctive concepts of valid or sane dissent. Worse, what looks like dissent in one culture at one time may not look so in another culture at another time. Let me give an example.

When Freud's ideas first came to India in the first decade of the last century, it was remarkable how little protest they aroused.[3] There was no frenzied opposition to it as there was in Victorian Europe. (I am using the term Victorian here in the wider sense in which Carl Jung used it, to capture the flavour of the middle-class culture in the whole of Europe in the late-nineteenth and early-twentieth centuries.) What offended Victorian sensibilities in Freud's work did not evidently offend the middle classes in India. Elsewhere I have mentioned Rangin Halder, a pioneering Indian psychoanalyst who did a classical Freudian interpretation of the Oedipal imageries in Rabindranath Tagore and his poetry in the 1920s, when Tagore was already being called a national poet and had become a revered figure in Indian public life. Such interpretations at the time meant primarily a heavy-handed exploration of psychosexuality. Almost nobody was offended, not even Tagore, so much so that Halder, who had first presented the paper to a small group of psychoanalysts, subsequently translated it into English

[3] Christiane Hartnack, 'Psychoanalysis and Colonialism in British India', PhD dissertation, Berlin, Freie Universitat, 1988; Nandy, 'The Savage Freud'.

and presented it at the annual meeting of the Indian Science Congress. It was a hit there, too.

What seems to us very naughty or defiant in one cultural context may not look so in another. A colleague once told me how her great-aunt—a seemingly house-bound, puritanical widow who had limited education and always wore white to conform to the traditional image of an austere widow in East India—helped her brother Sarasilal Sarkar, a first-generation psychoanalyst, to translate some of Freud's works into Bengali. She was not at all shocked by the newly imported, European theory of human nature, tinged with ideas of infantile sexuality and incestual fantasies. I remember in this context some Indian folktales about the Oedipal situation collected by poet and scholar A.K. Ramanujan. Many of them end rather tamely with the hero learning to live with the knowledge that he has unknowingly married or slept with his mother. There is moral anguish in them but not usually of the fierce, self-destructive kind found in the Greek myth. In one story that carries a touch of moral agony, the mother is the one who commits suicide.[4]

Contemporary Indian middle-class culture, however, has more in common with the global culture of common sense than with the folk tales Ramanujan had collected. We have to come to these alternative formulations in a different way, by examining the status of the post-Galilean world itself. Let me, therefore, look more closely at some elements in the critical apparatus of Enlightenment reason that the global triumph of the regime of rationality, sanity, and progress (encased in an expanding global culture of common sense and conventionality) should have given

---

[4] A.K. Ramanujan, 'The Indian Oedipus', in T.G. Vaidyanathan and Jeffrey Kripal (eds), *Vishnu on Freud's Desk: A Reader in Psychoanalysis and Hinduism* (New Delhi: Oxford University Press, 1999), pp. 109–36. See also Gananath Obeysekere, 'Further Steps in Relativization: The Indian Oedipus Revisited', T.G. Vaidyanathan and Jeffrey Kripal (eds), *Vishnu on Freud's Desk: A Reader in Psychoanalysis and Hinduism* (New Delhi: Oxford University Press, 1999), pp. 147–62.

us enough confidence to re-examine. Victory should have brought with it a new sense of self-confidence and responsibility, but evidently it has not.

The stalwarts who contributed to the Enlightenment vision tended to nurture one kind of critical attitude. That attitude used as its pivot, often creatively, the idea of demystification or unmasking. From Giambattista Vico to Sir Francis Bacon to Friedrich Wilhelm Nietzsche, it was the creation and unfolding of a new tradition of social criticism that sought to desacralize and demagicalize the world. That was the tradition on which the great critical theorists like Freud and Marx were to build. This tradition of demystification usually assumes that the manifest reality, after a point, is not trustworthy. If one tears the mask off that reality, one reaches closer to the truth, towards more justifiable certitudes. After the demystification, the certitudes that sustain the manifest reality and supply its standardized interpretations are shown to be unsustainable. Indeed, through this exegesis, one constructs a new reality closer to the truth, and that second-order reality provides one with a fresh bedrock of certitudes. It was the hope of the protagonists of this tradition that a new society, a new social vision, and even a new human personality could be built on these new hermeneutics.

The model of course was borrowed from modern science. There, too, the assumption is that once someone like Galileo dismantles common sense and everyday reality by proposing the idea of a heliocentric universe in place of the geocentric one; he demystifies or demagicalizes the universe and reaches closer to the truth. Likewise, the emergence of modern medicine can also be viewed as the emergence of a new narrative that sheds the earlier mystification of illness, and explains all diseases solely in the language of the body, as formalized in the science of biology. The assumption is that once one reaches the hard realities encrypted in the language of the body, one acquires greater mastery over ill-health. Likewise, there is a similarly with the Marxist idea of demystification leading to the certitudes of production relations and Freud's concept of psychosexuality.

There is another tacit assumption here. Namely, that there can be competing theories of knowledge, but not plural truths. Ultimately, one of the theories is expected to supersede the rest. Take the case of the Galilean discovery itself, which has served as a foundational myth of modern knowledge systems for nearly two centuries. Only two years ago, the Catholic Church recanted and apologized for prosecuting Galileo, a little too late in the day, some might say. Yet, a whole range of works, which rely on the actual arguments and exchanges between the two sides, make us suspect that the Church was not clear about the position it should take on Galileo's cosmology. Galileo was an influential person and had powerful friends in the Church. During his trial, he stayed in an abbey with a dignitary of the Church. The Catholic Church, never insensitive to political realities, was willing to compromise. In any case, it probably was less hostile to Galileo's heliocentric universe than to his belief that the Church should repudiate geocentricism and make heliocentrism a part of the official Christian dogma. In other words, the Church probably was willing to keep things vague and open and live with both the heliocentric and geocentric theories as contestants for the status of the truth. But the idea that there could be two co-existing, contesting versions of the truth was not acceptable to Galileo. In his world, one of the two theories had to win at the end.

Today, in the age of super-computers, it is possible to argue that in a relativistic universe, conceiving the sun as the epicentre is not that striking an improvement over conceiving the earth as the epicentre, if one chooses to confine oneself solely to the issue of the truth. A reasonably good computer can calculate the co-ordinates of the geocentric universe clumsily and inelegantly, but nonetheless *truthfully*. I emphasize the word truthfully, because Galileo's battle with the Church is described in school texts as a battle for the truth. I admit that the computations in the case of a geocentric universe will be more complicated; they will certainly not be aesthetic or parsimonious. But they will not be false. For heliocentrism and geocentricism are only two possible ways of viewing a relativistic universe. There could be other ways. Any modern physicist will agree with you on this as long as you do not bring in Galileo. He or she will be uncomfortable the moment you propose that Galileo was as right or as wrong as the dignitaries of the Church were. Galileo's dissent is a major myth of modernity, on which we have been brought up. To disown it is to disown a part of our selves.

The moral of the story is clear. What looks like radical dissent at one time, may look like a lesser innovation at another or become a lovely little story of dissent that has lost some of its rough edges. However, this also has the dangerous corollary that many ideas that were once instruments of liberation or parts of an emancipatory theory, which for decades came in handy for those battling social injustice or inequality, have ceased to be emancipatory. Perhaps for the simple reason that human beings, given long enough time, are perfectly capable of converting even the most radical theories of emancipation into sanctions for new forms of violence and oppression. It is probably better to be suspicious of all theories of emancipation after a point. Indeed, I believe that the coming generations may seriously demand that any significant psychological or political theory, to be so recognized, must have either an element of self-destructiveness or a subsystem of self-criticism built into it. It may not be good for the theorists; it will certainly be good for the rest of the world. There is no harm viewing all theories of liberation as transient instruments that retain the potentiality of becoming oppressive in the end.

Everyone knows of the demise of Leninism; few have noticed the demise of classical liberalism. Nothing reveals this twin defeat more poignantly than the changing language of the winners of the world. The new slogans of the victorious have gradually become those that the likes of Marx and Freud thought emancipatory. I have in mind the various theories of progress, science, rationality, social evolutionism, and development. The Nazis killed in the name of eugenics, the Soviet communists in the name of scientific history. The Khmer Rouge in Cambodia virtually acted out the dissertations that some of its leaders wrote for prestigious French universities. Values that at one time were associated with or indicated the defiance of authorities are the values of the authorities today. Values that at one time looked authoritative and dominant have become the values of the marginalized and the powerless. We are moving into a world where the nature of authority has changed. People at the heart of the Establishment today talk of the end of history, poverty, and human rights. Obviously so, because the end history has reached is not the one for which generations of dissenting intellectuals have worked. Poverty has become a billion-dollar multinational enterprise, and the idea of human rights is being exported by countries that have the shoddiest record of human rights in the Southern world. Nothing lasts forever; even dissent does not remain dissent after a point.

For us, who deal with human subjectivities, there is a more serious development in the wake of the crisis in modernity. The visions that presumed that individuality should provide the basic unit of social analysis and psychological intervention are themselves under severe stress. With individualism itself increasingly taking quasi-pathological forms, strengthening individuality no longer looks like a foolproof recipe for health. A few years ago, I was told that in large apartment complexes in some Scandinavian cities, electronic devices were fitted in the toilets of lonely, elderly persons. If a toilet was not flushed for a long stretch of time, the janitor came and broke into the apartment to check if the householder was alive. This was a response to instances of lonely senior citizens, deprived of community life, dying in their flats and the neighbours finding that out only after the bodies began to decompose and smell. This is individualism taken to its logical conclusion. It is my suspicion that all theories of consciousness—and if I may add for this audience, unconsciousness—will have to learn to look at the individual from a different point of view.

We do not have to give up the concept of individualism. We have seen what reified, overdone concepts of aggregates—such as race, class, nationality, and ethnicity—can do. In the last century, mostly deriving sanction from deified or demonized concepts of groups, we managed to kill 200 million of our fellow human beings. Their ghosts haunt all contemporary ideas of collectivity. I am suggesting that we re-examine individualism in societies where, in the name of individualism, certain basic dimensions of individuality have themselves been subverted. For most practical purposes, individualism has been reinterpreted as self-interest and consumerism. The Internet now threatens to reinterpret it as solipsism. The advertisement-driven individualism associated with consumer choices would have frightened even Sigmund Freud, whose individualism always had a Shakespearean dimension.

I once tried to calculate the shades of lipsticks available in the world. Within a short time, I arrived at a figure that ran into thousands. It is doubtful if physiologically the human retina is capable of registering that many shades of colour. I presume the width of this choice is partly bogus; it creates an illusion of wider choices than there actually are. It would have been a perfectly innocent illusion if the total cosmetic bill of American women had not over-stripped the total budgets of all the African countries taken together. For the moment, I am ignoring the quarter of a million animals sacrificed every year in United States (US) laboratories alone for scientific experiments, a significant proportion of them conducted for the cosmetic industry.[5] This is not a plea to abridge choices across the board; it is a plea to recognize that certain forms of absurd multiplication of choices can have psychosocial costs and can be considered puerile. I am merely taking seriously activist– scholar R.L. Kumar's proposition that the rhetoric of wider choices often hides that in modern societies an individual is increasingly left with only three substantive choices: to be a tourist, a voter, or a consumer. Other choices are usually either secondary or illusory. I am inviting you to extend to the favourite slogans of our times

[5] Shiv Visvanathan, 'Annals of a Laboratory State', in Ashis Nandy, *Science, Hegemony and Violence: A Requiem for Modernity* (New Delhi: Oxford University Press and Tokyo: UN University Press, 1988), pp. 257–88.

what Philip Rieff considers the heart of the Freudian enterprise, the analytic attitude.[6]

The very idea of the disenchantment of the world, so closely associated with the idea of demystification itself, is itself reaching the end of its tether. The world is getting so thoroughly secularized that the idea of a fully secular world has ceased to be an attractive dream, except to those still living in the nineteenth century. Two factors have contributed to the growing scepticism towards secularism. First, there is the growing environmental crisis, which seems intertwined with the secularization of the cosmos and the desacralization of nature and non-human life forms to many. If there is nothing transcendent or sacred, the final word on social morality becomes the aphorism of John Maynard Keynes, who has crucially shaped some of the major economic institutions with which we live: 'In the long run we are all dead.' If that is so, in a fully secularized, fully individualistic world, there is no reason why we should leave anything behind for the future. Certainly, institutions structured around self-interest, rationality, and hard realism have even lesser reason to do so. A conventional wit, W.C. Fields, puts it more directly and honestly than Keynes does: 'Why should I think about the future', Fields once asked, 'what has the future done for me?'

That is why many of the social formations that look like rebellions against secularism turn out to be, on scrutiny, offsprings of secularization. Disoriented by a changing world, they desperately seek meaning in the packaged versions of faith vended by charlatans, gurus, and bloodthirsty religious fanatics. I have been studying ethnic and religious violence during the last two decades. One of the most remarkable features of such violence, I find, is the element of secularization that has crept into it. Religious fanaticism now has little to do with faith, traditions, or communities. It is a product of uprooting, breakdown of community

[6] Philip Rieff, *The Triumph of the Therapeutic: Uses of Faith after Freud* (New York: Harper, 1968).

ties, and weakening of faith. Thus, expatriate Indians in the first world reportedly financed almost entirely the Ram Janmabhoomi movement that demolished the Babri mosque in India in 1992 and triggered countrywide violence. Likewise, mostly expatriate Tamils have bankrolled Tamil militancy in Sri Lanka, and the Irish Republican Army (IRA) has consistently received funding during the last seven decades from Irish Americans. It was almost as if individuals, feeling increasingly deracinated and uprooted, took up causes to battle their own sense of loss of traditions and community ties, to create what Hannah Arendt used to call pseudo-communities.

If this looks too facile an explanation, there is the fact that communal riots, in the whole of South Asia, are becoming a form of expertise and a profession. You can organize an ethnic or communal riot any time you like, provided someone gives you enough cash and political protection. You can order a designer riot to bring down a regime or change voting patterns or advance the cause of a political faction. The activists are known, so are their fees and their political patrons. The leaders who deploy these activists are also increasingly blatant about their profession. Organized religious and ethnic violence itself has become one of the most secular spheres of our public life. That is why, L.K. Advani, the leader of what many consider the world's largest revivalist formation, the Bharatiya Janata Party (BJP) and its allies in India, and the one who headed the movement that led to the demolition of the Babri mosque, could openly say in an interview with *The Times of India*, a national newspaper, that he was not much of a believer. As for his own religious sentiments, he added for good measure, that he felt closer to Sikhism than to Hinduism.

Advani is no exception. The Rashtriya Swayamsevak Sangh or the RSS, the steel frame of Hindu nationalism, was established in 1925. It supposedly has 1 million members now. Many of them are believers. Yet, for most of its existence and throughout all its formative years, the RSS has not had as its head persons who could be called believers. The first time the RSS chose a believing Hindu as its head was when M.S. Golwalkar took over in 1940. The earlier leaders were not diffident non-believers; they openly flaunted their disbelief, often trying to show how scientifically inclined they were, by attacking Hindu rituals and idolatry. They believed that they were fighting for the political cause of the Hindus, not defending Hindu religious traditions. Thus, V.D. Savarkar, who coined the term Hindutva and authored what has become the Bible of Hindu revivalism, *Hindutva,* declares himself an atheist in the same book. Evidently, the violent and venomous furies of religious fanaticism are not always associated with theories of transcendence in this century. They have been direct products of the modern, secular world, and the time has come for us to re-examine such fanaticism as the pathology of a modern ideology rather than that of a faith.

II

At the end, very briefly, I offer two theoretical proposals that might, just might serve as possible baselines for reconceptualizing forms of contemporary subjectivity, especially as they are reflected in the idea of individuality. I choose them because both are indirectly relevant to theories of healthy personality and psychotherapeutic practice.

First, healthy normal individualism is also possible when the boundaries of the self are not as sharply demarcated in terms of beliefs, faiths, or identities, categories that the moderns feel comfortable with. Our deepening cross-cultural experiences demand that we redefine health to accommodate a different concept of the boundaries of the self. Let me give two examples, one of them my favourite. I can confidently predict that in Japan, there will never be a religious conflict between the Shintos and the Buddhists, for the simple reason that a huge majority of the Japanese are Shintos and a huge majority of them are Buddhists. A similar prediction can be made about the Confucians and the Buddhists in China. Whereas in a country like India, where a periodic modern, scientific census has been conducted since colonial times, the percentages of different religious communities are so meticulously calculated that they always add up to exactly 100 per cent. The Hindus constitute 82.0 per cent of India, the Muslims 12.1 per cent, the Christians 2.3 per cent, the Sikhs 1.9 per cent, and so on.

Yet, when the Indian Anthropological Survey did a comprehensive survey in the early 1990s, not of individuals but of communities, it discovered that roughly 15 per cent of the 2800 communities studied had more than one faith. That does not only mean that these communities consist of people from different faiths; it also means that the communities include individuals who can be classified as belonging to more than one faith. This is not new to us. I have already mentioned Japan and China. Even faiths that have shed enormous blood to determine the fate of Jerusalem over the last two millennia evidently have other incarnations in the tropics. The Indian survey mentions 116 communities that are simultaneously Christian and Hindu, 94 that follow both Christian and the various 'tribal' religions, and 35 that are Hindu and Muslim. There are 17 communities which are followers of three religions; 11 can be classified as Hindu, Muslim, and Sikh; six as Hindu, Muslim, and Christian.[7] A colleague of mine has studied the Meos, one of the largest Muslim communities in northern India. They are devoutly Muslim, but also trace their origins to the Mahabharata clans. They have their own Mahabharata that they perform ritually. Even now, some elderly Meos have both Hindu and Muslim names, the way a huge majority of Indonesians do.[8]

It is possible to re-envision individualism, self-identity, and even the borders of the self. Some points of departure are available, and it is our responsibility to confront the violence of our age by pursuing these possibilities. We also have to remember that the communities that have kept alive these possibilities, despite enormous pressures to change or conform, are a beleaguered lot.

[7] K. Suresh Singh, *People of India: An Introduction*, Vol.1 (New Delhi: Anthropological Survey of India, 1994), pp. 82–3.

[8] Shail Mayaram, *Resisting Regimes: Myth and Memory in a Muslim Community* (New Delhi: Oxford University Press, 1997).

The forces of globalization and cultural homogenization threaten their lifestyles. Take the case of the Meos. Muslim fundamentalists, Islamic nationalists, and many modern Muslims have not been comfortable with Meo religious culture. Many Meos, too, having been victims of religious violence on and off during the last 50 years, now feel that their Islam is flawed. Indeed, Professor K. Suresh Singh, who headed the Indian Anthropological Survey's study of communities, tells me that such multi-religious communities revealed by his survey are the last remnants of a phenomenon that was once widespread in the region. They have ceased to be the norm in India, as in other parts of South and Southeast Asia. The official enumerative world in which we live has no respect for such traditions. It works with a more Cartesian concept of the individual self.

I reaffirm that there are possible ways of looking at the person to which the modern world has few clues. These possible ways cannot be explained away as mystifications or as romantic invocations of the past. Indeed, we are the ones who have been living in a make-believe world that ignores other concepts of the boundaries of the self with which a huge proportion, perhaps even a majority of the world, still lives. The new slave trade flourishing in our times, with full support from a large cross-section of the intellectual community, exports such people from our neighbourhoods to history, as a half-way stop on the way to a museum. We talk about such slaves in the past tense and accuse anyone concerned about them of being an incurable romantic.

Second, not only can the self be in dialogue with others, as most currently fashionable theories of multiculturism have come to acknowledge, the self can also be seen in the other and the other as telescoped in the self. This is not unheard of in clinical literature. There are studies that explain homicidal hatred towards outgroups as an attempt to exorcize alien parts of the self, the ghosts within. From the beginning, projection and displacement have been important defences in psychological studies of racism and ethnophobia. However, the healthier, more integrative possibilities in the story have not been explored. The same defences of projection and displacement can sometimes bond diverse communities within a shared cultural space.[9] As I have already said, the Enlightenment's tradition of demystification bares the material, the corporeal, the unhealthy, and the 'ugly'. It undervalues forms of second-order demystification that might reveal the sources of creativity and psychological health that underlie manifest ill health.

Recently, I studied a city in South India, Cochin, where at least 14 major communities have lived for centuries. It is a small city which was cosmopolitan and international much before the present idea of cosmopolitanism was imported into India during colonial times. The communities range all the way from two Jewish communities, one of which claims to have been in the region for more than two millennia, to Yemeni Arabs, who claim that they were in touch with Cochin since pre-Islamic days, to the Eurasian Parangis who came into being as a community within only the last 400 odd years. These communities live there and have lived there in peace. I studied the city to learn how.[10]

It took me some time to find out that the co-existence was not dependent on brotherly love. The communities were often ambivalent towards each other; sometimes they positively disliked some others. But while they did so, no person or community considered itself complete without the others. Cochin lives in what I have elsewhere called an epic culture, not with a linear, empirical, historical

[9] Shail Mayaram, 'Living Together: Ajmer as a Paradigm of the Asiatic City', in Kayoko Tatsumi (ed.), *Multiculturalism: Modes of Coexistence in South and Southeast Asia* (Washington: SPF, 1998), mimeo. This paper unwittingly, and therefore, unselfconsciously shows the involvement of two of the classical concerns of psychoanalytic anthropology—possession and psychic healing—in an Islamic mosque shared by the Muslims and the Hindus, and presided over by an unlikely Imam, a woman called Sushila Rohatgi.

[10] See Ashis Nandy, 'Time Travel to a Possible Self: Searching for the Alternative Cosmopolitanism of Cochin', *The Japanese Journal of Political Science* (December 2000), 1(2): 293–327.

concept of culture and communities. In that epic vision of life, you need villains to complete the picture, though these villains are usually fashioned out of the same defensive structures that students of ethnic and religious violence have come to fear.[11] Such a vision has to reaffirm, ritually and regularly, the existing configuration of the contests between the godly and the ungodly. You simply cannot do without the demons because you cannot even represent the gods without the demons. They are symbiotically related and are an unavoidable part of each other and your self. You do not have to love the demons, but you cannot nurture annihilative fantasies about them either. It is a bit like the story of the Jewish Robinson Crusoe who, I am told, *had to* build two synagogues, one to pray in and the other to set up as the one into which he would never step in. The second synagogue was important to him. He might have hated it, but his self-definition was not complete without it.

During the last two centuries, in the area of social knowledge and the knowledge of self, we have managed to destroy such visions by bringing in a peculiar evolutionary perspective on the relation between space and time. That perspective has drawn upon the various nineteenth-century theories of progress to convert geographies into histories, histories into geographies. At one time, one had the right to dislike other communities because they did not conform to one's ideas of morality and propriety. However, usually, one was forced to yield to the others, even if unwillingly, the same right to dislike one. It is no longer fashionable to exercise such rights or to own up to such prejudices. The triumphant culture of globalized cosmopolitanism has convinced us that we must pretend, even if we do not believe so, that everyone is the same. Yet, the same cosmopolitanism allows us to classify cultures according to the distance they have traversed on the timescale of history. So, I may not detest you—as representing a culture, a religion, a nationality, or ethnic group—but I retain

[11] Cf. Vamik D. Volkan, *The Need to Have Enemies and Allies* (New York: Jason Aronson, 1988).

the right to believe that you are what I was yesterday or in the last century. And if you behave well, if you obey the textbooks I have produced on self-improvement—through economic development, technological growth, acquisition of scientific rationality, or 'proper' political education—tomorrow you could be like me. It is what, according to Chinua Achebe, was Albert Schweitzer's idea of fraternity. 'The African: is my brother', Schweitzer said, 'but a younger brother'. Only apparently is this idea, which today infects virtually all liberal and radical theories of social change, an improvement on Immanuel Kant's or David Hume's belief in the natural inferiority of the Blacks, Browns, and Yellows. For in Schweitzer's view some cultures are only living out the pasts of others and are, to that extent, obsolete and redundant. A few cynics may claim that this is a way of pre-empting the future of some of the oldest civilizations of the world and annihilating the present of hundreds of humble micro-cultures that keep open our options by acting like cultural gene banks of alternative, dissenting, or even fantastic concepts of selfhood. But that is certainly not a popular view in the mainstream global culture of common sense.

Nonetheless, I remain optimistic enough to believe that the new century will define the capacity to listen as a major human virtue. An earlier generation of psychotherapists spoke of the need to listen with a third ear. Perhaps the next generation, less burdened by the ghosts of yesteryears, will not be embarrassed to speak of the need to listen with a second heart.

35

A Trialogue across Mortality*

Harilal Mohandas Gandhi (to Mohandas Karamchand Gandhi):
Tell us, why should we take you seriously?

Mohandas Karamchand Gandhi: (silent)

HMG: (in an insistent voice) You have to tell us. I have waited for
your answer all my life.

MKG: *You* don't have to take me seriously.

Ashis Nandy: That is no answer. You should know he has to take
you seriously but cannot do so.

MKG: Why?

AN: Because he is your son; he has to rebel against you. Sons are
always patricidal. But even that requires a serious, steady target
of demystification and violence.

MKG: But I have disowned him as a son. He has disappointed me.
He has lived a sinful life.

* Originally published as a Foreword to Makrand Paranjape, *Decolonization and Development: Hind Svaraj Revisioned.* © 1993. Makrand Paranjape. All rights reserved. Reproduced with the permission of the copyright holders and publishers. SAGE Publications India Private Limited, New Delhi.

AN: Sons are supposed to disappoint their fathers. They have to rebel. And that rebellion cannot always remain silent. Harilal may be saying something important when he rebels against the Gandhian worldview. Even if he does so in an odd or ham-handed fashion. There might be in him an implicit intellectual argument against your worldview.

MKG: Alcohol, meat, and women tell you nothing. They are his, a guttersnipe's idea of rebelling. Do you call that rebellion? Do they convey anything more than what they mean at the surface?

AN: They tell us that Harilal has objections to your moral universe. He may not be able to articulate his objections in your language but that is neither here nor there. It is your responsibility, as one who has brought up an entire generation, to decode what he wants to say. I know you will vehemently protest but, my dear Mahatma, you *are* a thinker. Harilal is not. You have to give him voice. Or are you going to argue that you are not your brother's, or in this case, your son's keeper?

HMG: (angry and defiant) I do not know what you are talking about. I only know that my father is a false Mahatma, a hypocrite. I have many faults, but hypocrisy is not one of them. What I do, I do openly. My father, on the other hand, is not transparent.

My father claims to be a saint but he has compromised with most of the evils he has fought. His non-violence worked because he had a liberal regime as his enemy, but he turned it into a universal panacea. He called himself a celibate but had to confirm his celibacy through sexual experiments with his own kith and kin, at the risk of what could have been horrendous cost to his innocent experimental subjects. He was supposed to be a saint in politics because few knew how shrewd a politician he was. Remember how he drove out Subhas Chandra Bose from the presidency of the Indian National Congress in the 1930s.

Above all, do not forget his attempts to sell a worldview that goes against the heart of the modern vision. As if he could take us back to some golden era of the past effortlessly and painlessly. As if anybody was going to listen to him and renege on hedonism and consumerism when he himself made so many compromises with contemporary tastes, demands of mass politics, the media, and with hard modernists such as Jawaharlal Nehru.

MKG: (evenly) I agree I have not led a consistently moral life. I have tried but failed. Harilal, you have a point.

AN: (impatiently to MKG) You are giving in too easily. Of course, despite being Gandhi, you are not a perfect Gandhian. You need not be. First of all, hypocrisy is better than sociopathy. Hypocrisy at least keeps values alive for the next generation; sociopathy does not. Gandhism, if you permit the use of the term for a few moments Mahatma, is the name of a worldview that is paradoxically larger than you yourself. It is part of the continuing human search for a more humane world, in the search for which critiques of progress, scientific rationality, hypermasculinity, and developmentalism have become vital at the moment. In fact, one can argue that what the wily Mahatma himself was, has become much less relevant to our times.

MKG: (shocked) That cannot be true. I have always believed that my lived life was an instrument and a vehicle of my thought. You are a Bengali. Actually the only serious Bengali sentence I ever wrote was: 'My life is my message.'

HMG: (quickly, to his father) According to Richard Grenier's well-known article in the *Commentary*, it is a bad message because your life was flawed.

AN: Forget Grenier. His argument suggests that we should not take Platonism seriously because Plato supported homosexuality and left instructions on the right way to bugger young boys. Would Grenier claim that Plato was the perfect Platonist, or had to be one, to qualify as a worthwhile read? Can we take seriously Beethoven and Milton who abused children? Or must we reject their art as contaminated? What about Thomas Jefferson who kept slaves? Do we or do we not take his ringing prose on democratic governance seriously? Tolstoy's life was not the best advertisement for his literary works or philosophy of life. Would Grenier as glibly reject Tolstoy?

Grenier has two standards. One for the Whites, the other for the Browns, Blacks, and Yellows.

MKG: Ashis, I am no thinker despite your claim. But in my way of looking at things, there is a continuity between life and thought, and between life and politics. So the principles you apply to Plato do not apply to me. I have to be responsible for my own life. Harilal and the American critic you mention are right. There is, I now suspect, something fundamentally wrong with my thought.

AN: Your highly personalized defence of your position bores me. Our generation has nothing to do with the purity of your image, grandfather. We are worried about being able to grapple with our world. We are not concerned with reconciling the contradictions, real or imaginary, in your life. Our fathers' generation, in the form of B.R. Nanda and his kind, has tried to do that for decades.

For our purposes we must begin with the axiom that the forces you represented were larger than you. And the enemies you identified or anticipated, unwittingly or otherwise, have now assumed more monstrous proportions. In that battle, your strategies, your thought, and even your controversial life constitute a master text. We reserve the right to read you according to our needs. From the American South to East Europe, where they have sometimes read you seriously, to Manila and Rangoon, where they have not done so but nevertheless carried placards bearing your name while facing army bullets, the story is the same.

HMG: Your argument is incomplete, Ashis. If Nanda belongs to your father's generation, so do I. My reading of the Mahatma has at least as much relevance as Nanda's. After all, as a son, I have known him first-hand. My reading of the man is different.

AN: I *have* pleaded for a voice for you. There should always be a place for a counter-player. Oedipal rebellion is nature's—if you like, culture's—way of ensuring that. The dialectics or, if you so prefer, adversarial encounter between a parent and a child is one way of sustaining the intellectual and moral renewal of a society through internal critiques and self-corrections. But my generation, too, has its Oedipal ghosts that it would like to exorcize. We, too, will like to defy the Gandhiana spawned by an entire range of self-certain figures—from Jawaharlal Nehru, on the one hand, to Harilal Gandhi, on the other. We cannot afford to get stuck with the inner demons of Gandhi's rebellious children who happen to be our intellectual parents.

MKG: Please do not mention Jawahar and Harilal in the same breath. Harilal has not seriously criticized anyone, not even me. He has merely lived out a life of sin in protest.

AN: But the protest has a cultural meaning, my dear grandfather. Harilal lived out a life that was contrapuntal to your preferred life. What Nehru did in a low-key, apologetic fashion, Harilal did flamboyantly and dramatically. He diagnosed perfectly what you were fighting within and occasionally failing to overpower or master. He embraced your counter-values and pushed them to their logical conclusion. He has actualized a defeated—some may say partly defeated—part of yourself.

Grandfather, to the extent you are relevant to our times as a social critic, Harilal is relevant, too, even if in a more metaphorical way. You might say that he represents modern India's critique of Gandhism in an idiom of cultivated absurdity. But it is no less serious for that reason.

MKG: (in a puzzled tone) This might look like a digression. Ashis, but I do not understand why you insist on calling me grandfather?

AN: Because the contradictions of one generation have a tendency to get resolved in the next. You can be more tolerant of your grandchildren and their 'odd' ways of assimilating or defying you than of your own children's 'oddities'. Likewise, your grandchildren acquire a perspective of you that is more seasoned or tempered by time—more benign, less judgemental and competitive, and more forgiving than the perspective of your children. Though I am a psychologist, it is no accident that your inner contradictions do not interest me beyond a point; your moral vision does.

HMG: (angrily) But it is his moral vision that is faulty. In public and private, he was a politician. His compromises have not been noted by his admirers.

AN: That also is a matter of interpretation. To us, your father's recognition of politics as a vital human activity is his main claim to immortality. Remember Arnold Toynbee's words: 'After Gandhi, humanity will ask all its prophets if they were willing to live in the slum of politics.' How much of a success the wily Mahatma has been in his politics is a secondary issue. That he was willing to enter politics and consider it a central human concern, something that allowed one to define one's *yugadharma*—ethics appropriate to one's own time—was itself a major intellectual dissent within a world where, in the name of rationality and secularism, politics has been artificially separated from morality and religion.

(Turning to MKG) To take up the specific example Harilal has given, you might not have considered Subhas Chandra Bose a scatter-brained crypto-fascist, but you considered Bose's masculinity strivings, unalloyed Statism, and his Eurocentric model of social engineering an adolescent compromise with the imperial West and a self-defeating internalization of European categories. You had to resist Bose and you chose to do so politically. Whether you were correct in your diagnosis or not does not interest us after 55 years.

HMG: (impatiently) You talk of the modern West and modernity as if they were cancerous growths. What was my father's alternative to them? For that matter, what are the alternatives offered by his young admirers pretending to be social oncologists? Do the Ashis Nandys and Makrand Paranjapes have anything concrete to offer? What is the point of talking in the air with vaguely worked out concepts like *Satyagraha*, village communities,

dharma, Ramarajya, self-help, *Swaraj,* intellectual decolonization, and other sundry utopian ideas?

AN: Harilal, we know what your father's ideas are. Shaken by
them, people of your generation have either rejected him as a
lunatic or tried to incorporate him within modernity as a hidden modernist. If you accept the second position—that is, if you
read your father as an odd internal critic of modernity pretending to be something different—you as a critic of his ideology
can be read either as a psychopath or as a lunatic. But I have
tried to give you your due; I have refused to accept your rebellion as psychopathic or demented. I have read you as a sane and
serious critic of the Gandhian worldview who, perhaps without
knowing what he was doing, carried the modernist scepticism
of Gandhi closest to Gandhi.

This means that I accept the first position: that by conventional concepts of normality, Gandhi was a lunatic. But when
necessary, like millions of others, I am willing to use his 'lunacy'
as a basis of political praxis.

One final point. Even if none of your father's ideas work,
his criticism of modernity will survive. This is because modernity is now about 400 years old and is showing the signs of
tiredness that all historical eras show after surviving for 400
years. Harilal, your father's critique of modernity allows us,
those who are living in societies where modernity has not
captured the minds and bodies of people entirely, to be better
prepared for the coming era. That this part of the globe still
has a majority of people who do not speak the language of
modernity gives us better options for a post-modern future
than have the fully modern societies. By default, we have
retained some of the non-modern foundations for looking
beyond modernity that they in the West are busy trying to
create, artificially, as new, manageable, internal critiques of
modernity. They recognize the vulnerability of their world,
but dare not break out of its embrace because that is the only
world they know.

HMG: But do we have the option to build another kind of world? Criticism is not the last word.

AN: Criticism, given the weight of negation it might carry, may not be the last word, but it deserves to be the first word. It forces us to admit that no worldview, no ideology, no transformative principle automatically becomes morally acceptable just because, at this point of time, no one has produced a viable or convincing alternative to it. That keeps intact our moral sensitivities and forces us to search harder for new alternatives. That also powers our struggle to retain available alternatives or diversities as possible foundations for the future.

MKG: (smiles at AN) I am glad that I can at least agree with that last comment of yours.

HMG: (happier but still sceptical) I have heard Ashis say some of these things earlier in different guises.

AN: As C.P. Snow once said, everyone has the right to his own clichés. In any case, we have to adjourn our debate. Makrand Paranjape is waiting. He has a different vocabulary, and he is not encumbered by our conversation. Let us hear his voice. Are you ready, grandfather?

36

Death as a Beginning*

In the sixtieth year of the murder of M.K. Gandhi, one must recognize the persistent ambivalence towards him in India's modernizing middle classes. Gandhi was not killed by British Imperialism or Muslim fanatics, but by middle-class Hindu nationalists committed to conventional European concepts of statecraft, progress, and diplomacy. He was not killed by a lunatic, as Nehru alleged, but by one who represented 'common sense', 'normality', and 'sanity.'

The middle-class antipathy to Gandhi cuts across ideologies. During one of her earlier tenures, Chief Minister of India's largest state and Dalit leader, Mayawati precipitated a first-class public controversy by attacking Gandhi. But she was only joining a lengthy line of distinguished critics of Gandhi, stretching from Mohammad Ali Jinnah, the classical liberal turned Muslim nationalist to Bal Thackeray of Shiv Sena fame. New, aggressive critics of Gandhi are now being thrown up by Hindu nationalists and the knights of globalization in India.

* This essay was originally written for *The Times of India*, 30 January 2008.

The fear of Gandhi has been consistent in India, and it has never been confined to the expensively educated Indians now flourishing in the global knowledge market. This fear overlies another, deeper fear: the fear of ordinary Indian citizens suffering from that incurable disease called Indianness, and suspicion of open politics that empowers them and allows them to bring into public life their strange, alien categories. It was this fear that Nathuram Godse took to logical conclusion on 30 January 1948. His was the third attempt on Gandhi's life by Hindu nationalists, the first of which was made in the 1930s (in which, too, Godse had participated). They made no such attempt against any other key secular leader in India or against Muslim leaders seen as enemies of the Hindus.

Godse thought he was executing Gandhi on behalf of a majority. Exactly as Mayawati, and before her, E.M.S. Namboothiripad felt that they were speaking on behalf of a majority—the *bahujan samaj*, the proletariat, the *Shudra*s, and the Dalits—when they attacked Gandhi. However, once the movement to which Godse belonged began to falter as an ideological formation and succeed as a political party dreaming of capturing power, it began singing a different tune. The Rashtriya Swayamsewak Sangh (RSS) included Gandhi's name in the daily prayers of its branches, and in the 1980s, the Bharatiya Janata Party (BJP) even adopted 'Gandhian socialism' as its official party ideology for a while. May be Mayawati's hostility to Gandhi had not waned because she was yet to make a genuine bid for a pan-Indian presence.

At the other end of the spectrum, despite some like E.M.S. Namboothiripad and Hiren Mukherji who were kinder, the Leninist hacks have always considered Gandhi a menace to progress, modernity, and rationality. The respect to Gandhi that some retired Stalinists have begun to show in recent years is a consequence of their political demise. The vendors of secular salvation now find that Gandhi has survived our times better than they have.

M.N. Roy, who broke away from Marxism, disagreed with the Leninists on many counts but not on Gandhi. His three essays on

Gandhi, read chronologically, show a declining hostility towards the Mahatma. The first is dismissive, the second ambivalent, the third mildly positive. As his confidence in being able to mobilize people for his version of revolution faltered, he came to grudgingly appreciate Gandhi's ability to touch ordinary Indians despite his 'irrational' credo.

Indian Maoists in the late 1960s and early 1970s were no less hostile to Gandhi. He with his toothless smile seemed to them a sly, scheming warhorse brainwashing rural India with his bogus ideology, whereas they, despite their direct communion with objective, scientific history and theoretical guidance from the great witch doctor at Beijing, had been exiled to urban India to survive as an ordinary terrorist outfit. As Gandhi was dead by then, they vented their anger against him by breaking his statues.

Within a decade though, from within the ranks of Indian Maoists emerged some who drew heavily, often creatively, upon Gandhi. Pushed to the margins of politics, with their dreams of an early revolution in tatters, the aging lions began to ruminate over their failures and take Gandhi seriously. Two steps backwards and one step forward, as the great helmsman might have said!

The liberals have never found Gandhi digestible either. Sir Shankaran Nair said that Gandhi was against everything that the great sons of nineteenth-century India stood for. Gopal Krishna Gokhale was even more forthright. He declared Gandhi's *Hind Swaraj* to be 'the work of a fool', and prophesied that 'Gandhi would destroy it after he spent a year in India'. Such honest estimates are now rare, because the liberals in the meanwhile have produced their own house-broken Gandhi—modern, nationalistic, progressive, statist, and secular. There is nothing left of the politically incorrect, intellectual maverick who took on the imperious Enlightenment vision and refused to accept that the vision's dominance was proof of its finality.

It is possible that Gandhi sensed his growing isolation in public life. The 200 years of Western domination had done its job, and the definition of normal politics had changed in India. Gandhi chose death, using as his accomplice the naïve, lost ideologue, Godse, to sharpen the contradiction that had arisen between the Indian civilization and the new-born Indian nation-state. Robert Payne understands this when he says,

'For Gandhi this death was a triumph.... He died as kings do, felled at the height of their powers.' And Sarojini Naidu put it more sharply when she chided a group of weeping women around Gandhi's dead body, 'What is all this snivelling about?.... Would you rather he died of old age or indigestion?'

Index